D0933353

A Thousand Years of *Czech Culture*

A Thousand Years of Czech Culture

Riches from the National Museum in Prague

Old Salem, Inc. • *Winston-Salem, North Carolina*

& the National Museum • *Prague, the Czech Republic*

Distributed by University of Washington Press

Published in conjunction with the exhibition, "A Thousand Years of Czech Culture: Riches from the National Museum in Prague," jointly produced by Old Salem, Inc., and the National Museum, which was held from September 14, 1996, to March 16, 1997, in the Gallery at Old Salem, Winston-Salem, North Carolina.

All rights reserved. No part of this book may be reproduced without written permission from the copyright holder.

© 1996 Old Salem, Inc.

All photographs © Ateliér Paul, Prague, except the following: fig. 71 on page 80, © Věroslav Škrábanek, Prague; figs. 79 and 80 on pages 89 and 90, © Jaroslav Jeřábek, Prague; cat. 199 on page 157, © Restaurátorské Ateliery, Prague. Fig. 2 on page 6 reproduced with permission of the Herzog August Bibliothek, Wolfenbüttel, Germany. Fig. 7 on page 10 reproduced with permission of the Nationalbibliothek, Vienna, Austria. Photographs of objects in the National Museum collections used with the permission of the National Museum.

LIBRARY OF CONGRESS CATALOGING-IN-PUBLICATION DATA

A thousand years of Czech culture / riches from the National Museum in Prague.

    p. cm.

  Includes bibliographical references.

  ISBN 1-879704-02-1

  1. Czech Republic—Civilization—Exhibitions.

DB2035.N37   1996

943.7—dc20   96-8564

          CIP

Edited by Cornelia B. Wright.

Designed and typeset by Kachergis Book Design, Pittsboro, North Carolina.

Color separations by All Systems Colour, Miamisburg, Ohio.

Printed and bound by Everbest Printing Company, Hong Kong.

Distributed by the University of Washington Press, P.O. Box 50096, Seattle, WA.

Contents

Contributors to the Catalogue

At the Historical Museum of the National Museum

HB   Hana Bretová
VB   Vladimír Brych
VK   Dr. Vlasta Koubská
JL   Dr. Jiřina Langhammerová
ML   Dr. Michal Lutovský
MM   Martin Mádl
JP   Jindřiška Patková
VPE   Vilemína Pecharová
MP   Milan Plášil
VPŘ   Dr. Věra Přenosilová
LR   Dr. Libuše Ruizová
MR   Dr. Marie Ryantová
PS   Petr Skala
EŠ   Evženie Šnajdrová
LS   Dr. Lubomír Sršeň
VŠ   Vítězslav Štajnochr
KŠ   Dr. Květoslava Štursová
PŠ   Petra Švehlová
AV   Dr. Alena Voříšková

At the National Museum Library

PM   Dr. Petr Mašek
ER   Dr. Eva Ryšavá
ES   Dr. Eva Stejskalová

At the Museum of Czech Music of the National Museum

BČ   Dr. Bohuslav Čížek
JF   Dr. Jana Fojtíková
MH   Dr. Markéta Hallová
MK   Dr. Markéta Kabelková
OM   Dr. Olga Mojžíšová
EP   Dr. Eva Paulová
ST   Dr. Stanislav Tesař
DV   Dr. Dagmar Vanišová

External Collaborators

LN   Lena Korba-Novotná, *Paris*
ZP   Dr. Zdeněk Petráň, *Czech Numismatic Society*
DS   Dagmar Stará, *curator emerita, National Museum*

Foreword

A country's cultural history may be influenced by political events, but its actual spiritual nature is formed through the centuries by the thoughts and creative work of individuals and groups of people. In other words, one can also say a culture springs from the internal spontaneous needs of man's own understanding and expression, and not from external psychic pressure. It seems that what is important for culture is this very excess by which it is raised above the material concerns of life. The internal spiritual charge contained in cultural works is then a wealth, the value of which greatly exceeds any material value. The yardstick of internal cultural maturity and strength has always been the ability to survive in times when its free blossoming is hindered, when spiritual life is artificially restricted to benefit the purely material needs of a certain privileged class.

If we look at a map of the world, we see that the Czech lands occupy a relatively small territory. However, their location in the center of Europe has marked the shape of their culture to an important degree. If we survey the Czech past, both ancient and more modern, we see that its cultural history was always directly or indirectly influenced by many sundry spiritual currents and orientations. Many apprentices and artists from other countries have worked in the Czech lands. In their works we shall often come across a pattern or form related to familiar works from Italy, Germany, or France. However, if we speak of a certain family relation and a closer resemblance, this does not mean a mere imitation of foreign work, since foreign patterns tended to be newly reconceived and re-evaluated in the domestic environment. They would often provide the impulse for an irreplaceable and quite distinctive new work.

This exhibition, jointly prepared by the staff of the museum of Old Salem in Winston-Salem, North Carolina, and the National Museum in Prague, has as its goal the representation, at least symbolically, of more than one thousand years of development in Czech culture. In recent times, the differences between American and European culture have usually been emphasized. We believe, on the other hand, that this exhibition will uncover for its visitors some common features from the cultures of the two continents. We trust that our American visitors, in their efforts to come to terms with our culture, will be helped by, among other things, the fact that in the eighteenth century the town of Winston-Salem was founded by members of the Unity of Brethren, a church whose first adherents once contributed to the spiritual revival in the Czech lands. Finally, we hope and wish that the exhibition not only inform, but also please.

Václav Havel
PRESIDENT OF THE CZECH REPUBLIC

Preface

A few years ago, the Trustees of Old Salem, Inc., decided that a changing-exhibits gallery would enhance Old Salem's ability to interpret history to the public and to attract visitors to the historic district with greater frequency. The project was the cornerstone of the 1992 Capital Campaign, "Old Salem: A New Direction."

Before the building was even designed, board members and staff began searching for a theme for its inaugural exhibition. We wanted something that would set a standard for future exhibits and help establish Old Salem as an important regional museum, but that would also relate to our historical and decorative arts mission. Someone came up with the thought, "Why not look to Old Salem's European roots?"

While the "Czech connection" is often mentioned in Old Salem, it it not well understood. The original town of Salem was founded by members of the Moravian faith, better known throughout the world as the Unity of Brethren, a religion that grew from early fifteenth-century religious reform efforts in Prague. For several centuries members of the Unity of Brethren in the Czech lands were persecuted; when the faith was declared illegal in 1627–28, many went into exile rather than give up their beliefs. In the 1730s, a small group of Brethren found a supporter in Count Nicholas von Zinzendorf in Saxony, Germany. He dedicated himself to spreading the faith, and his estate became the site of a community, Herrenhut, that embodied their religious principles. From Herrnhut, Unity of Brethren missionaries, now called Moravians, established several towns in the New World, including Salem, North Carolina. How Salem grew is another story, but this catalogue and the exhibition it accompanies explain the history and ideas that gave birth to the tradition that shaped it.

In 1992, with few contacts, a small group of Old Salem staff traveled to Prague in search of an exhibition. We found a wealth of materials and ideas. We also found a willing partner, the National Museum, a large, multifaceted museum of history, science, and culture. Dr. Milan Stloukal, the director of the National Museum, recognized the potential of a joint exhibition and the value of sharing a portion of the museum's rich collections with an American audience. Our staffs worked together to develop the theme, select the objects, write the catalogue, and design the exhibition. For these two museums from different cultures, working together on a common project has been a wonderful experience. At times there were frustrations caused by differences in language and methodology, but in the end we had more in common that we had differences. The result was "A Thousand Years of Czech Culture: Riches from the National Museum in Prague," an exhibition in which we both take great pride.

Please enjoy it.

Hobart G. Cawood

PRESIDENT,
OLD SALEM, INC.

In 1992, when representatives from Old Salem came to Prague with the idea of developing an exhibition from the National Museum's collections, I first viewed the proposal with a certain distrust. But when I saw the extraordinary effort with which our American partners embarked on the project, my doubts quickly vanished. However, one question remained: What would be the most suitable theme for an exhibition in the United States?

The National Museum, established in 1818, is the oldest museum in Bohemia. Over the years it has grown to be the largest and most important museum in the Czech Republic. Its five sections, the Natural History Museum, the Historical Museum, the Library, the Náprstek Museum of Overseas Ethnography, and the Museum of Czech Music, have collections totaling nearly fourteen million objects. Each of these museums has several departments devoted to specific fields of study, and our aim is that our staff includes the best scholars and curators available who can work as equal partners with other researchers, both within the country and abroad.

The National Museum has several permanent exhibitions in Prague and other locations in the Czech Republic, but they utilize only a fraction of our holdings. Thus every year we present between twenty-five and forty temporary exhibitions, both to display other objects from our collections and to share our curators' fine work with the community. It was not easy to select a limited number of items that would represent the full richness of the National Museum's resources and at the same time pique the interest of the American public. The theme we developed, "A Thousand Years of Czech Culture," represents the joint collaboration of fifteen departments in the National Museum. I sincerely hope it will be a great success.

Milan Stloukal

DIRECTOR GENERAL,
THE NATIONAL MUSEUM, PRAGUE

Introduction

The culture of a nation is exemplified by the achievements of its people and documented in a large part by the objects that survive. Using a careful selection of just over 200 objects from the marvelous collections of the National Museum in Prague, this book and the exhibition it accompanies attempt to illustrate the cultural achievements of the region historically referred to as "the Czech lands" or the "lands of the Czech Crown," now called the Czech Republic. Bohemia, Moravia, and part of Silesia make up this Central European country, with its capital in Prague. Through the centuries, despite changes to borders and political entities (the country's borders and name changed even during the course of this project), a distinctive Czech cultural identity has survived.

Geographically, the Czech lands are located at the crossroads of Europe, between north and south and east and west. The resultant streams of influence have produced a rich material culture, examples of which can provide an understanding of the Czech people. While most of the artifacts in this exhibition were made and used by Czechs, some were made in or near Prague by artisans from other countries such as Italy or Germany, and others were made by Czechs who had relocated to other parts of Europe. A few objects were imported to the Czech lands, rounding out the cross-cultural picture.

A thousand years of Czech culture, from the Middle Ages to the First World War, is an enormous topic, and it was necessary to pare it down to only the highlights. We concentrated, therefore, on five major themes: politics, religion, art and decorative arts, the performing arts, and folk culture. Because of space limitations, other themes, such as literature, science, and industry, have been touched on only briefly. This in no way reflects on their importance, and despite their omission, the story line presented here is a remarkably rich tale.

It begins with the first Slavic inhabitants of the Czech lands, whose daily life and conversion to Christianity are documented with a variety of archaeological finds. The history of the medieval Přemyslid dynasty and the Czech King and Holy Roman Emperor Charles IV follow. In the fifteenth century, simple relics of the

Hussite revolution stand out in contrast to masterpieces of late Gothic art. By the end of the Middle Ages, the Czech Kingdom was a well-developed state.

During the Renaissance, the Czech lands came under the influence of the Hapsburg Empire. Local artists followed the latest movements in Europe, looking predominantly to Italy for their inspiration. Meanwhile, religious unrest grew with the 1457 formation of the Unity of Brethren, the first organized Protestant religion in Europe. In the seventeenth century armed conflict broke out; the 1618 Battle of White Mountain outside Prague sparked the beginning of the Thirty Years' War. The Counter-Reformation that followed provided a fertile ground for the baroque styles seen in both sacred and secular contexts.

The eighteenth century saw dissatisfaction with Hapsburg domination and the resultant struggle to define a Czech identity. In the countryside, styles became increasingly regionalized, evolving into the distinctive folk customs of the nineteenth century. In cities and towns, the Czech National Revival was an intellectual and artistic movement, with some political implications. The effort to become independent of Austria came to fruition only after the massive upheavals of World War I. The selection of objects ends with this event, though an epilogue exists in the final essay of the catalogue, bringing the story up to the present day.

Each object presented here not only stands on its own, it also forms part of a larger story, whether historical, religious, or artistic. This is evident in the 1366 charter of Charles IV (cat. 26) that grants property to Charles University; or the Bible of Kralice (cat. 75), an early Bible printed in Czech, which was produced by United Brethren scholars and printers; or the 1895 sketch for the National Museum of Přemysl and the heralds of Libuše (cat. 187), an ancient legend that played a role in the National Revival. The same is true of the many examples of painting, sculpture, furniture, costumes, weapons, coins, books, music scores, instruments, and toys that make up this colorful mosaic of ideas, activities, and styles.

The objects in the exhibition are fully illustrated and described in the catalogue, thanks to the efforts of many curators of the National Museum. To complement the objects and their chronological presentation, we offer a series of essays written by Czech scholars that more closely explain the various themes that run throughout the exhibit and concentrate on history, art, religion, performing arts, and folk customs.

The great majority of these objects have never been exhibited outside of the Czech Republic. Some of them can be exhibited here for the first time in recent history thanks to the fine work of the Czech conservators who prepared them; most of them have never been published in Czech, and none of them in an English publication.

This exhibition and catalogue result from an interesting collaboration of two museums from two different continents. The extensive negotiation and planning this venture entailed were complicated by distance and differing expectations. While this experience was challenging and sometimes difficult, it resulted in increased appreciation for our respective curatorial philosophies and knowledge. Ultimately, the process of putting together this exhibition and catalogue will itself be part of the cultural history: a rewarding cross-cultural achievement between the Czech Republic and the United States.

The project would not have succeeded without the efforts and generosity of many individuals and institutions. The curatorial team would especially like to thank the following organizations for their support: the State of North Carolina; the John S. and James L. Knight Foundation; BB&T/Southern National Corporation; the Wachovia Foundation; Sara Lee Corporation; Winston-Salem Convention & Visitors Bureau; the Winston-Salem Foundation; the John W. and Anna H. Hanes Foundation; Loeffler Ketchum Mountjoy; Forsyth County, North Carolina; the City of Winston-Salem; USAir; R. J. Reynolds Tobacco Company; the Greater Winston-Salem Chamber of Commerce; Integon Corporation; Piedmont Natural Gas Company; the Mary Duke Biddle Foundation; Bowen, Hanes & Company; WXII TV, Winston-Salem; and ICL Czech Republic.

Support for a curatorial exchange was provided through the American Association of Museums' International Partnerships among Museums Program, funded by the Bureau of Educational and Cultural Affairs of the United States Information Agency. We would also like to acknowledge a generous contribution from the Samuel H. Kress Foundation specifically for the publication of this catalogue.

In addition, we thank the many contributors to the 1992 Old Salem capital campaign, "A New Direction," which funded the building of the new Gallery at Old Salem that housed the exhibition. Finally, we owe our immense thanks to the staff and boards of our museums for all their hard work and support.

Vladimír Brych   *Margaret Vincent*
Martin Mádl   *Paula W. Locklair*
THE NATIONAL MUSEUM,   OLD SALEM, INC.,
PRAGUE   WINSTON-SALEM,
                                    NORTH CAROLINA

The Czech Republic

GERMANY

POLAND

Děčín
Ústí nad Labem
Liberec
Teplice
Česká Lípa
Trutnov
Most
Litoměřice
Chomutov
Mladá Boleslav
Náchod
Karlovy Vary
Mělník
Kladno
Hradec Králové
Ohře
BOHEMIA
Labe
Cheb
Beroun
Prague
(Praha)
Kolín
Pardubice
Šumperk
Berounka
Kutná Hora
Opava
Ostrava
Plzeň
Sázava
Olomouc
Domažlice
Vltava
Havlíčkův Brod
Frýdek-Místek
Žďár nad
Klatovy
Tábor
Sázavou
Vyškov
Kroměříž
Písek
Jihlava
MORAVIA
Zlín
Strakonice
Telč
Třebíč
Brno
Slavkov u Brna
Uherské Hradiště
České Budějovice
Znojmo
Mikulov
Hodonín
Morava
Český Krumlov

AUSTRIA

SLOVAK
REPUBLIC

Essays

History of the Czech Lands in the Middle Ages

The term "Czech lands" is the name for the historical territory once known as the Czech kingdom, whose core—Bohemia, Moravia, and part of Silesia—forms today's Czech Republic. The Czech lands geographically belong among the Central European countries, while historically, politically, and culturally they have strong ties to the European West. This region's characteristic openness to outside impulses influenced contemporary political relations and contributed to the cultural identity and uniqueness of the Czech lands.

The Early Middle Ages from the Arrival of the Slavs to Great Moravia

The foundation for the gradual emergence of the Czech people, state, and cultural traditions was laid in the early Middle Ages. The historical significance of this lengthy epoch, known paradoxically as the Dark Ages, cannot be exaggerated. In the Czech lands the Middle Ages begins with the arrival of the Slavs at the beginning of the sixth century and closes with the elevation of the principality of Bohemia to a heritable kingdom at the end of the twelfth century.

The first centuries of the early Middle Ages are known as the old Slav period. The settlement of the Czech lands by the Slavs was part of the great Slavic expansion, which concluded the era of ethnic changes on the European continent known as the great migration. An ethnic group previously unknown to the ancient world, the Slavs came from the vast spaces beyond the Carpathians and spread over a

1. Floor tile with crowned, two-tailed lion, Zvíkov, South Bohemia, 1250–1275. According to legend, the two-tailed lion has been the emblem of the Czech state since the mid-twelfth century. This floor tile is from the royal chapel at the castle of Zvíkov. Cat. 1.

significant part of Europe and even into the territory of the Byzantine Empire. The Slav colonizers entering Czech territory probably encountered the remains of the previous Germanic (and older Germanicized) population, which were soon assimilated. Evidence from archaeological excavations suggests that this colonization effort occurred in two major waves during the sixth century and that both reached the agriculturally attractive area of Bohemia and Moravia.

The oldest western Slav political body to include the territory of the Czech lands was the Sámo Empire, with its probable center in Moravia. This tribal association was created in the 620s during the Slav uprising against the Avars, Turkish-Mongol nomads from central Asia. In 623–624, with the help of the Frankish merchant Sámo (d. 658) and his soldiers, the Slavs defeated the Avars. Sámo is without a doubt one of the most mysterious characters in Czech history. The lack of written sources prevents us from throwing greater light on his nationality or even his possible role in Frankish politics at the birth of the Slav Empire. The Slav chiefs elected him their leader, and he was able to defend the empire's independence not only against the Avars but also the powerful Merovingians, utterly defeating the troops of the Frankish King Dagobert I at the memorable battle at Vogastisburg in 631. From Sámo's death in 658 to the end of the eighth century, a fortified settlement near present-day Mikulčice became the most important center of power in Old Moravia, with an established warrior-baron class.

With the rise of the powerful Frankish empire under Charlemagne, crowned Roman Emperor in 800, a dangerous neighbor faced the central European Slavs. The expansion of his political empire, supported by the idea of a universal power in Western Christianity, strived to control the previously pagan tribes to the east, from the Baltic down to the Adriatic. Throughout the ninth century, one armed conflict followed another in which the Franks fought the Czech and Moravian Slavs. Even though the Frankish monarchs managed from time to time to force the Slavs into contributing a "peace tax"—in the early Middle Ages a rather common means by which one party protected itself against attack from an adversary—the Czech lands never submitted to any form of political dependence on the Empire.

Written sources from 822 refer for the first time to the Moravians, whose rulers had, with emissaries from Bohemia and other tribes, taken part in the negotiations at the Imperial Diet in Frankfurt. More socially and economically developed than the Czechs, the Moravians created a state whose internal organization was very similar to that of the Frankish Empire. The Mojmír princely family controlled the government in Moravia. Its first historically known representative was Mojmír I (r. c. 830–846), who accepted Christianity under the bishop of Passau, Bavaria, and who soon annexed the principality of Nitra to the east (now part of southwestern Slovakia). Prince Rostislav (r. 846–870) successfully defended the independence of Moravia in several armed conflicts with Ludwig the German, the ruler of the East Frankish Empire, but internal disagreements eventually led to his downfall. One significant success in Rostislav's diplomacy was the forging of ties with Byzantium, the eastern European power, which in 863–864 sent a mission to Moravia led by two learned monks, the brothers Constantine (Cyril) and Methodius. Rostislav's goal of obtaining ecclesiastical independence, which would have reinforced the political position of his state vis-à-vis the East Frankish Empire, was not fulfilled, but the cultural significance of this mission was far-reaching. Cyril codified the Slav alphabet and translated texts into Old Church Slavonic, laying the foundation for education throughout the Slav world. With the establishment of the Slav language for public worship, Old Church Slavonic reached the same status as Latin and Greek.

Svatopluk, Rostislav's nephew and successor, became a strong monarch under whose rule (870–894) Moravia reached its greatest power and territorial expansion. His political sagacity, apparent in his conclusion of a peace agreement immediately after his military success, allowed him to reinforce his position and develop his own conquest policies. Over the next several years, by direct use of arms or by threat of force, he came to control the territory of the Polish Vislans to the north, Czech and Serbs to the west, and eastern Slovakia and the former Roman province of Pannonia (now Hungary) to the south. Under his rule, a vast state developed that Constantine VII (Porphyrogenetos), a Byzantine emperor (912–959) and historian, later named "Great Moravia." Its core comprised the integrated territory of old Moravia, which extended beyond the borders of the present-day province to include southwestern Slovakia and Lower Austria north of the Danube. Svatopluk built a strong state infrastructure based on a network of castles that fulfilled the role of administrative, economic, and military centers. A looser association connected the newly conquered territories, whose princes could reign autonomously but who were required to recognize Svatopluk's sovereignty and pay a tribute. Svatopluk thereby united under his rule almost all the western Slav tribes. The bulwark of Svatopluk's policy was the Church, which was engaged in its own expansion. The appointment of Methodius as Archbishop of Moravia strengthened Great Moravia's independence from the Frankish Empire.

With Svatopluk's death in 894, Great Moravia's time in the limelight came to an end. His successor Mojmír II (r. 894–906) was unable to prevent the Czechs and Serbs from separating and was barely able to deal with the menace from the Finno-Ugric Magyars. In 906, the latter pulverized Mojmír's troops, and the state organization of Great Moravia collapsed.

Přemyslid Bohemia during the Era of the Princes

After 907, the center of political development shifted to Bohemia, where it splintered into several rival principalities. The most powerful of these was the central Bohemian principality of the Přemyslids. Their earliest historically corroborated ruler was Prince Bořivoj I (r. pre-872–889). With his consort Princess Ludmila (d. 921), Bořivoj supported Bohemia's conversion to Christianity and the construction of a state organized as a dynastic patrimony, both of which were

2. The Murder of St. Wenceslas, from the illuminated Wolfenbüttel manuscript of Gumpold's legend of the saint (before 1006). Here Prince Wenceslas stands in front of the church door at Boleslav. Denied sanctuary by a treacherous priest, he is set upon and murdered by his brother's henchmen. Wolfenbüttel, Herzog August Bibliothek, Cod. Guelf. 11.2 Aug. 2°; fol. 21r.

influenced by Great Moravia. Prague was probably founded by the Přemyslids in the 880s as a royal castle of Czech princes and later kings. By the early tenth century the Přemyslid dynastic domain was a well-organized little state, whose sovereignty was recognized by other princes living in pagan and tribal solidarity.

In terms of preserving the integrity of the land and its independence from the evolving Roman Empire, the decisive element was the achievement of a unification and state-generating process. At this fateful time, the government was assumed by Prince Wenceslas (Václav, ruled c. 922–935), an educated monarch who successfully worked to spread Christianity but was not able to build a power base strong enough to withstand the pressure from his dangerous neighbor. Wenceslas was murdered on September 28, 935, by his brother Boleslav at the latter's castle (fig. 2). Shortly after his death, Wenceslas began to be revered as a martyr; to this day he is considered the first national saint and the eternal protector of the Přemyslid dynasty and the Czech lands.

Boleslav I (935–972) instituted a number of fundamental changes in the Bohemian state, both internally and externally. Under his rule, Bohemia gradually acquired the characteristic features of a true state, including the beginnings of a unified administration throughout the entire territory, the collection of taxes, and the minting of money. In addition, Boleslav used territorial expansion as an essential means to obtain war plunder and new financial sources, from which a sizable and well-armed force could be maintained. By adding Moravia, Silesia, and the Cracow region to Bohemia, Boleslav created a Czech state that was now a power comparable to Svatopluk's Great Moravian Empire. One result of the rise of the Přemyslid state was the establishment of independent church dioceses, set up by Boleslav's son, Boleslav II (r. 972–999) in 973. With the massacre of the princely Slavník family (the brothers of Bishop Adalbert of Prague) at their palace in Libice in 995, Boleslav II definitively united the land under Přemyslid rule.

Disagreements within the Přemyslid dynasty and an unfavorable situation abroad soon led to a sharp decline in the state at the turn of the eleventh century. New elements in central European politics and dangerous new rivals to Přemyslid interests led to the loss of newly acquired territory. In 1019 Prince Oldřich of the Přemyslid dynasty (r. 1012–1033) reconquered Moravia. The strong reign of Prince Břetislav I (r. 1034–1055) brought a definitive reconsolidation of the state and a revival of the armed policy. The triumph of Břetislav's Polish campaign was the conquest of the church metropolis of Gniezno, from which he had the remains of Saint Adalbert, who had been martyred in 997, transferred to Prague. He used the ceremonial reinterment to advance his claim to establish an archbishopric there,

which to that time had been resisted by the Holy Roman Emperor. Břetislav also issued the Seniority Code governing succession to the throne, according to which the oldest member of the dynasty assumed rule over the entire land. The nonruling Přemyslids were entrusted with portions of Moravia, the main centers of which were Olomouc, Brno, and Znojmo, thereby giving them a special position within the Czech state. The fact that the law of succession allowed the Moravian Přemyslids to take power in Prague also guaranteed the territorial integrity of both parts of the state. The dexterous politics of Vratislav II (1061–1092), drawing from the support of German emperor Henry VII in his rivalry with the Papal Court (the investiture struggle), in 1085 made him the first Přemyslid to have the title of king, but only for his person, not his successors.

Of the princes who ruled after Vratislav's death, only Soběslav I (1125–1140) reinforced the central power of the state. The twelfth century was marked by the growing influence of the barons, with whose help Soběslav—in defiance of the law of succession—mounted the throne. He managed to defend his position even against Imperial King Lothair II, whom he defeated in a bloody battle at Chlumec in 1126. The barons' next choice for the princely throne was Vladislav II (1140–1172), who in 1147 led his soldiers on the Second Crusade as part of the army of Emperor Conrad III. Even though Vladislav did not reach Palestine, he was the only Czech ruler to take part in this significant—albeit unsuccessful—endeavor. After Vladislav's participation in the military campaign of Frederick Barbarossa against Milan, the Přemyslid state was elevated to a kingdom in 1158, and he ruled as King Vladislav I; however, Vladislav's successors were not strong enough to defend the royal office or to prevent increasing intervention by the Empire. This period of political instability and conflict for the throne ceased only under the reign of Přemysl Otakar I, which began in 1197.

At the end of the twelfth century, the Czech state was a fully constituted political entity with its own state ideology; its identity rested on the concept of Saint Wenceslas as the highest eternal ruler of Bohemia, from whom the members of the Přemyslid dynasty assumed temporary control of government. The concept of the Czech nation as a united "family of Saint Wenceslas" reinforced the influence of the princely retinue class, the barons, who shared with the monarch responsibility for government and defense of the land. These powerful men, known as the "shield of the Czech lands," had begun to exert themselves as an important internal authority and bearer of state sovereignty alongside the monarch. The gradual formation of the territorial nobility is one of the most significant results of social and economic change during the early Middle Ages. Population growth, new settlements, expansion of cultivated areas, and changes in settlement patterns accelerated during the second half of the twelfth century and reached a peak in the thirteenth century. The foundations of the vast Czech Kingdom under the last Přemyslids were thus laid in several restless periods of the eleventh and twelfth centuries.

3. *Silver denarius of Boleslav I, Prague, 965–972. This coin, the first to be minted in Přemyslid Bohemia for trade purposes, was produced in Prague under Boleslav I, who ruled from 935 to 972. Private collection. Cat. 22.*

4. *Silver denarius of Vratislav II, Prague, 1086–1092. The crowned bust of Vratislav II on the coin's obverse (shown) is rich in detail and may be an accurate reflection of the king's features. Private collection. Cat. 23.*

The High Middle Ages: The Rise of the Czech State under the Přemyslid and Luxembourg Kings

The beginning of the thirteenth century marks the threshold of the high Middle Ages, an era of great transformation. It coincided with the reign of Přemysl Otakar I (1197–1230), which was a milestone in the political development of the Czech state. In appreciation of the assistance Přemysl Otakar provided him in his struggle for the throne of the Holy Roman Empire, Frederick II formalized a number of rights and authorities of the Czech crown in a document signed on September 26, 1212, called the Golden Bull of Sicily. It confirmed all previous Přemyslid conquests, recognized the international authority of the Czech King, and formalized the relations between the Czech kingdom and the empire. It confirmed the right to domestic election of the monarch, as well as the right of succession of the royal title for Přemysl and his successors, the right to invest bishops, and the principle of the indivisibility of the Czech state. Some more or less formal obligations notwithstanding, the Golden Bull assured the Czech state a sovereign position within the Holy Roman Empire. The free allegiance to this vast supranational entity held many advantages for the Czech monarchs, including the right to participate in imperial elections. The Golden Bull became both the starting point for Czech monarchs' active international political activity and one of the pillars of Czech statehood.

The kingdom that Václav I (1230–1253) inherited was already a stable, recognized state. To strengthen his economic and military base, he encouraged the founding of towns (a trend that had begun later in the Czech lands than in southern and western Europe), the emergence of Prague as a fortified town, and the construction of a network of royal castles to replace the old strongholds. These efforts opened Bohemia to progressive economic and cultural influences from the west, including the Gothic style and a code of chivalry, which further stimulated development.

The expansionist foreign policy of Václav I's son Přemysl Otakar II (1253–1278), in combination with the weakening of the Holy Roman Empire, made the Czech state a major power in the Middle Ages. Dubbed the "King of Iron and Gold" for his military strength and his wealth, Přemysl Otakar II acquired Upper and Lower Austria through his marriage with Margaret of Babenberg. His defeat of Hungary's King Béla IV at the battle of Kressenbrun in 1260 secured Styria, and his occupation of the alpine lands of Carinthia, Carniola, and part of Friuli extended the Přemyslid empire to the Adriatic Sea. Another expedition, this one to far-off Latvia in the north, founded the town of Königsberg (present-day Kaliningrad).

5. Brass seal of the Land Court of Bohemia, 1250–1300. This seal's distinctive lion handle is welded to the stamp showing Saint Wenceslas, patron saint and symbolic leader of the Czech lands. It was used by the zemský *soud, or Land Court, the highest judicial body of the Czech aristocracy, from the mid-thirteenth century. Cat. 28.*

The power of Přemysl Otakar II rested above all on the economic potential of his royal towns, and a series of such towns emerged mainly because of his policies. In the structure of Bohemian society in the Middle Ages, there appeared a new class, the burghers, whose political ambitions grew in proportion to their economic strength. Mineral wealth and mining played a leading role, especially the veins of silver surrounding the royal town of Jihlava. Germanic settlers, now permitted to enter and do business in the country, contributed significantly to the development of this economic activity.

The growing power of the Czech king aroused concern among imperial princes and even on the part of the Pope. This resulted in the election of the insignificant (and thus more acceptable to the Imperial electors) candidate Rudolph of Hapsburg as Imperial king, whom Přemysl Otakar, who had sought the title himself, then refused to recognize. In the ensuing confrontation, Rudolph proved himself a skillful opponent, exposing the weaknesses of Přemysl's confederation and his methods of rule. The unwillingness of the self-confident Přemysl to find a compromise in his relations with the nobility and their political ambitions weakened his power. After losing the alpine lands and being abandoned by some of the Czech lords, Přemysl found himself pitted against Rudolph in a decisive battle at Marchfeld on August 26, 1278, where he perished. The defeat of the Czech troops had a catastrophic impact on the Czech lands in the subsequent period, termed the "evil years" by its chroniclers. Rudolph occupied Moravia, and Otto of Brandenburg assumed command over Bohemia as lieutenant to the underage successor to the throne, Václav. After the young prince was taken to Brandenburg and held in custody, a group of Czech nobles came forth with his ransom to guarantee state sovereignty. This ended the exploitative policy of the Brandenburgs and resulted in the prince's return to the country.

The Přemyslid state reached the peak of its territorial development and power under Václav II (1283–1305) who, having learned from his father's confrontational relationship with the nobility, launched a process of sharing political power, all the while relying on the towns and the church. His royal council, which was dominated by the voice of the clergy and included foreign diplomats in Czech service such as Peter of Aspelt, contributed to the creation of Václav's policies. Although the nobility foiled his attempts to codify the Crown Law and to found a university, Václav still managed to strengthen the authority of the monarchy. The opening of the Kutná Hora silver mines, the largest in central Europe, was of huge economic significance (fig. 7). It led to coin reform, the issuing of the Mining Law governing mineral rights, and the minting of the famous Prague grosch in 1300 (fig. 8). Václav continued his predecessors' aggressive foreign policy, this time oriented toward Polish territory to the north, which culminated in Václav's coronation as Polish king in 1300 in Gniezno. After the extinction of the Arpadian dynasty in 1301, Václav II successfully proposed his son Václav's candidature for the Hungarian throne. The Přemyslids, on whose heads three royal crowns now rested, stood at the peak of their power. The 1304 attack of the Imperial king Albrecht I on

6. *Charter of Přemysl Otakar II, Bohemia, 1264. This charter grants the abbey of Our Lady in Žďár rights to the gold and silver mined on the abbey's lands. Přemysl Otakar's seals were of high artistic quality. These fragments show the king on his throne. Cat. 25.*

7. Silver mining in Kutná Hora, from the illuminated title page of the Kutná Hora Gradual (1490s). This illumination shows an unusually precise depiction of the silver production process and the ore market. Nationalbibliothek, Vienna, Cod. 15.501.

Bohemia was repulsed by Václav with the help of the Czech lords; however, this large central European confederation did not survive his death in 1305. Within a year, his seventeen-year-old son and successor died at the hands of a hired assassin in Olomouc, where he was gathering troops for a campaign to Poland. In 1306, therefore, the Přemyslid dynasty ended.

The rise of the state's power under the last Přemyslids was supported by a dynamic period of development. The extent of these changes could be seen in the countryside (the large-scale deforestation that followed colonization), in settlements (new physical organization of villages and the creation of towns, which was an entirely new form of habitation in these regions), and society (the constitution of the feudal territorial noblemen, the establishment of feudal relations, and the birth of a new municipal society). The external colonization carried out by the Germans disrupted the ethnic homogeneity of the Czech lands. Progress was achieved in the economic sphere through innovations in agriculture, new technology and energy sources, and the development of market production and barter centers. Thus the picture of the Czech lands of the thirteenth century was completely different from that of a few centuries earlier, and the process of mutually influential changes that is generally termed the transformation of the Middle Ages reached its full extent. The Czech lands were approaching the status of more developed western Europe, which had already undergone similar changes.

The election of Rudolph I of Hapsburg (1306–1307), who died after reigning a year, was followed by that of Heinrich of Carinthia (1307–1310), but neither achieved general recognition or managed to stabilize relations. The growing anarchy prompted influential nobles and patricians, who supported the inheritance claims of Princess Eliška Přemyslovna, to terminate the reign of the incompetent Heinrich. After an initiative by Cistercian abbots and the diplomacy of Peter of Aspelt, the archbishop of Mainz and former Chancellor to Václav II, a contract was signed with the Holy Roman Emperor Henry VII whereby the Czech crown would be accepted by his son John, who would marry Eliška Přemyslovna. The choice was not arbitrary; in the background France, the new continental powerhouse, supported the rise of this hitherto obscure Luxembourg dynasty. A communion of political interests between the Czechs and the Luxembourgs was of great importance in strengthening the position of the Czech state, as well as for providing the agile Luxembourgs a power base that far exceeded, both in size and in significance, their dynastic dukedom on the western edge of the empire.

Thus supported, John set out for Bohemia with troops and expelled Heinrich.

8. Prague Grosch, Kutná Hora, 1300–1305. This famous coin, minted under Václav II, dominated the markets of Central Europe for almost 250 years. Václav brought about many changes governing mining, mineral rights, and coin reform. Private collection. Cat. 24.

9. Portrait bust of Czech king and Holy Roman Emperor Charles IV, flanked by the emblems of the Czech lion and imperial eagle, from the triforium of the cathedral of St. Vitus at Prague Castle. The artist Peter Parler was known for his outstanding and innovative Gothic architecture as well as his carved stone portraits.

The reign of John of Luxembourg (1310–1346), despite the extensive privileges granted the nobles, did not proceed without conflict; the Czech lords nearly stole the throne away from their new king. John, therefore, left the kingdom's internal affairs largely in the hands of the nobility and concentrated his energies on foreign policy, for which he exhibited exceptional talent. His most important territorial gains were the definitive acquisition of the Cheb region (formerly imperial territory), the Budyšín and Zhořelec areas, the core of Upper Lusatia, and even a large chunk of the economically important Silesia. John's diplomatic and military activity financially encumbered the Czech lands, leading to the mortgaging of Crown estates.

Among John's children, the one with the greatest significance for Czech and European history was his first-born son Václav, more commonly known as Karel or Charles IV (fig. 9). As a youth, Charles received an excellent education in France, and on the hot coals of the Italian Luxembourg domains, he acquainted himself with political practices and tested his mettle on the real battlefield. In 1333, bearing the title of Margrave of Moravia, he returned to Bohemia with his bride, Blanche of Valois, to help King John. The success of both Luxembourg rulers was tied to the existence of an independent Prague archdiocese, which extricated the Czech state from the ideological influence of the archbishops of Mainz.

With the heroic death of his father at Crécy, where the Czech and French troops battled the English and where Charles himself was wounded, he also assumed the crown of the Czech kings (1346–1378); Luxembourg diplomacy triumphed with Charles's election as Imperial king in 1346. As of 1355, when Charles was crowned in Rome, he could call himself Roman Emperor. In domestic politics, Charles consciously linked himself to the tradition of a domestic monarchic dynasty, which in previous periods had allowed a stabilized nation to expand economically and politically. Charles also strengthened his legal base. During his reign, the constitutional term "Czech Crown" referred both to the territory of the state (Bohemia and incorporated lands) and political representation abroad.

Charles's vision of a Czech state rested on the concept of the Czech crown lands as the unity of the monarch, noblemen, and clergy, and the unity took precedence over each group's particular interests. The crown of Saint Wenceslas was understood as the external symbol of this alliance (fig. 10). With the capital of the Czech kingdom and of the Holy Roman Empire in Prague, Bohemia and the Moravian Margravate (entrusted to Charles's brother Jan Jindřich) had a special position. Charles extended his empire to the Upper Palatinate, the remaining Silesian principalities, Lower Lusatia, and Brandenburg; under his reign the Czech state reached its greatest territorial extent and enjoyed its highest status as a world power. With the founding of the New Town in 1348, Prague under Charles became one of the largest metropolises of Europe.

Although, like his Czech predecessors, Charles IV was unable to codify Crown Law in his *Majestas Carolina*, as the lay head of western Christianity he did achieve considerable success in Imperial matters. His enduring 1356 Golden Bull served as the basic law of the Holy Roman Empire until the abolition of that political entity in 1806.

10. St. Wenceslas' crown, the most revered of the Czech crown jewels. Commissioned by Charles IV in 1346, the gold crown is set with precious rubies, sapphires, emeralds, and pearls from the historic Přemyslid treasury. Hidden in the cross at the top is a relic, a fragment of Christ's crown of thorns.

During Charles's reign, culture and education blossomed. In 1348, Charles founded in Prague the first university north of the Alps and east of the Rhine, which today bears his name (fig. 11). Charles himself was one of the most educated monarchs of the time and could speak and write five languages. With his support and that of the university, the Czech language began to take its place in literature alongside the dominant Latin. Charles had an unusual breadth of vision and considerable success in selecting political advisors (Archbishop Arnošt of Pardubice) and artists (the architect and sculptor Peter Parler), who turned Prague into a center of European artistic activity. It is characteristic of his statesmanship that the means Charles used to obtain his political goals were well-conceived diplomacy, a political marriage, and financial sacrifice if necessary; however, he avoided armed conflict. The label of *pater patriae*, first coined for Charles's person by Vojtěch Raňkův of Ježov (one of the leading scholars of the era and the former rector of the Sorbonne in Paris), captured not only the contemporary view of the Czech king, but also the significance of his life's work.

The long period of prosperity and peaceful development, however, was already being clouded near the end of Charles's life by signs of crisis, which only came fully to the fore under the reign of his son Václav IV (1378–1419). Worsening living conditions, private wars between nobles, and an increase in crime and in epidemics heightened social unrest in the Czech towns, already under strain from ethnic conflicts. The church too was in crisis; growing disparities between church theory and practice reduced its authority, just at the time that the insoluble rupture of the Church (the papal schism of 1378–1417) cried out for change.

Václav IV lacked the political breadth and tenacity of his father, but even his more capable predecessors would have been hard pressed to control the difficulties he encountered. Conflicts with the Archbishop of Prague and the high nobility led twice to the king's imprisonment, weakening his status at home and abroad. In 1400, Václav was deprived of his title as Imperial king. The rivalry with his brothers also did not help him. His ambitious brother Sigismund, king of Hungary and (from 1411) Imperial king, spoke out publicly against Václav and did little to hide his ambitions to obtain the Czech crown for himself.

From the Hussite Period to the Estates Monarchy

Under Václav IV, criticisms of social, economic, and political problems found a common cause in efforts to reform the church; gradually this united all the dissatisfied groups in Czech society. From this reformatory current emerged the Hussite movement, the predecessor of the European Reformation.

From the beginning, Charles University in Prague played a central role in the reformation movement. One of the first victories of the reformers was the Kutná Hora Decree, issued by Václav IV in 1409, which altered the voting proportions and thus the balance of power at the university in favor of Czechs. This provided a forum for reform ideas and was simultaneously an important step toward the secularization of the university.

At the head of the reformation current that criticized ecclesiastic and social wrongs stood the charismatic figure of John Huss, from 1402 a preacher in the Bethlehem Chapel, who held a master's degree from Charles University; he was a teacher and, from 1409, rector of the university. Václav and an influential group of Czech nobles supported Huss in his conflict with the Papal Court, which excommunicated the reformer in 1411. The situation culminated during storms of protest against the sale of papal indulgences: three young followers of Huss's teaching were

11. Foundation charter of a college of Charles University, Prague, 1366. With this document Charles IV donated a second house to the masters and students of Charles College, which he had founded in 1348. His signum is incorporated into the text. Charles University in Prague is the oldest university north of the Alps and east of the Rhine. Cat. 26.

12. The burning of John Huss from the Jena Codex (c. 1500). The illuminated illustrations in this book depict the well-known figures, events, and struggles of the Hussite movement against the established Catholic Church. Courtesy of the National Museum Library, Prague.

executed in Prague in 1412. Intensifying pressure eventually forced Huss to leave Prague to save the capital city from a papal interdiction, which would have prohibited all public worship in the town of Huss's residence. In the countryside, he continued his preaching activity and completed his pivotal writings.

In Prague in 1414, a fellow reformer, Jakoubek of Stříbro, first administered Communion to congregations *sub utraque specie* ("in both kinds," both bread and wine, the body and blood of Christ). The right to receive the wine as well as the host was a critical right for the Hussites, underscoring the equality of priests and laymen. The chalice as a symbol of this right became a symbol of the Hussite movement. In the same year, despite numerous warnings, Huss accepted an invitation from King Sigismund to attend the church council in Constance, where he was to get a public hearing. The council wanted not to hear his grievances, but to deal with a disquieting situation for the Roman Catholic Church, at whose head then stood three Popes. Although Huss's safety had been guaranteed by the emperor's letter of safe-conduct, he was not given the opportunity to defend his opinions. The council declared Huss a heretic and, after a summary trial, condemned him to death. Huss refused to recant his views, and on July 6, 1415, was burned at the stake (fig. 12).

Huss's adherence to truth at all costs made him a martyr, and his death ignited a storm of protest that cut across class lines. As only one example, 412 Czech and Moravian lords and knights appended their seals to a list of complaints sent to the Council of Constance, an act without parallel. In the years to come, the followers of Huss's teachings became more radical.

The revolutionary phase of the Hussite period began with the Hussite attack on the town hall of Prague New Town in 1419. It was led by the popular tribune and radical preacher Jan Želivský with the goal of liberating imprisoned fellow-believers. This first "Prague defenestration" resulted in several inimical town councillors being thrown out the Town Hall windows to their deaths, and gave control of the New Town to the Hussites. This and subsequent disturbances so upset Václav IV that he succumbed to a stroke. The heir to the throne at that moment was his stepbrother Sigismund, Imperial king and King of Hungary, to whom the Catholic Czech lords and the representatives of neighboring Crown Lands pledged their allegiance. In 1420, when the Pope launched a crusade against the Czech heretics, the Hussites united around two sites: Prague, which was the key to controlling the entire kingdom and the base of the moderate Hussites, and Tábor, founded by radical Hussites in Bohemia. The Táborites were for the most part simple countryfolk and artisans. Initially Tábor was a community without lords or serfs, where all wealth was shared communally. As well as Hussite priests, its members numbered some military commanders from the lower noble classes, without whose military experience and organizational skills, the Táborites would have been unable to repulse the enemies of the Chalice.

The leader of the Hussite forces who stands out was Jan Žižka of Trocnov, a one-eyed, undefeatable commander and strategist who served from 1419 until his death in 1424 (fig. 13). In revolutionary Prague, Hussite ideologists formulated their demands in the Four Articles of Prague, and made its acceptance a condition of accepting Sigismund as Czech king. Sigismund instead opted to acquire the Czech crown by force, but after being defeated at the battle at Vítkov Hill outside Prague in 1420 by Žižka's Táborites, he hurriedly let himself be crowned Czech king—the Castle guard had remained loyal to him—and then ingloriously fled the city that would not submit to him. From a military point of view, the decisive defeat of Sigismund's forces and liberation of Prague was brought about by the battle of Vyšehrad in November 1420. Soon afterward, the Czech Diet rejected Sigismund's claim to the Czech crown and endorsed the revolutionary changes. The delegates to the Diet now included not only lords but also representatives of the lower nobility and the towns.

All four subsequent campaigns to conquer Hussite Bohemia were defeated at Žatec (1421), Kutná Hora and Německý Brod (1422), Tachov (1427), and Domažlice (1431). The Hussites, soon splintered between the moderate Praguers and their allies, and the radical Táborites and east Bohemian "Orphans," as they were called after Žižka's death, were only able to unite under an external threat. When this passed, they engaged in internal armed conflicts in which none of the fighting parties was able to gain the advantage. The famous "flail-men" (cat. 33) of the peasent infantry, using the protection offered by mobile battlements and an unprecedented massive concentration of firepower, overturned the established knightly mode of combat. The impossibility of defeating the Hussites militarily, and the raids of the Hussites into neighboring countries, forced the Catholic world to negotiate with the so-called heretics. In 1433, Hussite theologians, led by Prokop Holý, gained a hearing at the Council of Basel, out of which emerged the Compact of Basel. In this document, the Catholic church recognized the Hussites' right to administer the Eucharist in both kinds, as well as more specific Hussite demands, and removed the label of "heretic land" from Bohemia. Among the inhabitants of a

13. Hussite warriors led by Jan Žižka and a priest carrying a monstrance with the sacred holy body (host) from the Jena Codex (c. 1500). Žižka, the one-eyed (later blind) military leader, one of the best known figures of the Hussite era, formulated the strategy and tactics of the Táborites during the Hussite wars. Courtesy of the National Museum Library, Prague.

14. *Shield, Prague, 1475–1500.*
This oblong shield, called a
pavis, bears a picture of the
gates of Prague, the emblem of
the city. It was one of several
that the shieldmakers' guilds
would supply the city to release
their members from military
service and various fees. Cat. 31.

kingdom weakened by long wars, the desire for peace began to dominate. The Hussite radicals, however, rejected compromise and once again arms were taken up. In a fratricidal battle at Lipany in 1434, the coalition forces of Prague Utraquist and Catholic units broke the Táborite and Orphan troops. The bloodbath also claimed Prokop Holý. Lipany did not mark the end of Hussitism in Bohemia, only the close of one revolutionary chapter linked with the radical brotherhoods.

When Sigismund accepted the subsequent demands, including those anchored in the Compact of Basel, nothing prevented his accession to the Czech throne (1436). However, he was unable to enjoy it for long; in 1437 this last of the Luxembourg dynasty died without a male heir. The short reign of Sigismund's son-in-law Albrecht of Hapsburg (1437–1439) was followed by fourteen years without a central ruler, during which the land was administered by regional associations of Utraquist and Catholic nobles. Finally, after the four-year reign of Albrecht's son Ladislav Pohrobek (1453–1457), the Czech nobleman George of Poděbrady was chosen king (1458–1471).

The "Hussite King" George, a recognized leader of the Utraquist nobles, was a contemplative and able politician, whose choice was even supported by the Catholic lords. George gained international fame for his project to peacefully unite the European rulers, ostensibly to repulse the Turkish menace in Europe, but actually to eliminate the role of the Pope in international politics. George's concept of a peace organization (in many ways a predecessor of the modern-day United Nations) was far too advanced for his time; in reality any throne or state sovereignty required an ongoing struggle. Pope Pius II's unilateral rejection of the Compacts of Basel in 1462 raised the specter of a new religious conflict, and soon George faced excommunication. George's troops suppressed the domestic resistance of the Catholic nobility (the Zelená Hora unit), only to face a crusade against Bohemia in 1468 led by Matthias of Hungary. By surrounding Matthias's forces at Vilémov, George forced a peace conference, but Matthias immediately reneged on the agreements and had himself elected Czech king in Olomouc.

Following George's death in 1471, the Czech Estates elected Vladislav Jagello as their king (1471–1516). The new king, from a Catholic Polish-Latvian dynasty, was at first only able to assume power in Bohemia, since the other Crown Lands were under Matthias's rule. The Olomouc Agreement of 1479 ended the war between the two monarchs with a paradoxical peace; the Czech kingdom, divided into two parts, had two kings. After Matthias's death in 1490, the Hungarian Estates offered his crown to Vladislav. The neighboring Czech Crown Lands—Moravia, Silesia, and Upper and Lower Lusatia—again joined with Bohemia, and the Czech and Hungarian kingdoms fell under Jagello rule. The Hungarians dominated the union, and Buda, their capital city, became the permanent residence of the Jagellos. (The loss of Prague's political prestige during the Jagello era was, of course, obscured to a certain extent by the exquisite expansion of Prague Castle, the seat of the Czech kings, by the architect Benedikt Ried.) The dynastic agreement with the Hapsburgs was of extreme importance for the future; it led to the engagements of Maria of Hapsburg and Vladislav's son Ludvík, and of Ferdinand of Hapsburg with Anna Jagello. The tragic death of Ludvík I (1516–1526) at the Battle of Mohács, where the king had been trying in vain to arrest the Turkish attack into Hungary, made the Czech throne available to the Hapsburgs.

Under the Jagellos, Hussitism achieved formal legitimacy, and Bohemia reached a position, quite extraordinary at the time, as a land of freedom and religious tolerance. The Kutná Hora religious peace in 1485 ensured the equality of both main churches—the Catholic and the Utraquist—and freedom of belief to all inhabitants of the kingdom, both lords and serfs. Only the minority *Unitas Fratrum* (Unity of Brethren) were excluded; this group carried on the spiritual legacy of Petr Chelčický, whose thoughts on the unjustifiability of violence, the rejection of official views on the organization of society, and other ideas were too radical for the two main religious trends of the time. In this, the Czech "kingdom of two peoples" differed completely from neighboring countries. The resolution of religious differences was politically significant. The Hussite period brought about serious changes in the structure of society and in the political system. The latter evolved from the absolute monarchy model to a more democratic form based on a dualism of power, the so-called Estates monarchy. The monarch was no longer an unrestricted ruler, but "first among equals"; he shared power with the Estates, which were made up of upper nobles (lords), lower nobles (knights), and the burgers elected by the free royal towns. The church, which had been deprived of its property during the Hussite wars, had a restricted role in political affairs, and in Bohemia it was later completely excluded. The main representative and legislative body of the Estates was the Diet. It had the right to elect the monarch and to decide on taxes, military matters, and domestic and foreign policy. That the feudal elite could no longer decide on these serious matters without the elected delegates from the free towns markedly distinguished the Czech state from the surrounding monarchies. The establishment of political rights for the so-called third estate was seen as the first step on the way to a modern European democracy; however, progress down this path was later to be slowed by the centrist policies of the Hapsburgs.

Vladimír Brych
HISTORICAL MUSEUM,
THE NATIONAL MUSEUM

Art in the Czech Lands from the Sixth to the Twelfth Centuries

17. Silver gilt belt mount and end piece from the second church site at Mikulčice, ninth century. One of the best-known archaeological finds of the Great Moravian period, this object bears an engraved figure of an orant (praying) figure, with hands raised in adoration. Courtesy of the Archaeological Institute of the Czech Academy of Sciences, Brno.

The culture and creative expression of the earliest Slavs (up to the sixth century) throughout the area of their expansion are characterized by simplicity and a high degree of uniformity. The half-recessed huts with a stone oven in the corner, and the austere vase-shaped undecorated vessels (called Prague ceramics) that served as articles of daily use and as funerary urns, typify the simple construction methods and handcrafted works of these people (fig. 16). When assessing the level of aesthetic sensitivity among the earliest Slavs, however, we must acknowledge that many objects that were used on a daily basis cannot be known from the archaeological record; articles of personal decoration were often lost as a result of cremation rites, and other objects made from organic materials disintegrated over the ensuing centuries.

The next settlers who came from the southeast at the turn of the sixth and seventh centuries produced technically more advanced ceramics; later still came pottery vessels with combed decoration of waves and bands, probably inspired by the manufacturing traditions they brought with them from former Roman provinces in the Danube basin. The Slavs' borrowing of techniques and creative impulses from more developed areas is the most striking feature of artistic creation in this early period.

Some of the most admirable examples of craftsmanship from the seventh and eighth centuries were cast-bronze decorative belt mountings. These were imported from the Avar Empire into the Czech lands and shortly thereafter were produced in the workshop of the Mikulčice castle. They form the only evidence to date for bronze casting in Slav Moravia during this time. The colorful range of decorative motifs produced—animal shapes, plants, and human forms—testifies to

16. *Slavic ceramics. Left: A pot of the Prague type from the vicinity of Mikulčice (sixth century); right, a decorated vessel from a burial in Prague-Motol (tenth century). Cat. 17, 18.*

Graeco-Roman, Byzantine, Iranian, and other influences. These cast belt decorations were originally worn by men; women's jewelry generally consisted of earrings inspired by Byzantine styles.

A great surge in craft production also occurred in the Great Moravian Empire during the ninth century. At first, during the Blatnica–Mikulčice period (early ninth century), western Carolingian art influenced local artistic traditions in Great Moravia, producing a very original style. Archaeological excavations of graves and princely tombs have revealed a series of exquisite works in this style, including decorated gilded spurs and ornately decorated sword hilts and horse trappings, that reflect the lives of the highest social milieu (fig. 17). Engraving, metal sheeting, and tausie (precious metal cold-pressed into the surface of the object) were among the techniques used. The quality and creativity of the Slav artists who produced these objects is unsurpassed. The most typical and the most attractive of the Great Moravian jewelry is the *gombíky*, a decorated round button made from thin sheet metal impressed with an embossed design, most often a plant motif (fig. 18, 19). Silver and gold earrings of various styles (crescent-shaped, grape bunches) were fabricated for women of princely society. *Gombíky* and earrings were decorated by delicate granulation (particles of precious metal heat-bonded to a surface) and filigree (delicate interwoven fibers of silver or gold), techniques whose perfection under the old Moravian masters instill respect to this very day (fig. 15). As Christianity spread across the region and was adopted by families of high rank, its symbols were also reflected in handcrafted jewelry, especially crosses, orant figures with their arms raised in prayer, fish, doves, and lambs (fig. 20).

The first monumental architecture of the Slavs can be considered the castles of

15. *Earrings, Bohemia or Moravia, ninth century. The fine filigree and granulation techniques used in these earrings, found at a princely burial ground at Stará Kouřim, reflect the advanced skill of the Great Moravian artisans. Cat. 2, 3.*

18. Button or ball brooch, Bohemia, 900–950. During the Great Moravian period, decorative buttons, called gombíki, were worn by men and women of high rank as clothes fasteners. This gombik of gilded bronze has a stamped bird motif. It was excavated at a burial site near Budeč, once an important Přemyslid stronghold. Cat. 7.

19. Buttons found in a burial at the archaeological site of Mikulčice. The position of these buttons in grave sites documents their function and use in both men's and women's dress. Courtesy of the Archaeological Institute of the Czech Academy of Sciences, Brno.

20. Lamb ornament, Central Europe, late tenth century. This silver lamb probably represents the Christian symbol of the Agnus Dei, the lamb of God. It is an example of Christian imagery being used in ornamental jewelry in Přemyslid Bohemia. Cat. 8.

the time. These extensive fortified strongholds, sometimes encompassing an entire town, were reinforced initially by wood and clay battlements and later by revetments and dry-laid stonework. The strongholds themselves, like the unfortified rural settlements, were constructed of wood, using techniques representative of the local Slav traditions.

In the late eighth and early ninth centuries, the introduction of Christianity led to the use of stone for churches and other religious architecture for the first time in the western Slav world. The knowledge of masonry construction, especially using bricks and roofing tiles, had been first brought to the Czech lands by Roman legionaries during the construction of outposts on the *limes*, the fortified boundary of the Roman Empire along the Danube in southern Moravia. The varied background of the Christian missions in Great Moravia resulted in a wide diversity of construction styles among the earliest churches. Western influences were at work here—Frankish, eastern Byzantine, and Dalmatian-Adriatic. (Suggestions of an Irish-Scottish influence are intriguing but have not been sufficiently documented.) A number of locales in the early period had a small, single-nave church with a rectangular presbytery or with a semicircular apse in the Byzantine style. Many churches were built on a central floor plan as rotundas with one or two apses; only one structure is known to have four internal apses. The basilicas that superseded the rotunda style required more demanding layout solutions.

The largest of the early known churches was a three-nave basilica in the Mikulčice castle, the probable center of Great Moravia and the old Moravian diocese. The eleven buildings of the castle and the settlement around it represented the largest concentration of religious architecture in Great Moravia at that time. The church complex at Sady near Uherské Hradiště (fig. 22), with its complicated

21. *Exterior of the tenth-century single-apsed rotunda of St. Peter at the early Přemyslid castle at Plzeň (today Starý Plzenec). The rotunda was a common structural form for Czech churches from the late ninth century.*

22. *Foundation plan of the ninth-century church in Sady near Uherské Hradiště. Archaeological research indicates this important Great Moravian church center consisted of a large church structure with free-standing baptismal font and burial chapel, and wooden dwelling structures. Courtesy of the Slovak Museum, Uherské Hradiště.*

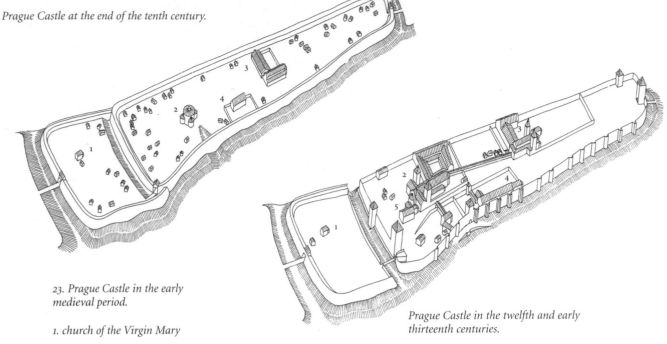

Prague Castle at the end of the tenth century.

Prague Castle in the twelfth and early thirteenth centuries.

23. *Prague Castle in the early medieval period.*

1. *church of the Virgin Mary*

2. *rotunda/ basilica of St. Vitus, with cloister*

3. *basilica of St. George with cloister*

4. *Přemyslid princes' court/ royal palace*

5. *bishop's palace*

Drawings by Petr Chotěbor.

layout, is of extraordinary significance because of a collection of early engraving tools (styluses) excavated there, which allows scholars to study religious architecture and the wider context of its functions, the most important being the educational activity of the missions.

The builders of most churches were princes, but barons also founded them in their residences. Archaeological discoveries also indicate that these church interiors were decorated with wall paintings, the earliest known in the Czech lands.

At the time of the first Přemyslids, the heirs to the expired Great Moravian state, Czech art was influenced by the cultural traditions of old Moravia. An excellent example is architectural design, where the adoption of the earlier style was deliberate. The first church in Bohemia, founded by Prince Bořivoj on his original castle settlement of Levý Hradec (around the 880s), had a single-apse rotunda, with obvious Moravian elements. The links between the Spytihněv rotunda of Saint Peter in the Budeč Castle and earlier architecture are controversial, but the significance of this monument is that it represents the only church from the late Great Moravian era that has been preserved intact.

Prague Castle, the seat of the Přemyslid princes, is of key importance to an understanding of tenth-century architecture (fig. 23). Whereas the oldest of Bořivoj's churches, dedicated to the Virgin Mary, was a typologically unique, although humble, structure, Vratislav's basilica of Saint George and the large rotunda of Saint Vitus (whose four horseshoe-shaped apses also indicate a continuation of the Great Moravian tradition) were creations worthy of a powerful princely seat. Later, under Boleslav II, the rotunda of Saint Vitus became the metropolitan church of the newly established Prague diocese, and the church of Saint

George became the location of the first Benedictine monastery in the Czech lands (973). The central church of the Slavník Palace in Libice (960s–995) is an example of an alternative architectural inspiration; its Latin-cross floor plan is an example of Saxon Ottonian architecture. Libice is also important because it provides an example of a princely palace's configuration in the tenth century. The Slavník Palace was a one-story timbered building connected by a bridge at the second-floor level to the gallery of the side nave of the neighboring church.

In Bohemia, the architecture of the early Middle Ages reached its peak during the Romanesque period. As in other parts of Europe, Romanesque architecture in Bohemia and Moravia either drew directly from the progressive centers of development in western and southern Europe or through the intermediating influence of neighboring German-speaking countries.

One important factor in the expansion of new artistic impulses was the international community of religious orders—at first exclusively Benedictine, and from the mid-twelfth century Premonstratensian. Monastery workshops introduced new construction techniques and concepts in the fine arts. Among the oldest monasteries on Czech soil are the Saint George convent in the Prague Castle complex (973); the monastery in Březnov (993), with an important early eleventh-century construction phase, and the monastery in Ostrov (999), where remarkable construction activity was carried out in the twelfth century. The characteristic mark of Benedictine construction was the basilica-church plan with three naves leading to a triple-apse eastern presbytery, a transept, and a pair of towers on the western facade. The resulting Latin-cross floor plan superimposed on the consecrated location symbolized Christ's suffering. An important element from an architectural point of view was the use of a large western tower with an arch at the ground level and a gallery on the first floor. Galleried "private" churches, built in the eleventh and especially the twelfth centuries by members of the feudal elite as part of their seats, became an emblematic, distinctive expression of Romanesque architecture in the Czech lands, leading one contemporary foreign visitor to comment that Bohemia was full of churches. While builders were influenced by the architecture of the large monasteries, in the ground plans of two of the simplest and most widespread variants, the rotunda and the longitudinal one-nave church, older traditions persisted on home soil.

The Premonstratensians played a significant role in the development of Czech Romanesque construction as well. Their monastery in Strahov (1140) is characterized by its monumentality and simple elegance; that in Doksany (1140s) has strikingly decorative architectural detail. The most impressive construction project of the early Romanesque period of the second half of the eleventh century was the Saint Vitus Basilica in Prague Castle, which replaced the original Wenceslas rotun-

24. *Interior of the Basilica of St. George at Prague Castle (after 1142). In this view of the main nave, the tomb of the church's founder, Prince Vratislav I, is seen on the southern wall.*

da. Out of respect for Wenceslas as saint and royal patron, his primary sanctuary, the southern apse of the old rotunda, together with his grave, was incorporated in the new construction. (Remnants of this basilica are preserved in the foundations of the standing Gothic Saint Vitus cathedral.) The two-choir ground plan of this flat-roofed three-naved basilica, with the transept on the west and a pair of huge four-sided towers, has crypts to the west and the east. The western crypt is a showcase of construction artistry, especially in the rich braided relief of columnar shafts, which owes much to Italian design influences.

The construction activity of the second half of the eleventh century spread to the second Prague castle of Vyšehrad, which Vratislav II made his residence. The number of churches—dominated by the basilica of Saints Peter and Paul and that of Saint Lawrence, with its relief-decorated terra-cotta flooring (fig. 25) and rich furnishings, as described by written sources—even exceeded those at Prague Castle.

25. Floor tile with griffin, Vyšehrad (Prague), late eleventh or early twelfth century. This mythological creature was one of several animals and monsters that were used to decorate the floor tiles of St. Lawrence Basilica at the royal residence of Vyšehrad. Cat. 20.

The Romanesque style was also used for secular buildings, the most important of which were are the stone castles of the monarchy at Prague, Olomouc, and Mělník and the bishopric at Roudnice. Here too there was a melding of old and new: while the construction technique is Romanesque, the ground plan reflects the older castle tradition. The first castle in the full medieval sense of the word was the border fort of Přimda from the early twelfth century, which represents the pure import of a *donjon*-type castle, with a large residential tower.

Romanesque Prague of the twelfth century formed an exceptional architectural and urban whole. The reconstruction of the castle under Soběslav I and King Vladislav I from the second to the fourth quarter of the twelfth century transformed the seat of the Czech monarchs into a vast complex, protected by stone fortification walls, by a series of turrets (predecessors to later bastions), and by tall towers to defend the gates (fig. 23). Dominating the enclosed area were the imposing Přemyslid Palace with its massive ground-level semicircular barrel vault, the independent palace of the Bishop, and the churches, whose gleaming white argillite towers crowned the Prague panorama in the early Middle Ages. Of these churches, the original shape of the monumental Saint George basilica has been essentially preserved to the present day. Other churches, monasteries, and seats of knights' orders (such as the Knights of St. John) grew up below the castle. The area that grew up under Prague Castle in the late twelfth century and early thirteenth century represented a memorable complex of pan-European significance. It was composed of dozens of Romanesque buildings, mostly mercantile houses. Some originally were components of the court compound; others were lined up to form streets. At this time the banks of the Vltava River were spanned by the first stone bridge, Judith Bridge, which represented the most demanding construction work of the early Middle Ages.

The striking atmosphere of Romanesque construction was also created by decorative elements. When composing external facades, blind arcades, and bow-shaped friezes (such as at the convent basilica in Doksany), special attention was devoted to sculptural decoration of column capitals and window jambs, which were often carved with elaborate acacia and palm-leaf motifs. Good examples of this ornament are the castle palace in Olomouc and the crypt in Doksany. Geometric diamond and dentil motifs exploited the contrast of light and shadow, as did complicated braided patterns found at the mona-stery basilica in Ostrov u Davle. The greatest wealth of sculptural decoration was applied to the entrance portals and their archivolts. One of the most beautiful Ro-manesque portals in the Czech lands, pre-served in the late twelfth-century church of Saint Procopius in Záboří nad Labem, com-bines plant, animal, and linear decoration (fig. 26).

Human figural sculpture was at first exclu-sively related to architecture. The oldest relief of Christ and his apostles is from a mid-twelfth century tympanum on the church in Oldříš. It reflects a motif used on Byzantine ivory tiles and is characterized by a flat, strongly schematic, and linearly subdivided relief. The figures of the Czech patrons on the facade of the church in Jakub, influenced by French style before 1165, are unique because

26. Church of Saint Prokopius in Záboří nad Labem. Detail of the portal (3rd quarter of the 12th c.) in the southern hall.

of the depth of their relief. The thematic decoration of these sacred buildings reflected their religious and moral function. At a time when the great majority of the population was illiterate, the Christian symbolism of the figures and scenes portrayed served as an intelligible and suggestive accompaniment to the spoken word, a sort of picture Bible.

In secular art, the sculptural decoration of the tower on the Lesser Town side of Judith Bridge, from around 1170, had a manifestly political goal. The two charac-ters portrayed, one of which was probably King Vladislav I, are among the best works of court art from that time. The oldest documented free-standing three-dimensional sculpture, called the Kouřim Lions, probably originally came from the church of Saint George at the Kouřim Castle and dates from the early thir-teenth century. The pedestal of this baptismal font or pulpit was conceived along the lines of a favorite theme, the sempiternal clash between the forces of good and evil, embodied in this case by roaring lions and winged monsters, either dragons or griffins.

Although Romanesque architecture and sculpture yielded to the Gothic style in the mid-thirteenth century, in painting the Romanesque endured until about 1300. The oldest example of an illuminated manuscript relating to the Czech environment is Gumpold's *Legend of Saint Wenceslas*, commissioned by Princess Emma before 1006. Produced in a German monastery, the manuscript is best known for its scene of the murder of Saint Wenceslas (fig. 2), which draws faithfully on the tenth-century Christianus legend. This Czech account tells a slightly different version of the stories of Saint Wenceslas and his grandmother Ludmila, patron saint of Bohemia and the first Christian martyr of the Czech lands. The peak work of medieval Romanesque manuscript illumination in terms of both content and artistic value is the *Vyšehrad Coronation Codex* (before 1085), which owes its origin to King Vratislav I. The remarkable works of Master Hildebert from the second quarter of the twelfth century include the oldest genre drawing, which captures the atmosphere of the medieval scriptorium with a surprising directness: while the master and his disciple are at work, a mouse gobbles up Hildebert's meal.

An interesting feature of early Czech paintings is the recurrence of themes relating to the patriotism of the time. The earliest depiction of the Czech nation appears in a pre-1200 illumination of Saint Augustine's *De Civitate Dei* depicting Heavenly Jerusalem: among the "chosen," Czechs can be identified by a banner and are symbolically represented in the persons of a bishop, a priest, a man, and a woman. The extraordinary cycle of wall paintings in the rotunda of Saint Catherine at the castle of the Přemyslid princes in Znojmo, dating from 1134, which captures the Přemyslid dynastic legend and genealogy, also has a pronounced political theme (fig. 27). The informational source for these paintings is Cosmas of Prague's *Bohemian Chronicle*, the first Czech history, written in Latin. The Znojmo cycle's enormous artistic value aside, the completely secular content of its paintings, relating to the Czech ruling dynasty and its roots, makes it of great European importance.

The minting of silver coins from the mid-950s exemplifies the Czech art of miniature coin pictures, which reached its peak on the denarii minted at the beginning of the twelfth century (see fig. 3, 4). Unusual in a pan-European sense is the depiction of a specific historic event, the coronation of Vladislav I in 1158.

The centuries of the early Middle Ages represent a long era in Czech fine arts. For the early periods, all that survives is archaeological material, which captures only one form of artistic expression—handcrafts—and only its most durable forms. The importation and interpenetration of style impulses and the search for individual expression are characteristic of the development in this region at this time, which had already achieved indisputable progress in applied arts and architecture by the time of the Great Moravian Empire. The true power of architectur-

al creation and of other artistic branches was attained during the Romanesque period, which culturally united Christian Western Europe. Given the church's role as primary patron of Romanesque art, the dominant ideological orientation of the works created is also made clear. In Přemyslid Bohemia, the Romanesque style was widespread by the twelfth century and reached a high level of quality. The distinctive value of Czech Romanesque art could, in a certain sense, be that certain works were not just works of art, but were also given deliberate political meanings. Architecture seems to have played the main role in the establishment of stylistic changes and influenced other fields of fine and applied art.

Vladimír Brych
HISTORICAL MUSEUM,
THE NATIONAL MUSEUM

27. The calling of Přemysl the ploughman to the princely throne, a wall painting from the rotunda of St. Catherine at the castle at Znojmo (1134). The princely dynasty of the Přemyslids took its name from this mythic figure.

Christianity in the Czech Lands

The Beginnings

The first mention of Christianity in Bohemia dates to 845, when fourteen Czech princes, probably the leaders of various tribes, were christened in Regensburg. The subsequent Christianization of the country meant that new places of worship had to be built, and by the end of the century Prince Spytihněv had the rotunda of Saint Peter built at the hill fort of Budeč. Ostensibly the earliest church building in the Czech lands, in both its dedication and its adherence to the Latin tradition it shows a possible Western influence, apparently that of the Regensburg mission.

In 863–864 Rostislav, the ruler of Great Moravia, invited Cyril and Methodius, two Byzantine monks and scholars from Thessalonika, to his land. The missionaries were the first to commit Old Slavonic to writing; Cyril developed the alphabet, named after him, that was used to record all Slavic languages. They translated fundamental ritual texts from Greek into Old Slavonic and introduced the Western liturgy in that language as well. Sites near present-day Mikulčice and Uherské Hradiště became the centers of the church in Great Moravia, and rotundas and basilicas were built. Methodius also christened the founder of the Přemyslid dynasty, Prince Bořivoj, and his wife, Ludmila. The royal couple founded the rotunda of Saint Clement at their fortified settlement of Levý Hradec. Pagan customs nonetheless survived among the common people; as late as 1092 Břetislav II of Bohemia issued a decree ordering the felling of groves and trees sacred to pagan ritual.

Early Patron Saints of Bohemia

The cult of saints since the early Christian era was widespread, and a number of "patron saints" were considered to have a special role in protecting the Czech lands. The most important was the pious prince Wenceslas (Václav) who ruled

28. Three reliquary crosses found at Opočnice, eleventh or twelfth century. From top to bottom, a cross with a Greek inscription and the figure of Christ in relief, probably from Kievan Russia; two enameled crosses with the figure of Christ, possibly from the Meuse-Rhine region. The origins of these objects reflect the varying religious influences at work in Czech lands in the early Middle Ages. Cat. 14, 15, 16.

Bohemia from 924 to 935 and was murdered by his brother Boleslav. The idea of Saint Wenceslas as the eternal ruler and protector of Bohemia soon became interwoven with Czech history. Wenceslas's grandmother Ludmila, who was murdered in Tetín and buried in the abbey of Saint George in Prague Castle, was also considered an important saint for the Czech people.

In 973 Rome established a bishopric in Prague, whose fame was advanced by Adalbert (Vojtěch), the second bishop. He and Boleslav II founded the first Benedictine monastery in Bohemia at Břevnov in 993. Adalbert, known as the apostle of the Poles, Prussians, Magyars, and Czechs, was martyred while on a mission to the East Prussians in 997 and was buried in Polish Gniezno. He too was soon honored as a patron saint. His younger brother, Radim, became the first archbishop of Gniezno in 1000. In 1003 five Polish and Italian Benedictines, called the Five Saintly Brothers, were martyred and their bodies were brought to Gniezno. In 1039 the remains of Saint Adalbert, Saint Radim, and the Five Saintly Brothers were brought to Prague as booty by Břetislav I.

Several other Czechs were elevated to sainthood. These include Saint Procopius, who founded the abbey of Sázava as a center for the Slavonic liturgy; the Dominican lay sister, Zdislava of Lemberk, who cared for the sick, the poor, and the suffering; Agnes of Bohemia, who founded the order of Knights of the Red Star, as well as abbeys for the Poor Clares and Minorites in Prague; and Ivan, or John, a hermit who lived in Bohemia.

Abbeys as Places of Education and Charity in Bohemia

The spread of Christianity resulted in the establishment of numerous medieval abbeys. The bishop of Olomouc in Moravia, Jindřich Zdík, founded the first Premonstratensian monastery in Bohemia. In the twelfth and thirteenth centuries several knightly orders established centers in Prague and Bohemia: the Knights of Saint John (1159, later the Knights of Malta); the Knights of the Teutonic Order (after 1200); and the Knights Templar (1232). These orders had a dual purpose; they founded hospitals, and their members were trained to fight in the name of the Church.

Also in the thirteenth century, abbeys of mendicant and missionary orders, the Minorites and Dominicans, expanded across Bohemia. In 1231 Saint Agnes founded Na Františku, the first convent of the Poor Clares in Bohemia, which had a fine scriptorium that copied and illuminated numerous manuscripts. Later in the same century, the Cistercians rose in importance. With substantial land holdings donated by the king and the nobility, the Cistercians built large abbey complexes at Sedlec, Zlatá Koruna, Vyšší Brod, Žd'ár nad Sázavou, Předklášteří u Tišnova, and Hradiště nad Jizerou. Cistercian abbeys were built according to strict rules. No towers, stained glass, or other costly decoration were allowed.

Harmony between the Church and the State under Charles IV

The reign of Charles IV was marked by political strength and a blossoming of the arts in the Czech lands. Charles's archbishop, Arnošt of Pardubice, helped consolidate the growth in power and glory of Charles's reign. In 1344, while John of Luxembourg, Charles's father, was still on the throne, Pope Clement VI removed the Prague and Olomouc dioceses from the authority of the Mainz archbishopric and raised Prague to an archbishopric. Shortly after becoming archbishop, Arnošt consecrated the foundation stone for Saint Vitus Cathedral in the presence of John of Luxembourg and Charles (fig. 29). Charles would later designate it as the burial place of the kings of Bohemia. In 1347 Arnošt crowned Charles IV as king of Bohemia and Blanche of Valois as his queen in the basilica of Saint Vitus. The same year Charles founded the Carmelite monastery, Our Lady of the Snows, and brought Slavonic Benedictines to Prague for the Emauzy Abbey, where they renewed the Slavonic liturgy. The Ambrosians he brought to the Abbey by the Powder Tower introduced the Ambrosian rite, a non-Roman rite that had been developed by Saint Ambrose of Milan in the fourth century.

Charles IV and Arnošt made Prague into a "second Rome" by gathering a great quantity of relics of saints that, from 1352, were regularly shown with the imperial relics to assembled pilgrims in the Corpus Christi Chapel. Charles greatly revered the Czech patron saints. To the traditional group (Wenceslas, Vitus, Procopius, Adalbert, and Ludmila), he added the King of Burgundy, Sigismund. Wenceslas, on whose skull the crown of Bohemia was supposed constantly to rest, enjoyed the greatest honor. His reliquary crown (see fig. 10), which contains a thorn from Christ's crown of thorns, was considered the property of Saint Wenceslas for all time; rulers could only borrow it. The term "the Lands of the Czech Crown" or "of the Crown of Saint Wenceslas" became a term of constitutional law.

Among the most important of Charles's acts were the foundation of the abbey of Augustinian canons, Na Karlově, dedicated to Charlemagne, who was favored by Charles, and the construction of Karlštejn Castle with its superb Chapel of the Holy Rood (fig. 49). Designed for the protection of the crown jewels and the holiest relics of the empire, the chapel was decorated with frescos and 129 pictures of saints from the workshop of Master Theodoric.

It can generally be said that Charles's success in government was achieved by the harmony of secular and spiritual powers, but late in his reign this balance broke down. Archbishop Arnošt's efforts clashed with the fiscalism of the papal curia. In addition, at the very end of his life, the preachings of the Austrian Augustinian, Konrad Waldhauser, which pilloried all the shortcomings of the church, spread through the Czech lands. In 1364 Arnošt of Pardubice died, shortly after he had been considered for election as pope by certain cardinals. His successor, Jan Očko of Vlašim, was the papal legate for the bishoprics of Regensburg, Bamberg, and Meissen. In 1378 he was made a cardinal.

Waldhauser's "successor" in the reform movement was Jan Milíč of Kroměříž. He established the "Jerusalem," a refuge for "fallen women," in the Old Town of Prague. Milíč continued to criticize the church and crown; once, in a sermon given in the presence of the emperor, he called Charles IV the Antichrist. Shortly before

29. Cathedral of St. Vitus at Prague Castle. The cathedral, begun in 1344 and completed according to the original concept in the late 19th and early 20th centuries, is the most important church in the Czech lands.

Charles's death in 1378, the French cardinals refused to acknowledge the election of Urban VI as pope and elected an antipope, Clement VII. This papal schism opened the Church to criticism and fueled ideas of reform among members of the clergy.

Charles's son, Václav IV, succeeded to the throne of Bohemia, but he could not maintain the balance between church and state that his father had. After initial concord between the king and his archbishop Jan of Jenštejn, their disputes began to multiply and in 1393 came to a climax with the murder of the archbishop's vicar-general, John of Nepomuk, by the king's forces. The archbishop, who did not find support among the leaders of the church, fled to Rome, where he submitted a complaint to the pope about the king. He died in Rome before receiving a reply. Under Zbyněk of Hasenburk, archbishop from 1403 to 1411, this crisis deepened. At the head of the reform movement were several professors and students of the university, in particular Matěj of Janov and John Huss. Another sign of change was the translation of the entire Bible into Czech at the end of the fourteenth century. Several copies of this version have been preserved, including the Dresden-Leskovec Bible and the Olomouc Bible.

The Hussite movement and the Reformation

Disputes in the church, the selling of dispensations, payments for Church offices, and nepotism evoked justified criticism among the reformers. They became especially outspoken after the papal schism. The writings of the English reformer John Wycliffe and his followers, the Lollards, reached Bohemia and were avidly read at Charles University. In 1403, however, the university banned their public or private reading because of several ideas they contained that were considered heretical. These included doubt over the transubstantiation of the Eucharist; the concept of the Church body as made up of those who are predestined for salvation, not necessarily the clergy, with not the pope, but Christ himself at their head; denial of the existence of purgatory; rejection of the sacrament of confession; and questioning the hierarchical organization of the Church and rejecting monastic orders. The eschatological mood grew and showed itself in several ways throughout the Czech lands—in apocalyptic predictions of the arrival of the Antichrist and, in South Bohemia, through the powerful influence of Waldensianism, which advocated the rejection of violence, prohibition of the death penalty, and an emphasis on humility.

In Prague, at the Bethlehem Chapel where Huss was appointed administrator and preacher in 1402, the issue of the laity being able to take communion *sub utraque specie* (in both kinds—both as bread and wine) became a unifying belief for the reform movement. This thesis, called Utraquism, was given a theological justification by a friend and fellow scholar of Huss's, Jakoubek of Stříbro. The chalice became the symbol of the entire reform movement. Originally with the support of Archbishop Zbyněk, Huss began to criticize the church and the clergy from the pulpit and translated Wycliffe's writings into Czech. His violent attacks were received with hostility in Rome, and he was excommunicated in 1411 by the new pope John XXII. Three years later, abandoned by Zbyněk and with his followers under an interdict, Huss was invited to defend his opinions before a general Church Council in Constance. He went there with an accompanying letter from Václav's brother, the emperor Sigismund, in which he was promised safe-conduct and a hearing before the council. After one of the meetings he was arrested and, after several interrogations, was sentenced to death as an incorrigible heretic. He died at the stake on July 6, 1415. Jerome of Prague, another scholar of the reform movement, suffered a similar fate a year later.

Huss's pyre set alight an inextinguishable conflagration in Bohemia. The nobles of Bohemia and Moravia sent a letter of protest to Constance, and in Prague Huss's enemies were persecuted. Charles University confirmed the validity of taking communion in both kinds and declared Huss a holy martyr. In 1419 the violence reached a climax. The people of Prague, led by a Carmelite from Our Lady of the Snows, Jan Želivský, hurled counsellors of the New Town of Prague from the windows of their town hall and occupied abbeys and churches. Václav IV died at the start of the Hussite revolution (in August 1419).

The Hussites broke up into several factions, including a moderate group in Prague and the Táborites, a radical group that left Prague to found the new town of Tábor, where they intended to fulfill their desire for social equality and freedom of confession of God's word. The demands of the Prague Hussites and the Táborites were summed up in the "Four Articles of Prague": (1) Freedom to preach the word of God, (2) communion in both kinds, (3) poverty of the clergy and expropriation of Church property, and (4) punishment of mortal sins. The Táborites went still further. Their priests said mass in Czech, they taught women and children to read the Bible, they rejected vestments, pictures, and music in church, and considered fine clothes, dancing, and other luxuries to be mortal sins. A smaller group of radicals, of whom a leading member was Petr Chelčický, rejected the shedding of blood and appealed to Christ's love and his injunction not to judge and not to kill. Chelčický argued that Christians should not rule "by worldly law."

Within the kingdom two parties were clearly defined: those who took communion in one kind (the Catholics) and those who took it in both kinds (the Hussites). The Hussite sects had united under the famous Hussite warrior, Jan Žižka, in the war against the emperor Sigismund and the Catholics from 1419. The important clash at Domažlice in 1431, in which the Catholic forces fled on hearing the song of the Hussite army, led to the realization that no military solution could

30. Chalice, Sezimovo Ústí (near Tábor), before 1420. This simple earthenware chalice embodies the core beliefs of the Hussite religion: a congregation's right to partake of the Eucharist as both the body and blood of Christ and the rejection of ostentatious rituals and objects, focusing instead on the essential meaning of the liturgy. The chalice became the symbol of the Hussite movement. Cat. 32.

be reached, and the Hussites were invited to the Council of Basle. There the Hussites were represented by Prokop Holý and a priest, Jan Rokycana. In 1437 the Compact of Basle was ratified, which guaranteed that the Czechs could receive communion in both kinds.

In September 1448 George of Poděbrady seized Prague and in 1452 was elected administrator of the land. In 1451 Aeneas Silvius Piccolomini, later Pope Pius II, visited Prague. In his "History of Bohemia," he praised the level of education of the people of the country, suggesting that "in Bohemia every old woman knows the holy scriptures better than certain prelates in Rome." The adherents of Utraquism sent a mission to Constantinople in 1452 to propose the union of the Utraquists and the Orthodox, although this never came about.

In 1457 at Kunvald u Žamberka, the Czech Brotherhood or Unity of Brethren was founded. Its spiritual progenitor was Petr Chelčický, and its foundation was connected with the progressive decline of the Utraquist party. The core of this emerging Protestant reformed church was composed of Brother Řehoř and his friends. In 1467, at its first assembly in the village of Lhota u Rychnova the separation of the Brotherhood from the Catholic Church was completed. The Waldensian bishop Štěpán consecrated their first bishop, giving the new faith apostolic succession. The basic teaching of the Brotherhood was the authority of the scriptures resting on certain opinions of Chelčický, Huss, and the Táborites. From 1535, the formulation of their confession of faith was influenced by certain elements of Martin Luther's teaching. The development of printing allowed the Bible to reach more of the population; in 1475 the New Testament was published for the first time in Czech, and in 1488 the entire Bible appeared in Czech. In 1579 the Czech Brotherhood began to publish a superb Czech translation of the Bible known as the Kralice Bible (fig. 31).

In 1526 Ferdinand I of the Hapsburgs was elected king of Bohemia, and from that point to 1918, with only brief interruptions, the house of Hapsburg ruled the Czech Lands. At the start of his reign Ferdinand acted toward the Utraquists with forbearance. His reinforcement of central power caused revolt in 1547 among the nobility and towns. Shortly after putting down this unrest in 1548, Ferdinand issued a mandate against the Czech Brotherhood that closed down congregations of Brethren and banished the Brotherhood from the country. Some of those Brethren who resisted paid with their lives.

From 1545 to 1563 the Council of Trent reaffirmed the doctrines of the Catholic Church, with the goal of restoring the predominance of Catholicism in Europe and soon in Bohemia. The Compact of Basle was no longer considered binding, and many Utraquists adopted the teachings of Luther as Huss' successor, producing a trend called New Utraquism. Despite persecution, the Czech Brotherhood maintained its centers in the country, first at Litomyšl and then at Mladá Boleslav. Among the Czech Brotherhood, in whose theology elements of Calvinism began to dominate in the second half of the sixteenth century, important figures such as

31. Bible of Kralice, Kralice, Moravia, 1579. One of the most important books ever printed in the Czech language, the Kralice Bible was the first complete translation of the Bible from the original-language texts into a vernacular language. Translated by Unity of Brethren scholars and printed by a Unity of Brethren press, it served for several centuries as the basis for codifying the Czech language. Cat. 75.

Jan Blahoslav and Jan Augusta were active. At the end of the sixteenth century more than 85 percent of the population were members of the Old or New Utraquists. In 1555 the German Protestants and Catholics signed the Peace of Augsburg based on the unfortunate principle of *cuis regio, eius religio* (whose is the kingdom, his the religion). This meant that subjects must adopt the same faith as their ruler. Ferdinand, a devout Catholic, began to implement this principle in Bohemia by filling important leadership positions with Catholics.

The arrival of the Order of the Society of Jesus, or the Jesuits, had great influence on the renewal of Catholicism in the country from as early as 1556. The Jesuits first concentrated on education, and their pupils in following generations became fiery defenders of the Catholic faith. In 1561 a new archbishop of Prague, Antonín Brus of Mohelnice, was once again appointed. The right to appoint the archbishop was transferred from the papacy to the king of Bohemia. The Prague archbishops took up residence in a palace in the very shadow of Prague Castle. In 1564 the new archbishop declared a program of Catholic revival in the country. Three years later the Compact of Basle was removed from the state records. Driven onto the defensive, the Czech Estates, many of whom were Utraquists, requested Emperor Maximilian to allow the Augsburg Confession, the Lutheran confession of faith, in the Czech Lands. Their request was, however, dismissed. In 1575 representatives of the Lutherans, New Utraquists, and the Czech Brotherhood agreed on a "Czech Confession" (a compromise declaration of faith), but even this the emperor would not sign.

These disputes came to a head during the 1576–1612 reign of the art-loving

32. Chasuble, Central Europe, after 1500. The chasuble is an overgarment worn by a Catholic priest during the celebration of the Mass. The rich materials and elaborate embroidery and appliqué of this chasuble reflect the late Gothic idea that material richness and beauty mirrored the perfection of God's heavenly kingdom. Cat 51.

Rudolph II. Under his rule, a party of radical Catholics, closely connected with the Spanish court, came to power. In 1584 the papal nuncio Giovanni Francesco Bonhomini presented a program of re-Catholicization to the king; Rudolph, being lukewarm in religious matters, did not implement it. He did, however, order the closing of congregations of the Czech Brotherhood. The first serious clash was in 1609 when the Protestant Estates, under the leadership of Václav Budovec of Budov, elected directors from among their own ranks and began to gather an army. In fear, the emperor signed an imperial charter in which he allowed the Czech Confession and the occupation of the Lower Consistory. It granted even serfs in Bohemia the right to choose a different faith from that of their lord.

The Battle of White Mountain and Its Consequences

In 1618, the Utraquist Estates, angered at decrees closing Protestant congregations in Hroby and Broumov, broke into the Chancellery of the Czech Court in Prague Castle and hurled the hated Jaroslav Bořita of Martinice, Jáchym Slavata of Chlum and Košumberk, and his secretary Fabricio out of the window in what came to be known as the Prague Defenestration. This act sparked the beginning of the Thirty Years' War, which was to convulse the whole of Europe.

The Czech Estates deposed the Hapsburgs from the throne and drove the Jesuits from the country. They elected as their king Frederick, elector palatine, a Calvinist, but were defeated at the Battle of White Mountain near Prague in 1620. The Hapsburgs reoccupied the throne, executed rebels in Prague's Old Town Square, and declared Catholicism the state religion. Non-Catholics, including teacher and bishop of the Czech Brotherhood John Amos Comenius, were forced into exile. None of the results of the Battle of the White Mountain were changed by the 1648 Peace of Westphalia, which ended the Thirty Years' War and placed the Czech Lands in the Hapsburg sphere. The university was handed over to the returning Jesuits and renamed the Charles-Ferdinand University. Both established and newly arrived religious orders joined in the Counter-Reformation. Cults of the saints and the Virgin Mary were revived. As a votive offering for the end of the sufferings of the Thirty Years' War, a Marian column was raised in Prague on the Old Town Square, complete with a statue of the Immaculata (an iconic depiction of the Virgin Mary). Statues and pictures of medieval origin connected by legend with the glory days of Catholicism in the Czech Lands were honored, and the cult of

33. Interior of St. Nicholas Church in Prague's Lesser Town (1703–1751). Designed by Christof and Kilian Ignatz Dientzenhofer and built for the Jesuit order, this baroque church exemplifies the relationship between high artistic expression and the spiritual movement of the Catholic Church.

Czech patron saints, which combined patriotism with religious fervor, thrived. Catholic piety reached its peak with the beatification (1721) and subsequent canonization (1729) of John of Nepomuk, perhaps the most familiar of Czech saints. More bishoprics were founded: In 1655 at Litoměřice, in 1664 at Hradec Králové, and later, in 1785, at České Budějovice.

A second wave of persecution of non-Catholics began after 1700 and came to a climax in 1717 with the patent of the *zemský sněm* (the Diet of the Land) against non-Catholics. The last remnants of the Unity of Brethren found a refuge at the estates of Count Nicholas von Zinzendorf in Saxony. He was sympathetic to their cause and granted them permission to found their own community in nearby Bethelsdorf, which they called Herrnhut (Ochranov). Through Daniel A. Jablonský, episcopal consecration was passed to the Unity of Brethren in Herrnhut, thus continuing the tradition of the Czech Brotherhood. Zinzendorf became a member of the Brethren and was later consecrated as a bishop. Under his leadership, the Unity of Brethren became an international religion. He sent missions from the Brotherhood throughout the world, to England, Greenland, Labrador, Africa, and to the American colonies, where its adherents are known as Moravians. In his concept of the Tropus, Zinzendorf developed the idea that all forms of Christianity could contribute to recreating the kingdom of God on earth, and that they would be bound together by love of the Lamb, the symbol of Christ.

34. Monstrance, Moravia, 1789. The rich yet unified decoration of this monstrance, which held the consecrated host during special religious ceremonies, is typical of metalwork produced in the rococo period. Cat. 95.

The reforms of Emperor Joseph II

The waxing of rationalism in the second half of the eighteenth century had a strong effect on religious thought and observance. The number of religious holidays was progressively reduced, and the spiritual and material power of the Church was limited by the state. In 1773 Pope Clement XIV abolished the Society of Jesus, and its members were subsequently banished from the Czech lands. In the 1780s Joseph II disestablished abbeys that did not do educational or charity work and issued decrees against pilgrimages. Through a 1783 decree he established a general seminary for educating priests that was under state control. (This authority was returned to the archbishopric in 1790 under Leopold II). Joseph's most important decree, however, was the Patent of Tolerance, issued in 1781 (see cat. 107). This document legalized Lutheranism, Calvinism, and the Eastern Orthodox faith.

Religion in the Nineteenth and Twentieth Centuries

After the Napoleonic Wars, there was a renewal of pilgrimages and interest in religious life. The Redemptorist Clement Maria Hofbauer, who died in 1820, was canonized in 1909 for his activity in strengthening the church. From the beginning of the nineteenth century, many priests, including Josef Dobrovský and Stanislav Vydra, worked to support literary activities and arts relating to the the National Revival. The later nineteenth century saw the revival and formation of several Protestant sects. In 1870, the first Vatican Council declared the dogma of papal infallibility, leading to the formation of the Czech Old Catholic Church. In 1880 members of the Unity of Brethren came from Herrnhut to the Czech lands to renew the Czech Brotherhood there. At the end of the nineteenth century, as a result of the work of American missionaries in the Czech lands, the Free Reformed Church was established (renamed in 1918 the Brotherhood Church). In 1895 the preacher Jiří Novotný left the Free Reformed Church and founded the first Baptist congregation in Prague, the domestic branch of the Baptist World Alliance. The Baptists accepted Petr Chelčický's teachings and baptized only adults.

After the creation of an independent Czechoslovakia in 1918, the Czechoslovak Hussite Church broke away from the Catholic Church, taking with it around two million believers. During the four decades of Communist rule, all organized religions were persecuted. The abbeys were dissolved, and many priests were imprisoned or executed. In 1989 the head of the Catholic Church in Czechoslovakia, Cardinal František Tomášek, played an important role in the downfall of the Communist regime. In the post-communist era, all churches have been able to operate with greater freedom and have contributed a moral balance in the new democracy.

Jan Royt
CHARLES UNIVERSITY,
PRAGUE

The Cultural History of the Jews in the Czech Lands

Bohemia and Moravia long have been a cultural crossroads on which the civilizations of East and West clashed and mingled. Among the specific cultural groups that settled in the Czech lands and significantly influenced their character were the Jews.

Although archaeological evidence of the earliest Jewish settlement is lacking, Jewish traders probably entered Central Europe as early as the second century, following the A.D. 70 collapse of the Jewish state, to trade with the Celtic, German, and later Slavonic tribes there. The first direct evidence of the presence of Jews in Bohemia and Moravia comes from the ninth and tenth centuries, though only Cosmas of Prague's *Bohemian Chronicle* from the early twelfth century describes the status and activity of Jewish society within the Czech feudal state. Jews had settled mainly in Prague, where they participated in the development of domestic trade, crafts, and finance and were generally a part of the Czech milieu. This came to a brutal end at the time of the First Crusade (1096), with political and social changes in feudal society and the Roman Catholic Church's efforts to reinforce its role as a power in Europe over the course of the twelfth century. The segregation of Jews, declared officially in the Fourth Lateran Council in 1215, led to their expulsion from the centers of Christian towns and relegated them to a subordinate status. Czech Jews could not, however, be entirely isolated from the cultural mainstream of the Czech environment. In the Middle Ages, numerous towns in Bohemia and Moravia (for example Brno, Cheb, Kolín, Mikulov, Mladá Boleslav, Ostrava, Roudnice nad Labem, Tachov, and Teplice), had become centers of Jewish life, and in them important ghettos were established. The largest and most important center of Jewish culture and religious life through the centuries was Prague's Jewish Town, which came to be known as the "City and Mother of Israel."

The life of the community within the ghetto walls was regulated by a liturgical calendar based on the Torah (or Pentateuch) and codified by the Mishnah and the Halakic parts of the Talmud. These codified regulations defined the membership in the Jewish faith in the diaspora and became the foundation of community law-making. They included all aspects of relations between the individual and the collective and covered general religious rules of Judaism, ranging from prayers, the Sabbath, and annual festivals to intimate aspects of daily life such as ritual cleanliness, but they never became dogma. Instead, in the lands of the diaspora, commentators (*tosaphists*) worked to explain the enigmas of the Talmud and to attune Jews to the specific realities of life in their individual community. In the Czech lands, the first known commentators of the Talmud, such as Isaac ben Jacob ha-Laban and Isaac ben Mordechai, lived as early as the twelfth century. Abraham Isaac ben Moses spread the fame of the Talmudic School of Prague in the thirteenth century through his work *Or Zarua* (Diffused Light), which had annotations in Old Czech. The massacre of Prague Jews in 1389 and the social and political disturbances related to the Hussite revolution a few decades later stifled Jewish education. Jewish literature next flourished in the second half of the sixteenth century with the establishment of a Hebrew printing house that became a mainstay of Jewish religious life in the Czech Crown Lands. Supported by such important personalities as Mordechai Meisl, the favorite of Rudolph II, it became one of the most important in Europe and contributed to the general cosmopolitan character of the

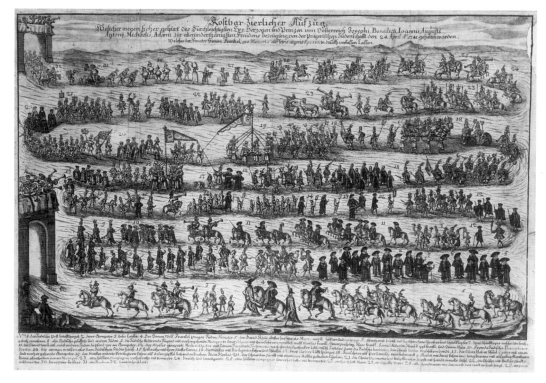

35. *Parade of Prague Jews, Prague, 1741. This engraving commemorates a procession by members of the Jewish community of Prague to honor the birth of Hapsburg archduke and prince Joseph, who later became Emperor Joseph II. A number of individuals are identified in the legend accompanying the print. Cat. 105.*

Prague Jewish community in the sixteenth and early seventeenth centuries. Its fame was spread by Rabbi Jehudah Loew, called Maharal (1520–1609), not only through the legend of the Golem, in which the rabbi brought a human figure of clay magically to life, but also through his profound theological, philosophical, social, and pedagogical knowledge that became the basis of his publications. In his teaching, he united traditional Judaism with Renaissance humanism and reached beyond the boundaries of the ghetto and the Jewish faith. Rabbi Loew, whose humanistic approach is comparable to that of John Amos Comenius, was the most important figure ever to have lived in Prague's Jewish Town.

In the seventeenth century, although Prague remained a center of Jewish culture and many important scholars worked there (such as Loew's successor and famous commentator of the Mishnah Jomtov Lipman Heler, and Italian Josef Salomon del Medigo), spiritual life and with it the literary output of the community stagnated, in part because of the Thirty Years' War. Soon afterward, Sabbatarianism and its Ashkenazi form, Frankism (named after its founder, Polish trader Jakob Frank), gained numerous adherents in Moravia and, to a lesser extent, Bohemia. Both movements, condemned by rabbinical tribunals as heresy and apostasy, were based on messianic ideas of Judaism and on mystical elements of the Cabala; both strove to explain the miserable situation of the Jewish population in the Hapsburg state during the Thirty Years' War. The Frankists paradoxically became a mass secret sect and found an adherent even in the person of Rabbi Jonatan Eybenschutz of Prague. Several Frankists penetrated the imperial Hapsburg court and influenced aristocratic circles with connections to Freemasonry. Despite the efforts of Prague's orthodox rabbis such as David Oppenheim, Ezechiel Landau, and Eleazer Fleckeles, who tried by their erudition to prevent the spread of Frankism and the associated enlightenment ideas, it proved impossible to stem new directions in thought and action.

The reforms of Joseph II, the influence of the French Revolution, the *haskalah* (Jewish enlightenment), and the mid-nineteenth-century abolition of the ghettos formed the basis for emancipation and assimilation of the new Czech Jewish and German Jewish cultures, a trend that continued until 1938. Along with emancipation and assimilation, which were strongly supported by Salomon Jehuda Rapoport, one of the last great rabbinical authorities of the nineteenth century and the cofounder of Jewish science, the era of traditional Jewish scholarship came to an end. New opportunities, however, opened up for a more profound penetration of Jewish feeling and for scholars to relive the historical experience of the "wandering Jew" in the context of Czech and German cultures in the second half of the nineteenth century and first half of the twentieth century. Artists such as Vojtěch Rakous, František Gellner, Richard Weiner, Karel Poláček, Jiří Langer, Otto Gutfreund, and Alfred Justitz, and authors such as Franz Kafka, Max Brod, Oskar Baum, and Franz Werfel explored Jewish mysticism, with its faith in humanity and its struggle for survival, and became prophets of the deep existential changes of the twentieth century.

Prague's Jewish Town was a monument to and a treasure house of the Jews' tangible heritage. An early nineteenth-century paper model by Antonín Langweil gives evidence today of its original form. Despite repeated onslaughts from the floods and fires to which the poorly situated Jewish Town often fell victim, the late nineteenth-century slum clearance that destroyed much of the old "Josefov" (the post-ghetto name for the Jewish Town), and the ravages of the Nazis (who, of all synagogues in the countries they occupied, spared those in Prague), several structures survive; they bear witness to Jewish history and exemplify the influence of mainstream Czech art on Jewish architecture.

The essential building of any Jewish community was the synagogue (from the Greek *sunagoge*, "place of assembly"). Although since ancient times it had been a place for common prayer and religious ceremonies, it differed markedly from Christian churches. As a rule, town synagogues were built among residences and were not distinguishable by their exterior appearance. Without decoration, towers, and bells, the synagogue did not evoke the awe of a Gothic cathedral or the mysticism of a baroque church; it called instead for a friendly gathering in the name of God. It also housed economic and judicial meetings.

The oldest Prague synagogue, the Old School, probably dates from the midtwelfth century but was rebuilt in the nineteenth century in a pseudo-Moorish style. The Old-New Synagogue (fig. 36), a Gothic building, has been preserved; it dates from the thirteenth century and today is the only example of a medieval twonaved synagogue in the Czech lands. The similarity of architectural details in this building to those of the Cistercian abbeys in South Bohemia and the Convent of Saint Agnes in Prague suggests that stonemasons from the same workshop worked on both Jewish and Christian buildings.

36. Old-New Synagogue in Prague's Old Town. Built at the end of the thirteenth century, this is one of the oldest preserved synagogues in Europe.

37. The Jewish cemetery in Prague's Old Town was the burial place for Jews from the fifteenth to the eighteenth centuries. The graves of many renowned figures can be identified here.

During the Renaissance, several interesting buildings were constructed in the ghetto. The High Synagogue together with the Jewish Town Hall was founded by Mordechai Meisl, mayor of the Jewish community in the second half of the sixteenth century. Originally the house of prayer for the town hall and the meeting hall of the rabbinical courts, the High Synagogue is remarkable for its richly decorated Renaissance vaulting. The Pinkas Synagogue was also built in the second half of the sixteenth century, but as a private house of prayer for the Horowitz rabbinical family of Prague. The Meisl family had a private synagogue built during the Renaissance that was renowned for the beauty of its interior. It burned at the end of the seventeenth century and was never renewed to its original state; it was subjected to radical renovation several times in the nineteenth century and took on its neo-Gothic form at the end of the nineteenth century. The Klaus Synagogue is unique. It was built at the end of the seventeenth century in an early baroque style on the site of three smaller, earlier buildings, called "klauses," that had served students as classrooms, places of prayer, and ritual baths. In the eighteenth century, it became the second most important synagogue in Prague after the Old-New Synagogue.

Prague's Jewish Town Hall, built in the sixteenth century at a time when the community was flourishing economically, burned down in the great ghetto fire at the end of the seventeenth century. It was restored in a baroque style and, after the mid-eighteenth century, underwent a fundamental renovation in the rococo style that it still exhibits. Since its founding, the town hall played an important role in the life of the community and took on the economic, judicial, and administrative authority of the synagogues.

Another notable monument of Prague's Jewish Town is the Old Jewish Cemetery (fig. 37). It was established in the first half of the fifteenth century and was used for burials until 1787. Its more than twenty thousand tombstones are a valuable resource for the study of the history and prominent figures of the Jewish community.

As well as important architectural monuments, valuable collections of Jewish artifacts are preserved in Prague. The first impulse for gathering these was the destruction of the Prague ghetto at the turn of the century. Under the management of M. S. Lieben, a Jewish museum was created to preserve objects of the Jewish past. Paradoxically, the collection was vastly extended during the catastrophic Nazi occupation. The Nazis collected all the valuables of 136 Jewish communities in Bohemia and Moravia, whose inhabitants they had transported to concentration camps, and stored them in Prague.

Liturgical items and family heirlooms are both evidence of the development of Jewish crafts and often the only witnesses to the history, culture, and life of the Jewish communities. The specific character of Jewish art stands out: it cannot be compared with the art of Christian churches, for example, because the emotional nature of Jewish art does not rest in the depiction of an ideal, but in the authentic reflection of the joys and woes of ordinary and festive days. The Jewish textiles, silver, porcelain, and other objects in the Jewish museum tell of the festivals, ceremonies, and religious expression of many generations (fig. 38). The collection of curtains *(parochet)* that covered the tabernacle *(Aron-ha-Kodesh)* in the synagogues, as well as the symbolic silver and textile decorations of the Torah—such as covers *(mé il)*, swaddling *(mappa)*, cover bosses *(tas)*, crowns *(kéter)*, winding rods *(rimonim)*, and reading pointers *(yad)*—bear witness to the rules of Jewish monotheism, the profound respect in which the rules were held, and their meshing with the lives of individuals and the community (fig. 39).

Liturgical life and family life were closely connected because the family is the basis of Judaism. The family circle was integral to the experience of the Sabbath and the chief holidays of the year, such as Passover, Shavuoth, and Sukkoth; important days, such as New Year's (Rosh Hashanah) and Yom Kippur; or festivals, such as Hanukkah and Purim. Table settings, silver candlesticks, festive textiles, fine Sabbath spice boxes, and many other gems tell of this. They are witnesses to the faith and hope of the thousand-year-old Jewish community of Bohemia and Moravia.

Lena Korba-Novotná

PARIS

38. Menorah, Bohemia, late eighteenth century. Designed to hold oil for burning during the eight days of Hanukkah, this menorah shows the figures of Moses and Aaron from the Old Testament and the six-pointed Star of David representing the Jewish people. Cat. 102.

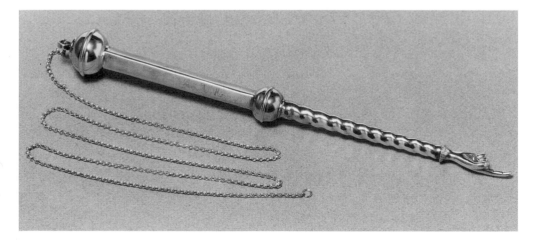

39. Torah pointer, Bohemia, late eighteenth century. Reading the Torah is an essential part of every Jewish religious gathering. Because the Torah scroll in a synagogue is treated as a sacred object, it can only be touched by a ceremonial pointer like this one, never with the hands. The pointer was made of a precious metal, often silver. Cat. 101.

Czech History in the Early Modern Period

The Estates Monarchy in the Hapsburg Era

The death of the young King Ludwík Jagello at the battle of Mohács on August 29, 1526, began a new era for the development of the Czech state. In autumn of the same year, the Czech Estates elected Ferdinand Hapsburg as their king, and the Estates of the neighboring Czech crown lands accepted him on the basis of the inheritance rights of his wife Anna, a daughter of Vladislav Jagello. Although Ferdinand I (1526–1564) promised to fulfill the numerous requests of the Estates, soon after his coronation he began to reinforce his sovereign power and create a centralist monarchy. His absolutist efforts met with resistance; the Estates had no intention of giving up their established privileges and opposed him by forming an alliance with the townships. Disagreements focused mostly around questions of money, especially tax collection, which was in the powers of the Estates Crown Diet, and on religious matters; while the majority of the Estates community was Utraquist, Ferdinand was an orthodox Catholic.

The conflicts came to a head in 1546–1547 in connection with a war waged by Ferdinand's brother Charles V, Holy Roman Emperor and king of Spain, against the Schmalkaldic League that had united Protestant princes throughout the empire. When without prior consultation Ferdinand called up the Crown army, the Estates refused to take part and martialed their own army against the monarch. They counted on the support of the neighboring Czech crown lands and of the Elector of Saxony, but the latter was defeated on April 24, 1547, by the Imperial forces at Mühlberg. The reprisals that followed included the execution of several people and the confiscation of Estate property; restrictions were also placed on the townships' autonomy, their privileges and rights to real estate were denied, and they were placed under the supervision of royal officers. In addition, a court of appeal with the power to reverse decisions of the municipal courts was

also established. Ferdinand, who became Holy Roman Emperor in 1556, later softened some of the measures. Although he took steps to re-establish Catholicism as the dominant religion by introducing the Jesuits to Prague in 1556 and reviving the Prague archbishopric in 1561, Ferdinand made one concession to the Utraquists in 1564 when he succeeded in persuading the Pope to accept the distribution of the Eucharist *sub utraque specie* (in both kinds) in Bohemia and Moravia.

Ferdinand was succeeded by his son Maximilian II (1564–1576) who, although not a strong monarch, expressed sympathy for non-Catholic denominations. The Estates took advantage of this in the end and tried to introduce their own religious program to resolve the complicated situation in the Czech lands: apart from the various Utraquist groups, there were significant groups of Lutherans and Brethren, and the Catholics had to be taken into consideration as well (the Old Utraquists retained many beliefs of the Catholic faith, while the New Utraquists adopted many principles of Lutheranism). The Lutherans, new Utraquists, and Unity of Brethren eventually agreed on a new confession of faith, the Bohemian Confession, to anchor religious tolerance, and at the 1575 Diet submitted it to Maximilian as a condition of their accepting his son Rudolph as the Czech king. Maximilian agreed verbally, but never confirmed it in writing. Faced with this inconclusive vic-

40. View of Prague, Cologne, 1572. This handsome copper engraving by Georg Höfnagel illustrates the city's beauty during the Renaissance period. The upper half shows Prague Castle; the lower, a panorama of the city from the north. Cat. 54.

41. Tolar of Rudolph II, Kutná Hora, 1588. This striking likeness of Emperor Rudolph II was the work of the Italian artist Antonio Abondio. Cat. 69.

tory, the Estates proceeded to elect fifteen "defensores" (defenders) to safeguard their religious freedoms. Thus unresolved, the religious question was to bring further problems in the future.

Rudolph II (r. 1576–1611), who had been brought up at the Catholic court of Spain, transferred his seat from Vienna to Prague in 1583. The move made Prague an important cultural center, attracting major artists and scholars. The city was drawn into an increasingly complex political situation, on both an international and a domestic level. The Turkish threat had increased, and the Hungarian Estates had to be guaranteed religious and political freedom in 1606; in Bohemia the highest offices passed into the hands of Catholic supporters (the "Spanish party"), and the Catholic party was reinforced in Moravia.

The resurgence of Catholic power brought about several changes: it opened the door to the Counter-Reformation and the persecution of Unity of Brethren members, strengthened the centralist and absolutist efforts of the monarchy, and weakened the position of the Estates. Gradually, the Estates formed a non-Catholic opposition. At the same time relations between Rudolph, whose declining mental state complicated his performance of government duties, and his brother Matthias became heated. Matthias was able to win the Austrian, Hungarian, and eventually the Moravian Estates to his side, and in 1608 achieved the Libeň peace, on the basis of which he took over the government of Hungary, Moravia, and the Austrian lands. Rudolph retained Bohemia, Upper and Lower Lusatia, and Silesia, but was required to accede to the requests of the Czech Estates who had remained loyal to him and to abandon his radical pro-Catholic policy. The Imperial Charter for Religious Freedom, issued on July 9, 1609, enforced the Bohemian Confession and guaranteed that no one would be forced to observe a religious faith against his or her will. To protect non-Catholic sects, a committee of thirty defenders was established, and the charter legally took effect despite the objections of the Lord High Chancellor Zdeněk Vojtěch Popel of Lobkovice. Rudolph II, whose authority had declined with the issuing of the charter, tried to retaliate by inviting the army of his relative, Bishop Leopold of Passau, to Bohemia. The rampage of the Passau units in Bohemia, especially in Prague, at the beginning of 1611 sparked strong resistance and eventually forced Rudolph to abdicate the throne to Matthias, whom the Estates then accepted as king.

The Battle of White Mountain

The reign of Matthias I (1611–1619) was marked by increased tension between Catholic nobles and their opposition, ultimately leading to the Estates Uprising. The actual hostilities commenced with the Prague Defenestration on May 23, 1618, when members of the Estates threw the unpopular vice-regents of King Matthias from the windows of their office in Prague Castle. (The king had relocated his seat to Vienna upon becoming Holy Roman Emperor in 1612.) The rebels elected a government of thirty Estate directors, recruited an army, and, at the general Diet of the Estates of all Czech Crown Lands in July 1619 after Matthias's death, declared the

42. Morion helmet, Central Europe, late sixteenth century. The morion, a visorless helmet with a ridged brim, was used in many European countries. The engraved decoration on the crown represents Mucius Scaevola, the mythological figure Perseus, and birds and angels. Cat. 66.

formation of a confederation. The Diet also forced Matthias's successor Ferdinand of Styria from the throne and chose a Calvinist, Frederick V, Elector Palatine (r. 1619–1620), as their monarch. In initial military clashes between the Imperial and the Estates armies, the Estates were successful, but later the relative numbers of the forces changed, leaving them at a disadvantage. In a final clash at White Mountain, near Prague, on November 8, 1620, the Imperial army devastated the Estates army (fig. 43). The new monarch, Ferdinand II (r. 1621–1637), launched a series of reprisals: many rebels were imprisoned, and twenty-seven Czech leaders were executed in Prague's Old Town Square. The property of other individuals was confiscated, and many fled the country to avoid punishment.

The defeat of the uprising and the repression that followed allowed Ferdinand to further push for centralization and re-Catholicization. He issued the Renewed Establishment of the Crown (1627 in Bohemia, 1628 in Moravia), which codified the inheritance rights of the Hapsburgs to the Czech throne, restricted both the authority of the Diet and the importance of the Czech offices, gave the German language equal standing with Czech, and made Catholicism the only permitted religion. Many non-Catholics, including the bishop of the Unity of Brethren and educator John Amos Comenius (fig. 44), emigrated rather than assume another faith.

The Czech hostilities of 1618–1620 also marked the beginning of the Thirty Years' War, a pan-European conflict that involved many Protestant princes and foreign powers and the Holy Roman Empire. The Czech lands suffered further under several armed clashes and military campaigns, especially the Swedish campaign in the late 1630s and the 1640s. The war was finally concluded by the Treaty

TAB. II. BOHEMORVM ACIEI Á CÆSAREANIS ET BAVARICIS DIE VII. NOU: AN. 1620. PROFLIGATÆ DELINEATIONEM EXHIBENS.

A. Nachtruck der völligen Keyserl: vnd Bayr: Armee vnd ledstes treffen.   B. Einnehmung der Schantzen.   C. Statt Prag.   D. Flucht der Vngarn.
E. der Böhmen Reutterei.   F. Böhmisch fußvolck.   G. Thiergarten.   H. Gr. vom Thurn Regiment so sich am langsten gewehrel.

43. The Battle of White Mountain on November 8, 1620. The battle, one of the most fatal battles in the history of the Czech nation, was depicted in a series of prints by J. Sadeler. Here we see the last phase, after the collapse of the Estates army while trying to defend access to the capital of the slopes of White Mountain. Prague is visible in the background.

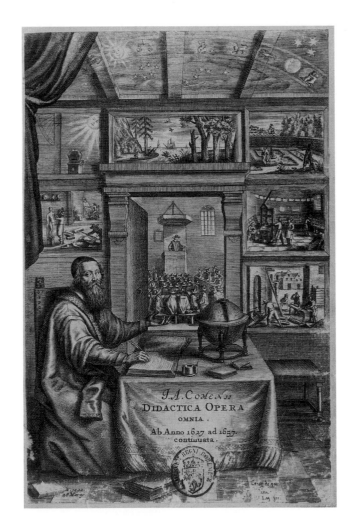

J. A. Comenii
DIDACTICA OPERA
OMNIA.
Ab Anno 1627 ad 1657.
continuata.

44. Title page from John Amos Comenius's Opera Didactica Magna. *Comenius, an important figure of the post-White Mountain era and bishop of the Unity of Brethren, was a scientist and world-renowned pedagogue. Engraving by David Loggan after Crispin de Passe.*

of Westphalia, signed on October 24, 1648, in Münster and Osnabrück. This treaty, which confirmed and reinforced Hapsburg power, was a disappointment; since it prohibited Protestant religions in the regions under the Hapsburg monarchy, it quashed Czech emigrants' hopes for return.

In Bohemia, the emperor's confiscation policy led to great changes in property ownership and allowed foreign nobles to establish themselves in important positions. The growing economic importance of the land-owning nobility increased the burden on the serfs, with predictable results. Widespread expressions of dissatisfaction and rebellion among the rural population, the greatest of them in northern and western Bohemia in 1680, led Leopold I (r. 1657–1705) to issue an imperial edict reforming serf relations.

The ascent of Charles VI (r. 1711–1740) to the throne signaled an end to reform and a return to a policy of absolutism. However, the abysmal state of the economy forced the emperor to attempt an economic revival, even as he strove to consolidate the dynasty's waning power. The wars of the Spanish succession had ended the Hapsburg claim on Spain, and since Charles VI had no male heirs, the monarchy's foreign policy was significantly influenced by the problem of succession. In 1713, he issued a Pragmatic Sanction that allowed the crown to pass to female descendants. Enacting this law required significant effort and several concessions, especially territorial. The monarchy was further weakened by military failures in the Balkans, where the Turks regained their lost positions. Within the Czech lands, the emperor further weakened the remains of the Estates monarchy (the Diet), lessened the position of the Czech nobility at court, and increased Counter-Reformation efforts by issuing several anti-reformist edicts and establishing severe punishments for heresy.

For the first time since the Thirty Years' War, the Catholic Church systematically worked to re-establish the Catholic faith. It engaged in missionary activity, provided an adequate number of Catholic priests to serve the parishes, and founded new bishoprics. It placed a renewed emphasis on religious celebrations, attending mass, and the observance of the sacraments and holy days, and published Catholic literature. The church also encouraged respect for the saints; it developed the cult of Mary and in 1729 canonized a new saint, John of Nepomuk. The new baroque style played an important role in this development, not only in architecture and the fine arts, but also in music and literature.

Changes during the Period of Enlightened Absolutism

Charles VI's daughter, Maria Theresa (r. 1740–1780) was greeted by a number of problems when she ascended to the throne (fig. 45). Neighboring monarchs, led by Frederick II of Prussia and Charles Albrecht, Elector of Bavaria, were laying claim to the Austrian inheritance. By the end of 1740, the Prussian armies had marched into Silesia, in 1741 the Bavarian-French-Saxony army occupied Bohemia, and in the same year Charles Albrecht was accepted and crowned emperor as Charles VII.

Maria Theresa decided to conclude a disadvantageous peace with Prussia that involved the appreciable economic loss of most of Silesia and all of Klodzko. She then settled with her Bavarian opponent and in 1743 had herself crowned in Prague. She was recognized as the queen of the Austro-Hungarian Empire, and upon Charles VII's death in 1745, her husband Francis of Lorraine was crowned emperor. Conflicts with Prussia reoccurred, however, in 1744 and above all in the Seven Years' War (1756–1763). During this conflict Prussian military units came within a stone's throw of Prague, and the Austrian monarchy suffered the definitive loss of industrially developed Silesia.

The situation of the Czech state was not reassuring. Maria Theresa adopted a policy of enlightened absolutism in various areas of political and economic life, bringing about a number of reforms that strengthened the centralized monarchy. The initial changes involved the state administration. In 1749, the highest authority of the Czech and Austrian state, the Court Chancellery, was abolished and replaced by new joint offices for both countries that combined their political and financial agendas, while the court administration was organized independently. This represented a fundamental shift in the legal position of the Czech crown lands within the framework of the Hapsburg monarchy. In addition, other institutions were reorganized or created, regional authorities were re-established, and even tax collection was reorganized under a new framework, the Theresian Land Registry. A new currency was introduced, together with a new system of measurements and a united customs tariff system. A new criminal code was implemented, and the

45. *Mart. Tyroff,* Coronation Parade of Maria Theresa as Czech monarch, *Prague, 1743. The coronation procession is making its way through Prague, entering Charles Bridge on the way to the castle. The print shows both Gothic (Old Town Bridge Tower) and baroque (the Church of St. Francis and the Jesuit college of the Clementium) structures.*

court system was reformed. The development of industrial commerce also received increased attention.

Educational reforms supplemented the existing isolated schools with a network of primary schools throughout the countryside, providing basic education to a broader segment of the population. In 1773, the Jesuit order was driven out of the Austro-Hungarian Empire. One important problem that remained was the legal and social standing of the serfs, whose poverty and large payment obligations had led to low, unsatisfactory agricultural production. Unrest among serfs peaked with the peasants' revolts of 1775, which affected almost the entire Bohemian territory and led to the issuing of a new edict regulating serfs' duties (see cat. 106). The final solution to these problems remained a task for Joseph, Maria Theresa's son and successor, who had been emperor and co-ruler with his mother since 1765.

After Maria Theresa's death in 1780, Joseph II (1780–1790) sought a fundamental solution to the serf question and in November 1781 issued a decree abolishing serfdom. This allowed serfs to marry, to move, and to have their children educated without the permission of the lord; it represented a significant transformation in serfs' legal standing, but not their duties. He next established the Joseph's Land Register to keep track of land ownership. He also announced tax and urban reforms that changed the existing work system into a salaried pay structure and significantly reduced the tax burden on serfs. Because of the nobility's resistance to these changes, however, they were abolished after Joseph II's death.

Joseph's second important step was the issuing of the Edict of Tolerance in October 1781, officially recognizing the Lutheran, Calvinist, and Eastern Orthodox faiths. For economic and strategic reasons, members of these faiths had been tolerated in the developing industrial sector and in the army, but the edict gave them the freedom to worship openly (fig. 46, cat. 107).

Joseph II carried out other reforms affecting many areas of public life, which did not always receive unanimous support. However, during his reign scientific and literary exploration flourished. The blossoming of enlightenment ideas under Maria Theresa and Joseph had a beneficial influence on the development of the Hapsburg state.

Marie Ryantová

HISTORICAL MUSEUM,
THE NATIONAL MUSEUM

46. "Tollerance" tobacco box, Bohemia, after 1782. The figures on this tobacco or snuff box, a Lutheran, a Calvinist, and a Catholic bishop, represent the freedom of confession granted by Joseph II's 1781 Edict of Tolerance. Cat. 108.

Fine Art from the Thirteenth to the Nineteenth Centuries

Gothic Architecture and Art in the Czech Lands

In the thirteenth century, political and economic growth stimulated the development of the Gothic style in the Czech lands, which after a century's development in its native France was at its zenith. An important mediator of this new style was the Cistercian order; with the help of the Přemyslid dynasty, it founded numerous abbeys. The simplicity of Cistercian architecture determined many characteristics of the Czech Gothic style for the remainder of the thirteenth century. Buildings of this strict, well-organized order are distinguished from the Gothic style of most French cathedrals by their lack of vertical emphasis, restrained use of ornamentation, and emphasis on unadorned wall areas. Interior spaces are harmoniously composed by the rhythm of simple piers, arcades, and robust elements—piers, ribs, transverse ribs, and load-bearing diagonal vaulting. Unlike the French cathedral Gothic, Cistercian basilicas had no complex external system of flying buttresses and towers. One of the most refined examples of Cistercian architecture is the c. 1240 Capitulary Hall in the northern Bohemian abbey of Osek (fig. 47).

The thirteenth century was also marked by the development of towns, where the Gothic style was connected with the work of the mendicant and preaching orders, the Franciscans and Dominicans. In the 1230s, the Order of Poor Clares founded an abbey in Prague where the churches of Saint Francis (1240–1250) and Saint Salvator (c. 1285) were built. In the town of Jihlava, the Dominican and parish churches (post-1250) were important for the development of a triple-nave hall-church with nave and aisles of the same height. Cistercian architecture began to influence the form of other structures, including the Old-New Synagogue in

Prague (c. 1290), several town houses, and royal castles at Písek, Zvíkov, and Bezděz.

In the second half of the thirteenth century, elements of high Gothic appeared in regional architecture. In Kolín at the church of Saint Bartholomew (post-1270), a pair of high towers and flying buttresses were used apparently for the first time in the Czech lands. At the end of the century, high Gothic characteristics became more pronounced, with an increased emphasis on verticality. Walls were perforated by large windows decorated with ever more complex tracery. The fragile piers and ribs holding up the heightened vaulting were made substantially more slender and lost their round form. Piers in the walls were transformed into ribs without the interruption of capitals, and previously lively, realistic foliate decoration became schematic. These tendencies are apparent in Cistercian abbeys at Zlatá Koruna, Vyšší Brod, and Sedlec, built with the support of Václav II.

The fourteenth-century attempt at unifying the internal space of buildings further neutralized the mass of the walls and structural components, and often filled the hall spaces with diffused light. This was a departure from the basilica style, which had a raised central nave that put to use the contrast of light and shadow.

Sculpture dating from the first half of the fourteenth century was also influenced by this high Gothic trend. It is marked by a calligraphic style, in which plasticity is repressed and rhythm is imparted by shallow cuts that organize the surface yet do not reflect the internal movement of the figure. Examples of this linear concept include the Přemyslid cross, a mystical crucifix of exaggerated sensuality; the Pietà of Jihlava; and a group of Madonnas that probably came from a sculptor's workshop in Brno. In painting, the Passional of Abbess Cunigunde, an illuminated manuscript from 1313–1321, is a masterpiece of this style.

47. Capitulary Hall in Osek Monastery, 1240. This room, where monks met for readings and discussion, is one of the best examples of Cistercian architecture in the Czech lands. Its style was influenced by Cistercian architecture in Burgundy.

48. Interior of the Chapel of the Holy Rood at Karlštejn Castle. The chapel's gilded ceiling with ruby glass stars, the series of panel paintings of Jesus and the saints, the wall frescoes, and the stone-inlaid walls all combine to produce the impression of a "heavenly Jerusalem."

A general blossoming of culture occurred during the reign of Charles IV (1346–1378), king of Bohemia and Holy Roman Emperor. This gifted and energetic ruler, who had lived at the French royal court and had traveled in Italy, established close diplomatic relations with Germany, Italy, France, and England that ensured rapid exchange of the latest artistic trends. He commissioned work from artists of exceptional skill. The greatest development occurred in Prague, which, as the new imperial metropolis, gained an unprecedented prestige. Prague's New Town was laid out according to a grand plan, and many fabulous examples of architecture were built there. Other parts of the city were significantly extended, making Prague one of the largest towns in the world. The banks of the Vltava River, which flows through the center of the city, were connected by a new stone bridge with stately tower gates at either end. Prague Castle underwent an extensive renovation. The cathedral of Saint Vitus was rebuilt in the Gothic style, which in its dimensions and artistic decoration exceeded all that had yet been seen in the Czech lands. French architect Matthias of Arras designed and built a long choir and a ring of polygonal chapels rising to the height of the triforium in the manner of the southern French cathedrals of Narbonne, Rodez, and Toulouse. After Matthias's death, the work continued from 1356 under the young German architect Peter Parler, who finished some of the cathedral's chapels and built new ones, including the particularly fine chapel of Saint Wenceslas; he also built the upper story of the central nave, which is surmounted by technically and artistically perfect vaulting with a network of intermeshed ribs. Parler's work, in contrast to Matthias's linear approach, is characterized by the sculptural development of elements and by clearly conceived forms (fig. 29).

The sculpture of Saint Vitus Cathedral in the 1370s and 1380s is marked by a move from linearity toward plasticity and increased volume, as the tombs of the Přemyslid kings in the chapels and a series of portrait busts in the triforium demonstrate (fig. 9). Figures are characterized by the relation of inner form to movement of drapery; their depiction is marked by a certain realism. This tendency, which was also evident in fourteenth-century philosophy, reflects an interest in illustrating how the visible world reflects higher truths.

Karlštejn Castle (1348–1357) occupies a unique place in the art of Charles IV's time. It was built as a repository of royal and imperial crown jewels and holy relics, which Charles sought and collected passionately. The architecture of the castle and its lavish interior decoration correspond to its importance. In the Chapel of the Holy Rood, the rich surface treatment, the wall paintings, and the unique cycle of 129 panel paintings by Master Theodoric and his workshop in the 1360s turn the room itself into a giant reliquary and an earthly evocation of the heavenly Jerusalem (fig. 48).

After the death of Charles IV in 1378, court patronage declined; the interests of various groups or individuals led to a plurality in artistic concepts and to a certain mannerism. A renewed tendency toward emotionality also appeared in fine art, connected with the current of new piety (*devotio moderna*) aimed at the internalizing of spiritual life, and with the Czech religious reform movement.

In architecture, a spiritual aesthetic created new possibilities for enclosed spaces. Hall churches were designed with attention to unity and harmony that could facilitate contact between the congregation and the priest in the pulpit. Elements that would distract worshippers from prayer, such as wall paintings, decorated capitals, and sculptures, were eliminated. The idealized spirituality of these buildings was woven into their geometry; these churches were frequently built on a square or multiple-square plan. Their walls are made up of large, uninterrupted areas, and the vaults are borne on cylindrical columns so slender they give the impression of fragility. A further step toward unified space was achieved by double-naved plans, in which the central axis has only one row of piers or even a single pier; examples of this include the Augustinian church (post–1380) in Třeboň and the church of Saint Vitus (pre–1400) in Soběslav (fig. 49). Around 1400, interest in the artistic design of vaulting was inspired by Saint Vitus Cathedral in Prague.

49. Interior of St. Vitus Church in Soběslav (pre-1400). One of the best examples of the hall church style, a typical form in the Czech region. It differed from Gothic cathedrals in that the intention of the architect was to build a united space with regularly diffused light and a lack of surface decoration or wall texture and other decorated architectural elements. Such a space was suitable for preaching and praying; it offered a peaceful space for contemplation.

Around the same time, a deepening sense of social and spiritual crisis led to both a reform movement condemning the existing social order and a self-imposed isolation on the part of the court circle, which created its own ideal world. Within this milieu the "beautiful style" of art was developed, the Czech counterpart of the European international style. The beautiful style was distinguished by an extreme aestheticism that promoted the creation of lyrical works and stressed absolute beauty. Characteristic examples include statues of the Madonna that possess fragility of form, subtlety of proportions, an ethereal sweetness in the depiction of parts of the body (especially faces and hands), and finely executed detail, particularly in clothing. Shortly before the Hussite wars (1429), the Master of the Týn Calvary abandoned the beautiful style in favor of expressive, sharply realistic elements, a shift that influenced Czech sculpture for half a century.

In painting, the lyrical and poetical spiritualizing tendency appeared earlier than in sculpture. The most important representative of this current is an anonymous artist known as the Master of the Altar of Třeboň, whose three remarkable panel paintings from an altar group for the Augustinian church in Třeboň (c. 1380) depict Christ on the Mount of Olives, the entombment of Christ, and the Resurrection on the front side, and pictures of saints on the reverse. In each, the artist used realism to convey the psychological state of the men and women depicted, particularly the minor characters, but relied on a certain unstable fragility to

50. Panel painting, Ecce Homo, *Bohemia, c. 1450. In its depiction of the human figure and the use of gestures to convey emotion, this panel painting reflects the style of the late Gothic. Cat. 50.*

express the spirituality of Christ. His use of colors to achieve soft, sensitive modeling of forms also distinguishes this artist from his predecessors. Transitions from shadow to golden light have the character of chiaroscuro.

Bohemia played an important role in the cultural development of Europe and influenced the art of neighboring countries in the fourteenth century and the first quarter of the fifteenth century, but this cultural ascendancy was halted by the Hussite revolution, during which many works of art were destroyed.

After the mid-fifteenth century, construction began anew under the influence of Austria and Bavaria. The climax of Gothic vaulting, an intermeshing of ribs known as a cellar vault or diamond vault, was introduced from Saxony. Sculpture from this period was based on the domestic, pre-Hussite tradition and drew on both Parler's work and the beautiful style. The realistic art of the Low Countries, introduced to Central Europe by followers of Nicolaus Gerhaert, became increasingly influential (fig. 51). In the final phase of development of Gothic sculpture in the Czech lands, the 1500–1510 work of the Master of the Žebrák Lamentation, and in Moravia the work of Gerhaert's successor, Anton Pilgram, distinguished by strongly realistic elements, are important.

Painting was influenced for a long time by the beautiful style. Elements of late Gothic art also appeared: figures became more solid and rested on a more realistic base, sharply folded drapery gained a plastic form, and the range of colors and hues increased. The Master of the Litoměřice Altarpiece (post-1500), classified as a member of the Danube School, exemplified the close of Gothic painting in the Czech lands. He concentrated on the structure and geometry of the composition rather than on descriptive details. Pictures by this master possess the expressiveness of the Middle Ages and the reflection of perceived experience of late Gothic style, as well as the intellectualized approach to composition typical of the Renaissance.

Renaissance Influences in Czech Art

The Italian Renaissance pervaded Central Europe in various ways in the last quarter of the fifteenth century. While many Italian masters worked north of the Alps, individual Central European artists also traveled to Italy. Various works of art, graphic models, and books that were imported to Central Europe from Italy influenced the sensibilities of local artists and patrons. In court circles, an exag-

51. Madonna and Child, Southwest Bohemia, before 1500. The dynamic energy of this statue's drapery, with the calm beauty of the facial features of mother and child, makes this one of the finest late fifteenth-century madonnas produced in Bohemia.

53. *Vladislav Hall in Prague Castle (1493–1502). This knight's hall, designed by architect Benedikt Ried for King Vladislav Jagello, was one of the largest secular spaces of its day. It is remarkable for the combination of dynamic late gothic vaulting supported by circular ribbons and early Renaissance windows.*

52. *Candleholder, central Europe, fifteenth century. This candleholder is in the shape of a torchbearer dressed like an aristocratic dandy of the late fourteeth or early fifteenth century. Cat. 41.*

gerated sense of spirituality was gradually supplemented by an interest in empiricism.

Renaissance elements in the arts were introduced to the Czech lands in Moravia through the Budapest court of Matthias Corvinus and first influenced decorative elements of medieval Moravian castle architecture at Tovačov (c. 1492) and Moravská Třebová (c. 1495). The earliest penetration of the Renaissance into Bohemia is connected with the reign of Vladislav Jagello, who succeeded Matthias to the Hungarian throne in 1490. Vladislav ordered another extensive rebuilding of Prague Castle; the knights' hall (1493–1502), built under the direction of architect Benedikt Ried, was one of the largest secular interiors of its time in Europe (fig. 53). Its dynamically formed space, whose insubstantial vaulting is supported by a maelstrom of spiraling ribbing, is balanced by the static calm of its Renaissance features such as large tripartite windows and portals.

At the beginning of the sixteenth century, Renaissance masonry features appear more frequently. Portals begin to be topped with a semicircular arch, flanked by columns or pilasters at the sides that in turn are topped by a straight lintel. Later a tympanum might be added. This formal composition, as well as newly conceived ornamental motifs, was used in other areas of fine and applied art.

Monumental painting of the period begins to exhibit a formal calm, supple-

54. Belvedere designed by Paolo della Stella and Boniface Wohlmut (built 1538–1557). The summer house, ordered by Czech King Ferdinand I for his wife, was one of the purest examples of the Italian Renaissance style. The characteristic arcade open to a garden, though common in Renaissance Italy, was unusual and new for Prague.

menting the tension of the late Gothic style, as is apparent in the decoration of several chapels of Saint Barbara in Kutná Hora or in the Saint Wenceslas Cycle in the chapel in Saint Vitus Cathedral in Prague (pre-1509). Renaissance perspective and proportion found a voice, but in many areas, until the sixteenth century they were confronted by and often subordinated to a stronger Gothic tradition. Panel paintings for altarpieces were the dominant art form, later to be replaced by painted epitaphs. In sculpture, epitaphs made of sandstone, argillite, or red marble also became prevalent. While these were generally produced in a craft rather than an artistic tradition, they possess a sense of dignity and balance (cat. 70).

A massive influx of Renaissance art to the Czech lands followed the 1526 arrival of the Hapsburgs, whose broad cultural vision and humanist education made them important collectors and patrons. They initiated the construction of the most refined structures of the Czech Renaissance, such as the royal summerhouse built in the 1530s in the newly founded Italian garden near Prague Castle (fig. 54), and the 1567–1569 "Jeu de Pomme" (ball court) by architect Boniface Wohlmut.

In 1551, many representatives of Bohemian and Moravian aristocratic families traveled to Genoa and other towns of northern Italy to welcome King Maximilian of Bohemia and his wife, Maria of Castile, on their arrival from Spain. Their stay

55. *Renaissance town houses in Slavonice. Note the sgraffito decoration on the surfaces of the burgher houses in this Southeast Bohemian town.*

in Italy influenced these aristocrats' tastes in art and architecture, and a boom in the building trade, on the part of nobles and burghers alike, followed. Among the important examples of local architecture in the second half of the sixteenth century are the castles of Nelahozeves, Pardubice, Opočno, Horšovský Týn, Náměšť nad Oslavou, Litomyšl, Telč, Moravský Krumlov, and Bučovice. Fashionable Italian gardens were established near several castles. The Renaissance also influenced the appearance of particular houses and sections of the towns of Prague, Plzeň, Slavonice, Český Krumlov, Telč, Nové Město nad Metují, Chrudim, and Olomouc.

Building facades were often decorated with sgraffito, a graphic technique in which the drawn motif is carved into two layers of dark and light plaster (fig. 55). Frescos gained a new character; they changed not only their form but also their themes. In addition to biblical themes, allegories and scenes drawn from classical literary sources such as Ovid's *Metamorphoses* became popular.

Interior decoration was differently conceived, emphasizing the artistic treatment of ceilings with paintings, stucco, or carved wood panels. Doors and furniture (chests and cupboards) were decorated with inlay. Colorful tiled stoves became popular (fig. 56). Local and imported collections of art and decorative objects furnished both castles and palaces.

Although the Czech Renaissance lacked the heroic élan of Italy, it closed on the

exuberant note of mannerism. In the 1580s, for political and personal reasons, Rudolph II moved with his entire court from Vienna to Prague. The art-loving ruler, one of the greatest patrons of all time, gathered in Prague gigantic collections of art that included works by Titian, Correggio, Parmigiano, Bassano, Bruegel, Bosch, Dürer, and others. He also attracted artists from all parts of Europe, including painters Bartolomaeus Spranger, Joseph Heintz, and Hans von Aachen, and sculptor Adrian de Vries. Throughout the city, the many artists and craftsmen working in varied fields made Prague the artistic metropolis of Europe.

The Rise of the Baroque

The political and religious crisis that grew into the Thirty Years' War precipitated a general cultural decline. Many artists left Prague. Rudolph's collections were dispersed, with the greatest losses occurring during the 1648 looting of Prague by the Swedish army. Yet cultural developments in the Czech lands did not stand still. The new political situation brought new obligations. The Catholic Church and Catholic nobility appointed by the emperor became patrons who extracted vast property from the state. Baroque art, although based on the same sources of inspiration as the Renaissance, carried a new ideological charge. It extravagantly conveyed the strength of the victory that the Catholic Church and Catholic nobility

56. Stove tiles of a nobleman and noblewoman, Opočno, Bohemia, 1538. In the Renaissance, the original designs of stove and floor tiles gave way to imported motifs that spread across Central Europe. So-called noble tiles, with high-born men or women framed by architectural elements, were popular. The multicolored glazing was also a change from the monochromatic tiles of the medieval period. Cat. 59, 60.

57. *Decorated beakers, Bohemia, mid-eighteenth century. In the eighteenth century, Bohemia was famous for its beautiful crystal and glass products. These beakers are examples of the Zwischengoldglas technique, whereby a design in gold foil is sandwiched between two layers of glass. Cat. 136, 137.*

had won. While initially it was characterized by a certain brutality and ruthlessness, it gradually acquired more cultivated features.

Baroque decoration appears in all areas of fine and applied art. It is marked by a striving for the maximum illusory and organic connection between various fields of art in a single object. Some excellent examples of baroque richness can be seen not only in architecture, but in interior design and decorative arts as well. The architecture of churches, palaces, and castles was complemented by sculpture, frescos, paintings, stucco, furniture, wall hangings, wallpaper, embroidery, glass (fig. 57), art collections, rhetoric and music, and even perfumes. In contrast to the intellectual principle of the Renaissance, baroque art appealed to the senses. This lasted from the seventeenth through the eighteenth century, although over time refinement, delicate playfulness, and a picturesque quality came to replace monumentality.

In the seventeenth century, many Italian master craftsmen came to work in the Czech lands, particularly builders and masons from the north Italian Lake District; some of them settled permanently. During the building activity at the end of the Thirty Years' War, the Society of Jesus—which on the one hand was connected with the Counter-Reformation in the Czech lands and on the other brought a new level of culture and education—commissioned builder Carlo Lurago to construct religious houses and churches similar in character to Il Gesu, the Jesuit church in Rome. Francesco Carrati, who was influenced by the work of Palladio, was involved with the construction of Černín Palace. A third important builder was the Italian-trained Frenchman, John-Baptiste Mathey. The sensitivity with which this architect composed the wall surfaces and the mass of his poised and refined buildings prefigured the subsequent trend in Czech architecture. The artistic quality of Mathey's work is best illustrated by the church of the Knights of the Cross in Prague Old Town, and in the castle of Troja near Prague. Among the Italian architects working in seventeenth-century Moravia was Imperial engineer Giovanni Pietro Tencalla, whose vast and varied, albeit conservative work made an important contribution to baroque art in that region.

Czech painting was also influenced by Italian art. Karel Škréta, the most important Czech artist of the seventeenth century, spent several years in Italy, becoming conversant with several schools of painting. He produced numerous religious pictures, portraits, and sketches for graphics. Škréta's chef d'oeuvre is the meditatively conceived passion cycle executed toward the end of his life for the church of Saint Nicholas in Prague Lesser Town. One of his successors, Jan Jiří Heintsch of Silesia, lacked Škréta's invention and masterful ability in more complex composition, but was able to draw on Škréta's baroque realism in direct, sensitive religious scenes and portraits (see cat. 83). The work of another, Amsterdam- and Antwerp-trained artist Michael Leopold Willmann of East Prussia, was also important for the development of Czech baroque art.

The creation of a new iconography of saints spawned new cultural forms, such as Marian and plague columns. The most widely used materials for Czech baroque sculpture were sandstone (exterior) and wood (interior), generally polychromed. Around the mid-seventeenth century, sculpture exhibited a more realistic robustness and a rhetorical cogency of gestures and emotional engagement, as a figure of a Jesuit saint illustrates (see cat. 89). The influence of Roman baroque sculpture, exemplified by Bernini, also increased, mediated through the work of Jan Jiří Bendel, a South German sculptor in Prague.

As it developed in the last decade of the seventeenth century, high baroque was so assimilated in the local environment that it lost its foreignness and began to be shaped by local impulses. It was also supported by an improving economic situation. New artistic tendencies were reflected strongly in architecture; the influence of Bernini, Borromini, and Guarini was of great importance in the creation of Czech high baroque architecture, as was a Viennese group, represented by Johann Bernhard Fischer of Erlach, Domenico Martinelli, and Johann Lucas Hildebrandt, that passed on certain Italian ideas of classicist monumentality and elegance, illusory decorative features, and the composition of space.

The artist Christof Dientzenhofer, who came to Bohemia from Bavaria around 1676, designed and built a group of radically original churches that in their bravura mastery of proportions and in their dynamically created spaces surpass their Italian models. They were built on a complex plan of interpenetrating ovals and other shapes, defined by smoothly undulating walls and by systems of vaulting that give the illusion of movement. Dientzenhofer built the Church of the Epiphany in Smiřice, Saint Joseph in Obořiště, Saint Clare in Cheb, Saint Margaret in Břevnov,

58. Cherub, Bohemia, c. 1720. Small painted statues of cherubs were frequently used in decorating baroque churches. Cat. 90.

59. Church of St. John of Nepomuk on the Rock in Prague's New Town, designed by Kilian Ignatz Dientzenhofer and built from 1730–1739. In the eighteenth century churches began to be not only monumental but also sensitive to the scale of their urban surroundings. Monumentality was achieved not by size, but by the use of stylistic elements.

and the nave of Saint Nicholas in Prague Lesser Town. They represent the climax of European radical baroque architecture.

Christof's son, Kilian Ignatz Dientzenhofer, was an architect of equal importance. In his palaces and religious buildings he continually strove to achieve an organic synthesis of central and longitudinal space. He frequently combined the south European dome church style with the characteristic northern longitudinal layout. Among his most important churches are Saint John of Nepomuk on the Hradčany, Saint John on the Rock (fig. 59) in Prague New Town, Mary Magdalene in Karlovy Vary, the church of Saint Nicholas in Prague Old Town, and the completion of the church of Saint Nicholas in Prague Lesser Town (fig. 33). Through his designs for village churches, Kilian Ignatz influenced the development of Czech rural church architecture; he also had an impact on the formation of late baroque architecture in neighboring countries.

The third most important architect of the Czech baroque, who came from a family of Italian artisans who settled in Prague, was Jan Blažej Santini-Aichel. Like Christof Dientzenhofer, he strove for a dynamic conception of space. Unlike Dientzenhofer, who stressed the structural elements—columns, beams, and footings—and suppressed the expressiveness of the walls, Santini modeled walls in an expressive manner by employing structural morphology with a picturesqueness and compositional virtuosity that demonstrated his training as a painter. His most original buildings are those in the baroque Gothic style. Churches designed by Santini harken back to a pre-Hussite tradition; for example, he restored the five-naved Cistercian basilica of the Assumption of Our Lady in Sedlec near Kutná Hora. Santini also worked in Moravia, where he created the baroque pilgrimage church of Our Lady in Křtiny. One of his most important, imaginative buildings is the pilgrimage church of Saint John of Nepomuk on Zelená Hora near Žd'ár nad Sázavou (fig. 60), in which he successfully united the two styles, Gothic and baroque.

Czech baroque painting reached its zenith at the beginning of the eighteenth century. Silesian Jan Kryštof Liška stands out for his indisputable artistic qualities. The Austrian painter Michael Václav Halbax spent a brief but important time in Prague. These two artists and an older tradition of painting influenced the master of baroque tenebrism, Petr Brandl, a painter of impassioned altarpieces and evocative portraits with lively, robust presence and energetic brushwork and use of color. A Czech painter who became famous for his portraits beyond the bounds of the kingdom was Jan Kupecký. Another superb artist was the fresco painter Václav

Vavřinec Reiner, whose dynamic compositions, filled with a spirit of abandon and local color, lend a most valuable final touch to Czech baroque architecture. Reiner's altarpieces are unusual, as are the landscapes in which he laid the foundations of the local landscape-painting tradition.

The two most important baroque sculptors are Ferdinand Maxmilian Brokof and the Tyrol-born Matthias Bernard Braun. Braun's work, drawing on the pattern of Bernini, is imbued with dramatic pathos, and his statues are characterized by their open composition, expressive movement, and whirling drapery. Brokof's work is majestic in its balance, monumental composition, eloquent gestures, and realistic treatment of the human figure. Braun and Brokof worked on the sculptural decoration of Charles Bridge and a number of churches. Both created various monumental sculptures in open spaces in towns. In addition, Braun and his workshops produced numerous statues for town and country residences of the nobility, including the most important sculptural group for the residence and hospital of Count Špork in the spa of Kuks.

Although there were artistic parallels between Bohemia and Moravia, baroque art and architecture in Moravia evolved differently, primarily as a result of its proximity to Vienna. A classicist tendency in architecture was reinforced by Martinelli, who built castles at Lanškroun, Slavkov near Brno, and Buchlovice, and Johann Bernard Fischer of Erlach, builder of the castle church of the Holy Trinity in Vranov nad Dyjí. Austrian influence is also evident in Moravian painting. For example, the mid-century development of frescoes was spurred by several graduates of the Viennese Academy, under the influence of the artists Paul Troger and Franz Anton Maulbertsch. In pre-1750 Moravian sculpture, the classicist influence of Austrian Georg Rafael Donner is already reflected in the work of the German Josef Winterhalder and the Silesian Gottfried Fritsch, who came to Moravia around 1740.

In the mid-eighteenth century in both Bohemia and Moravia, there was a general move away from high baroque pathos. Rococo decorative motifs—band ornament and, later, rocaille—appeared in architecture and applied art (see fig. 34, cat. 142). Painting was influenced by Venice, although elements of domestic baroque endured. The palace architecture of Jan N. Palliardi and the sculptural work of Ignác František Platzer (fig. 61), a pupil of the Viennese Donner school, united classical and baroque themes in an original manner. A lively baroque tradition survived in small towns and in the country well into the nineteenth century.

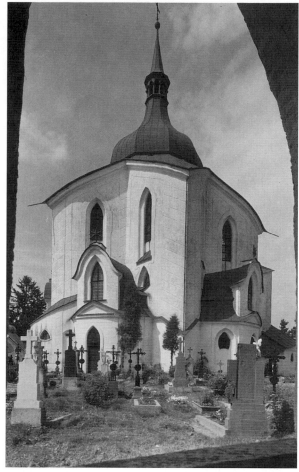

60. Church of St. John of Nepomuk in Žďár. Designed by Jan Santini and built from 1719–1722, this central building has a star-shaped ground plan. It combines high baroque trends with a revival of Gothic elements and the Gothic understanding of space.

Czech Nationalism in Eighteenth- and Nineteenth-Century Art

In the second half of the eighteenth century Czech culture experienced a gradual decline as powerful patrons, drawn by the centralizing efforts of Empress Maria Theresa, moved to Vienna and as Joseph II's secularization movement reduced church patronage. The lamentable cultural atmosphere elicited efforts on the part of the educated public to advance national culture. Czechs promoted the fine arts and struggled to raise the status of the Czech language to that of German. The 1796 formation of the Society of Patriotic Friends of Art led to the building of the first public gallery in the Czech lands and to the founding of the Academy, a school of fine art in Prague. The works of its early nineteenth-century graduates like František Tkadlík, Antonín Mánes, or Josef Navrátil, reflected late classicism, romanticism, and an emerging interest in the Czech countryside. The portraits from their contemporary Antonín Machek stand out in Central European art. Josef Mánes, a painter of great natural talent, appeared on the Czech cultural scene at the end of the 1830s. His paintings from the mid-nineteenth century are characterized by a lively and stylistically unshackled form of expression. His excellent portraits include *Luisa Bělská* and *Josefina,* an idealized depiction of feminine beauty. Through his pure and direct yet cultured art, Manes became one of the greatest of Czech artists, and his work pointed the way to subsequent artistic development. After the mid-nineteenth century, a tendency toward realism and the influence of French art came to the fore, reflected in the work of Soběslav Pinkas and Karel Purkyně. The paintings of Adolf Kosárek celebrated the Czech landscape.

61. Statue of a bishop, attributed to Ignatz František Platzer, Bohemia, after 1750. This small statue probably served as a modelletto, *a small model of an artist's to show potential customers. The energy of the figure's movement and the rich effect created with paint and gilding are characteristic of the rococo period. Cat. 94.*

Early nineteenth-century architecture was conventional and dependent on foreign models. After mid-century, Czech architecture began to draw level with the modern emphasis on harmony between a building's artistic concept and its internal purpose. The architectural and decorative vocabulary was substantially enriched by the appearance of the neo-Renaissance style, which was employed in the construction of prestigious public buildings and town villas. The decorative arts of this period combined a reliance on conservative motifs and ornamentation with technological innovation and a striving for perfection.

In 1868, the foundation stone was laid for the new National Theater in Prague. Its construction was a symbolic victory for Czech cultural self-determination, and an entire generation of leading Czech artists shared in its building and decoration. Architect Josef Zítek drew his inspiration from the late Renaissance of north Italy

62. František Ženíšek, Přemysl and the Heralds of Libuše, c. 1895. This pastel cartoon for a wall painting in the Pantheon of the National Museum in Prague shows Přemysl at his plough being greeted by messengers from the princess Libuše, who ask him to be her consort and prince of the Czechs. This legendary character gave his name to the Přemyslid princely dynasty that ruled the Czech lands from the late ninth to the fourteenth centuries; this myth was a favorite theme of the national revival of the nineteenth century. Cat. 187.

to design a building that is marked by a refined clarity of style, softness of form, original composition, and strength of expression. The works of sculptors Antonín Wagner, Bohuslav Schnirch, and Josef Václav Myslbek and painters Josef Tulka, František Ženíšek (fig. 62), Mikuláš Aleš, Václav Brožík, Julius Mařák, and Vojtěch Hynais, among others, contributed to an ambiance that celebrated the Czech spirit. Some artists of the National Theater generation also worked together on other important projects, including the National Museum, which was designed by Zítek's partner, Josef Schultz, and completed in 1891. This generation of artists laid the foundation for modern Czech art, which at the end of the nineteenth and beginning of the twentieth century, had attained a firm, particular, and irreplaceable niche in European art.

Martin Mádl

HISTORICAL MUSEUM,
THE NATIONAL MUSEUM

63. Cup and saucer, Březová, 1820–1840. Produced as a souvenir of the spa Karlový Vary (Carlsbad), this cup and saucer are richly decorated with gilt motifs. The hand-painted scene on the cup shows a romantic mill site near the town. Cat. 207.

One Thousand Years of Czech Music

In 1868, at the laying of the foundation stone for the National Theater in Prague, composer Bedřich Smetana coined the elegant motto, "In music, Czech life." His phrase embodied the national fervor of the nineteenth century, which saw Czech songs as a source of revival for national life. There was certainly more than a grain of truth to this; during periods of oppression, the Czech language had thrived, far from the towns, through folk literature and songs, thereby preserving a corpus of typical intonations and melodies. Perhaps Smetana also wanted to allude to Czech musical history, which in certain periods could boast of illustrious names, and its influence on European musical development, both of which were just beginning to be recognized.

In the early Middle Ages, the means and education necessary to assemble a music collection were only at the disposal of the Catholic Church, which strove to defend its interests against the pagan inhabitants of the Czech lands. It is easy to understand why both the Catholic Church and the later reform movements were the most important musical producers and consumers. Music was a part of mystery and celebration: it also represented those who had commissioned the music and propagated their ideas. Thanks to the position of the Czech lands in between East and West, the Christianization movement became intertwined with Slavonic influences, such as the Byzantine liturgy, which shaped the oldest recorded written music in the country (from around 900). The western influence of the Latin liturgy was also important. Spiritual music of the Czech lands, as was the case elsewhere in the regions dominated by the Roman Catholic Church, was sung in Latin. Gregorian chant, a form of music sung throughout the western Christian world, reached Bohemia relatively quickly in the ninth and tenth centuries, thanks to the network of monasteries across Europe; in a similar way, multi-voiced compositions known as "organum" traveled eastward at the end of the twelfth century.

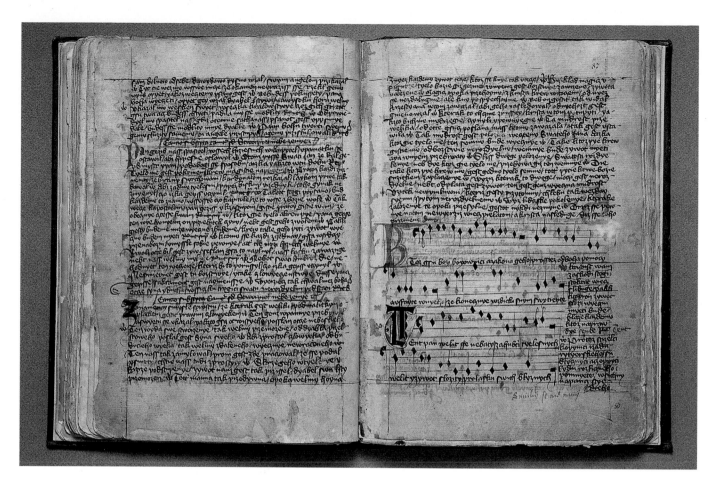

Czech composers put many Latin texts to music, some of which, like the liturgical singing for the feast of Saint Wenceslas and other Czech saints, occupy an important place in Czech music. However, what is more important is that they composed music for texts written in the Czech language. The clergy generally rejected the notion of Czech songs, claiming these were beyond the scope of the liturgy. This situation had its consequences. For example, the oldest known Czech spiritual song, the late tenth-century "Hospodine pomiluj ny," (Lord, have mercy on us) which was in its own way a state anthem, was not set down in writing until the end of the fourteenth century. Not until the beginning of the fifteenth century was the use of the Czech language permitted in religious services, even in Gregorian chant. The change was due primarily to the Hussite reformist movement that emphasized the significance of Czech songs and thus paved the way for the emergence of future Czech hymnals during the Renaissance and baroque periods (fig. 64).

Cantiones bohemicae (Bohemian chant) was an original Czech musical form of the Middle Ages that fused melodic elements from polyphony, folk music, and various styles of spiritual and secular music. In the second half of the fourteenth century these songs spread to other countries, sometimes as far away as Finland. In their educational wanderings through the universities of Europe, seminarians and students captured medieval society in songs that ranged from the serious to the most carefree. Less concrete documentation survives for medieval music of anoth-

64 Jistebnice Hymn Book (mid-15th c.). The manuscript is a songbook in the broadest meaning of the word. It contains the sum total of sacred songs of the Hussite era: songs suitable for prayer, Christmas, Easter, the adoration? of Mary, etc. The two Hussite chorales, "Ye warriors of God," and "Arise, arise great city of Prague," illustrate that the hymns included are not only spiritual but military in tone.

er form, *laboratores* (music of the working people), which was for the most part orally transmitted; when it did infiltrate higher genres, it was more or less only tolerated and rarely written down.

For reasons that we now recognize as politically and philosophically expedient, nineteenth-century Czech historians and artists overrated the influence of the Hussite era on the fine arts, drama, and literature. Although the reflection of Hussitism was still evident in the 1458–1471 reign of George of Poděbrady, little is known of the music from either that era or more generally the entire Czech Renaissance. New musical organizations typical of the Reformation did emerge in this period, which in Bohemia were called *fraternitas litteratorum* (literary brotherhoods). Some of these associations of musical laypeople had great fortunes at their disposal and could afford to commission magnificent single-voice and multi-voice hymnals. Literary brotherhoods possessed a certain amount of social prestige; members performed various rituals during religious services, both Utraquist and Catholic, and enjoyed some economic advantages. The Czech burghers' contact with business partners in other countries also facilitated transmission of popular compositions of the day. Although there was no lack of Czech composers among the humanist-educated literati, regrettably their merits were not recognized beyond the boundaries of their native land.

The sixteenth-century choirs of the brotherhoods were closely linked to town and city schools that provided singers in the upper ranges, as well as persons who functioned as teachers and choir directors. The breakup of the Catholic monopoly on education, which had extended to the purchase of sheet music collections, brought an increase in commissions for secular compositions; ranging from the mildly spiritual to the openly secular, these were vocal and instrumental pieces. The Unity of Brethren celebrated its concern for education, the Czech language, and the quality of printed works with two works that rank with the best Czech hymnal literature of all time: the *Hymnal of Szamotuly* (1541) and the *Hymnal of Ivančice* (1564; see cat. 73).

The Prague court during the reign of Rudolph II (1576–1612) formed one of the most significant centers of mannerism, and the names of the musicians who worked there, including Phillipe de Monte, Charles Luython, and Jacob Regnart, are among the foremost representatives of late Renaissance music. The orchestra of Rudolph's court had seventy-four members, the overwhelming majority of whom were of Dutch and Italian origin; it performed during religious, ceremonial, and festive occasions.

Although the emperor's residence and the city stood at different levels physically as well as religiously, some of the court compositions crossed this barrier and appeared in the town, for example in adapted form as musical scores for lute solos *(in tabulature)*. Performances in private and secular spaces increased during the Renaissance; music was performed in pubs, during theatrical performances, and at weddings, as well as in traditional environments like churches, schools, and at court. At various civic celebrations, trombonists blared from gates and town hall towers. Special Jewish ensembles played in Prague's Jewish Town. The successful Prague sheet music printer J. Nigrin served a select clientele, such as Jacob Handl-Gallus, the director of a Prague parish church, who had the majority of his works printed there.

The uprising of the Czech estates in 1618 signaled the outbreak of the Thirty Years' War, which for Bohemia ended tragically on the plains of White Mountain two years later. Among the Czech lords executed in 1621 was the talented composer Kryštof Harant of Polžice and Bezdružice, a politician, traveler, and military commander; one of the few Czech nobles with an interest in period music, he had a large collection of musical instruments. However, the role of aristocrats in musical circles was less pronounced than in other countries such as Italy, with the one exception of the southern Bohemian Rožmberks. The aftermath of the Battle of White Mountain had a wide-reaching impact on Czech music through the emigration of the non-Catholic population, epidemics, economic depression, and the relocation of the imperial court from Prague to Vienna.

During the Counter-Reformation, the Czech baroque, in fine arts, architecture, and music, was an important element of the Central European cultural climate. People of the seventeenth century were surrounded by dramatic, exalted music that seemed to challenge and embody the contrasts of daily life: light and dark, sainthood and sinfulness, life and death. Music was most often heard in church, with mandatory attendance estimated to be four times a week. In its own way, the ceremony of the mass with its orchestra, choir, and soloists took the place of public musical productions, which were generally inaccessible to the lower classes. The opera performances in the Moravian domain of the Questenberk family in Jaroměřice, where the lower classes participated as both performers and audience, were apparently a rarity in Europe at this time.

The burgher class, so important for the development of opera and secular music in general, lost many of its privileges after 1620, including its role as an important music promoter. The immensely costly baroque events could at that time only be afforded by the Church, which spared no expense. The 1729 canonization of Saint John of Nepomuk in Prague's Saint Vitus Cathedral was celebrated with three hundred musicians and was designed to affect the consciousness of as many people as possible. Ignatius of Loyola, the founder of the Society of Jesus, advocated the value of seeking to strive toward a higher spiritual plane through the

65. Baroque guitar, 1754. This six-stringed guitar was made by the renowned Prague instrument maker, Tomáš Ondřej Hulínský, who also made violins, lutes, harps, and other stringed instruments. Cat. 124.

senses. Both the Jesuit and Piarist orders offered theatrical performances set to music and performed oratorios in church and parish chapels. These included the works of both foreign (Antonio Caldara, Antonio Lotti, Johann Josef Fux, J. G. Reinhardt, and Antonio Vivaldi) and Czech (Jan Dismas Zelenka, František Ignác Tůma, Bohuslav Matěj Černohorský [see cat. 120], and others) composers, who today are of equal importance in music history. *Musica navalis,* a celebration held on the Vltava River usually in the twilight of mid-summer night's eve, was until the eighteenth century an important Prague attraction. It is a good example of the baroque "water music" composed and celebrated, for example, by Georg Friedrich Händel in England.

The tradition of Czech religious songs was drawn upon for many baroque hymnals. Non-Catholics who practiced their religion in secret used old Czech Unity of Brethren hymnals as well as the hymnal of John Amos Comenius, published abroad after his emigration in the mid-seventeenth century. The poetic and melodic forms of these songs, such as Michna's carol "Chtíc, aby spal" (Let him sleep; see cat. 118), are yet another important aspect of the baroque, and some of them continue to be sung to this day.

At the beginning of the eighteenth century in Bohemia, opera was still considered exceptional: Fux's *Costanza e Fortezza* (see cat. 129), was the highlight of the 1723 coronation of Charles VI as king of Bohemia. The domestication of opera was brought about by more regular performances by traveling Italian opera companies, held at the summer spas in Kuks and during the winter season in Prague. In the 1780s and 1790s, the operas of Wolfgang Amadeus Mozart met with great acclaim, especially *Don Giovanni,* which had its 1787 world premiere in the Nostic Theater in Prague, and *The Marriage of Figaro.* Mozart's relations with the people of Prague has become legendary, but there is no doubt about the wide influence of his compositions, which spread, in various adaptations, into the countryside. Operatic arias (not only Mozart's, but also Josef Mysliveček's) with new spiritual texts rang out from church choirs, and piano extracts from Mozart's operas were adapted by Czech artists (see cat. 133).

Secular musical forms and types—instrumental, sonata, suite, concert, secular cantata, and opera—did not develop as quickly in Bohemia as church music. The Czech lands in the following period became a literal reservoir of cheap, professionally competent musicians for the rest of Europe, a fact reflected in music historian Charles Burney's claim that Bohemia was the conservatory of Europe. Emigrant Czech players and composers created several centers abroad in the eighteenth century. In Germany, Mannheim became the home of Johann Stamic and Franz Xaver Richter, and Berlin of František Benda and Jiří Antonín Benda. Czech musicians lived and worked in other major European cities: Vienna (Legold Koželuh, Jan Křtitel Vaňhal, Jan Václav Voříšek, and the Vranický brothers), Paris (Antonín Rejcha and Jan Křtitel Krumpholz), London (Jan Ladislav Dusík), Mainz (Jan Zach; see cat. 123), and others. A second wave of emigration was still to come in the nineteenth century with Czechs traveling abroad, but this time toward the east (St. Petersburg) and to the north (Smetana's stay in Sweden).

In the final decades of the eighteenth century, the reforms of Joseph II limited the performance of orchestral masses, but fortunately this was not strictly enforced. Around this time, the Czech National Revival, commonly understood as the period from late eighteenth to the mid-nineteenth centuries, had become central to contemporary life. In the nineteenth century, the Czech music director was idealized as a leader of rural choirs and a patriot. Czech texts, including pastoral compositions (see cat. 121) and Christmas carols, became a mainstay of church choir repertoires. They carried on the tradition of the Christmas mass *Hej, mistře!* (Hey, master!) from Jakub Jan Ryba, the Rožmitál teacher, choral director, composer, and musical theoretician (see cat. 190). The compositions of František Xaver Brixi (fig. 66) were widely played, as well as those of choir directors and organists Jan Antonín Koželuh, Jan Lohelius Oehlschlägel, Josef Praupner, František Václav Habermann, and others. Church music gradually began to imitate the Viennese style, becoming more and more conservative, and in the mid-nineteenth century succumbed to the in-fluence of the Cecilian movement, which strove to purge rampant musical, orchestral, and secular elements from religious services.

66. *Musical score for František Xaver Brixi's* Missa, *1760. Cat. 119.*

Instrumental music in the eighteenth century appealed to the aristocracy, many of whom, including Franz Joseph Haydn, were leading composers and musicians. The chamber orchestras of Counts Pachta (see cat. 131, 132) and Clam-Gallas and the Nostic, Lobkovic, and Schwarzenberg groups were renowned as fine musicians. As well as playing for private occasions and functions, they also performed the works of the Vienna masters, including Ludwig van Beethoven's symphonies. After their social and economic prestige flagged, around the time of the French Revolution, the nobles began to support financially less demanding wind ensembles (harmony), and piano pieces became the mainstay of aristocratic and burgher salons.

In the nineteenth century, the music scene first acquired the character we recognize today. It began to be supported by a range of organizations—schools, music publishers, rental shops, and music agencies—and regular music criticism in the press began to appear. Public concerts changed substantially as cities and organizations took on a greater role. Before 1860, the situation was complicated by the Austrian monarchy's refusal to grant the Czech population the right of association.

67. Photographic portrait of Bedřich Smetana.

68. Portrait of Antonín Dvořák, painted in the studio of Macháček in the 1880s.

Once this right was granted, however, there followed a literal explosion of artistic activity, including the founding of the Umělecká Beseda and the Association of Chamber Music, and several hundred singing associations. High standards were demanded of public orchestral productions, including theatrical and school orchestras, as well as of military bands and dance ensembles.

Romanticism entered Czech music from abroad through the efforts of Carl Maria von Weber at the Estates Theater in Prague. It is also evident in the work of Czech composers Václav Jan Tomášek and František Škroup. It synthesized classical and romantic aesthetics with traditional Czech folk music. These works can be favorably compared with those of other contemporary European composers such as Franz Liszt, Richard Wagner, and Hector Berlioz, and the movement that created them also appeared in other countries as part of the broader trend toward nationalism of the nineteenth century. Bedřich Smetana (fig. 67) and Antonín Dvořák (fig. 68), two of the most distinguished Czech composers of this time, created precedents for their contemporaries and successors in all genres: the former in opera and symphonic poems, the latter in chamber works, songs, symphonies, cantatas, and oratorios. In addition to composing, both men devoted themselves to other activities, especially teaching. Smetana performed as a pianist and conducted theater orchestras; Dvořák, in addition to performing as a pianist and concert violinist, traveled around the world as a conductor. During his stay in New

York from 1892 to 1895, he served as director of the New York Conservatory and had a major influence on new American music, concert performances, and conducting.

Dvořák lived to receive academic honors and acclaim from abroad, and until today he is the most widely performed Czech composer. On the other hand, Smetana's greatest fame was achieved in his native land. The early twentieth-century assessment of the works of Smetana and Dvořák led to undignified political struggles, tearing these men from the context of their time and pitting them against one another; however, Smetana and Dvořák, each in his own way and in his own field, crowned the developments in Czech music that had been building for centuries. If any Czech artists of the nineteenth century truly balanced an awareness of Czech musical history and trends in world music culture, Smetana and Dvořák did.

Composers of the early twentieth century followed in the tradition of Smetana and Dvořák, further exploring new creative polemics. This new generation, called the "Czech musical modern," was represented by Josef Suk, Vítězslav Novák, Leoš Janáček, and Otakar Ostrčil. In the flood of diverse artistic styles and formats that followed, society became less accepting of "serious" contemporary music, and the role of music in society became more complex. The establishment of the Czechoslovak Republic in 1918 was a milestone not only from a political point of view, but also provided a psychological break, ushering in what we now consider the modern music movement.

Dagmar Vanišová
MUSEUM OF CZECH MUSIC,
THE NATIONAL MUSEUM

69. Silver and gilt wreath presented to Antonín Dvořák at the gala premiere of his opera Dimitrij *at the National Theater, Prague, on April 5, 1884.*

Czech Theater

In the Czech Lands the earliest form of theater evolved from the dances or movements that were a part of pagan rituals and seasonal ceremonies. The ninth-century introduction of Christianity disrupted the natural development of these forms, because the Church sought to suppress all pagan traditions. The custom of turning religious rites into drama survived, however, and the Christianized Slavonic tribes developed new theatrical forms based on both the earlier traditions and the newly adopted Latin liturgy and scripture. The story of the three Marys at Christ's tomb was the inspiration for the oldest documented Czech theatrical celebration, held at the end of the twelfth century in the monastery of Saint George in Prague Castle.

The development of religious drama had a major effect on the use of theatrical space, which previously had been undefined. The stage for passion plays was usually divided horizontally into three to four parts or zones representing scenes in hell, on earth, at Christ's tomb, and, on occasion, in heaven. Subsequently, at the turn of the fourteenth century, the form and content of church theater were influenced by secular medieval theater, particularly performances by wandering jesters (joculators). Religious dramas moved from church buildings to public spaces like the graveyard, the market, and the town square. Actors spoke Czech more frequently than Latin, portrayed humanized versions of biblical characters, and incorporated contemporary events into biblical stories.

The oldest theatrical texts in Czech are two fourteenth-century fragmentary versions of the "Quack" story, a popular episode in medieval passion plays. In the traditional story of the three Marys, the women are on their way to Christ's tomb to anoint his body when they discover that he has risen from the dead. In the "Quack" version, as the three Marys stroll through a medieval market and buy ointments to anoint Jesus's body, their commentary is developed into an entertaining and critical look at contemporary life. In one version, the scene where they meet the quack, a familiar figure in West European theater, is complemented by a bold parody of the church ceremony of the resurrection of Christ (a scene of the

resuscitation of Isaac, the son of Abraham). Fragments of other Czech texts of the fourteenth century, such as *The Resurrection of Christ and Its Celebration* and *The Play of "Merry" Magdalene,* have similar characteristics, especially the incorporation of secular elements, the use of Czech rather than Latin, and the satire of religious material.

In the fifteenth century, the Hussite revolution relegated both secular and liturgical drama to the fringe of the arts, hindering the blossoming of Czech theater. Stability in the fifteenth century during the reigns of George of Poděbrady and the Jagellons renewed the tradition of late medieval theater, encouraging both its further secularization and the increased use of Czech. A new character that first appeared in the mid-fifteenth century was the fool or court jester, of whom the best known was Jan Paleček, jester to King George of Poděbrady and a member of the Unity of Brethren.

Humanism and the Reformation influenced mid-sixteenth-century Czech theater. The Renaissance interest in classical culture appeared in performances by university students, generally held at the end of freshmen convocation ceremonies. Plautus's comedy, *Miles Gloriosus* (The Boastful Soldier), was the first of a series of

70. Set design by Tobias Mössner, c. 1850. In this design Mössner, the foremost designer for the Estates Theater, combined an ability to show the reality of country life in a way that suited nineteenth-century romanticism. Cat. 194.

71. Český Krumlov Theater from c. 1720. This building has the oldest theater interior in Europe to be preserved not only with its original decor, but also its original mechanical stage equipment.

Latin school plays performed at the Town Hall of Prague's New Town in 1535. Plays with purely secular themes were soon replaced in school dramas by those with biblical themes (*Susanna*). With the arrival of the Jesuits in Prague in 1556, the school theater began to compete with the pomp of the spectacular Jesuit theater, which was supported by the imperial court and served as a means of education and agitation for the Counter-Reformation. The first Jesuit performance in Prague was held in 1558; as further houses were founded, Jesuit theaters opened in Olomouc, Brno, Znojmo, Český Krumlov, Kutná Hora, and elsewhere.

Alongside the productions of the university and the Jesuit houses, an unofficial exclusively Czech humanist theater developed. In addition to popular farces such as *The Country Carnival* and *The Adulteress Caught* by Václav Kocmánek, it featured the works of Pavel Kyrmezer and Šimon Lomnický of Budeč. These playwrights continued to employ a characteristic device of Czech Gothic and baroque drama, religious themes set in a contemporary Czech environment. The climax of humanist attempts to link theater and education was John Amos Comenius's play cycle *Schola Ludus,* written in exile in the 1640s and 1650s.

In the baroque and early classical periods Prague became a center of European theater, with German, English, and Italian theater and opera companies in residence. In 1723, a famous performance of the opera *Costanza e Fortezza* by Johann Josef Fux, arranged by Giuseppe Galli da Bibiena (see cat. 129), was held at Prague Castle and led to the baroque theater's subsequent embrace of opera. The dominant position of drama in the eighteenth century instigated the construction of the first permanent theater buildings. After the closing of the Špork Theater, which had been leased to Italian opera groups, the 1738 Kotce Theater was the most important Prague playhouse until the opening of the Nostic Theater in 1783. A permanent theater was also built in Brno. The space demands of the grandiose baroque style suited the aristocratic castle theaters built during the seventeenth and eighteenth centuries; the castle theater preserved in Český Krumlov is an especially good example of baroque decorative arts and stage technology (fig. 71). The Nostic Theater in Prague (after 1789 called the Estates Theater), a classical edifice designed by Antonín Hafenecker and completed in 1783, is the oldest stone building in the Czech lands to serve from its founding to the present day as a theater. Josef Platzer, a famous Viennese stage artist who came originally from Prague, designed a group of twelve basic sets for the theater. In 1787, the Nostic Theater hosted the world premiere of Wolfgang Amadeus Mozart's opera *Don Giovanni*.

The second half of the eighteenth century saw the first professional theater performances in Czech. The first of these, an intermezzo with Czech songs, called *The Amorous Night Watchman*, was staged in Kotce in 1763. The 1771 performance of a translation of a German comedy, *Prince Hansel*, is widely acknowledged as marking the beginning of the modern Czech theater.

In contrast to the aristocratic baroque theater, amateur theater was performed throughout the countryside. Rural drama evoked medieval traditions, with religious plays (*The Comedy of the Martyrdom of Our Lord and Savior, Jesus Christ*) as well as secular dramas (*The Comedy of the Turkish War, Salome,* and *The New Comedy of Libuše and the Maidens' War in Bohemia*). In only a few cases are the authors of these local plays known; village scribe, František Vodseďálek, or schoolmaster Jan Antoš, who wrote *The Opera of the Peasant Revolt*. In the eighteenth century, puppetry, most frequently using marionettes, also developed in the country. Puppet troupes performed the repertoire of Prague theater, but on a level that the less educated country people could appreciate. In all contexts, the theater played an exceptional role in shaping the history of the Czech nation and the Czech language.

The Czech National Revival that began in the 1780s had a major impact on Czech theater. Until that time, theater performances in Czech in the Nostic Theater had been successful but rare. From 1776, there were regular Czech performances in a wooden building called Bouda ("The Hut") near the present Wenceslas Square, and after it was demolished in 1779, at the U Hybernů theater. The leading figure of the patriotic theater was the dramatist, translator, director, and actor Václav Thám. The repertoire consisted of translations of German comedies, complex classical plays (Friedrich von Schiller, William Shakespeare), original plays taken from Czech history (Thám's *Vlasta and Šárka* and *The Swedish War in Bohemia,* and Antonín Josef Zíma's *Oldřich and Božena*), light musical plays, pantomimes, and ballet. The first attempts at farces set in Prague were Prokop Šedivý's *The Butchers' Shops* and *The Brewers of Prague.*

In 1812, occasional amateur productions were held under the leadership of the dramatist Jan Nepomuk Štěpánek, who wrote plays based on Czech history (*Břetislav I, The Czech Achilles,* and *The Swedish Siege of Prague)* and comedies (*Czech and German* and *The Brewery in Sojkov*). When he was appointed co-direc-

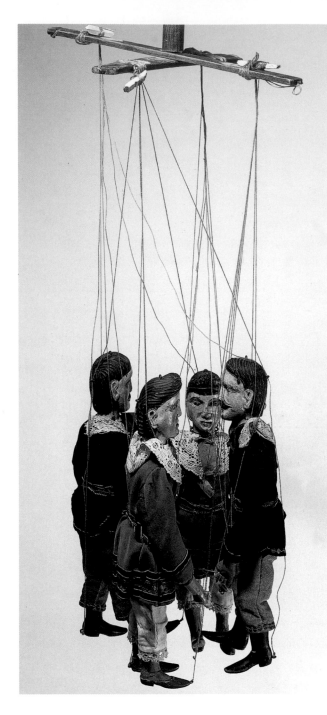

72. Group of four dancing puppets by puppeteer Arnoštka Kopecká, mid-nineteenth century. This type of puppet group frequently appeared as a finale to a performance. Its apparatus was adapted so that pairs of dancers could move in unison. Cat. 195.

tor of the Estates Theater in 1824, Štěpánek introduced regular Czech productions on Sundays and holiday matinees. Aside from his own plays and adaptations of popular Viennese farces, he staged Václav Kliment Klicpera's plays of chivalry (*Blaník, The Bell of Loket*) and comedies (*The Magical Hat, Four-Horned Rohovín, Comedy on the Bridge*). He also offered operas translated into Czech (*The Swiss Family* by the Austrian composer Joseph Weigl and Mozart's *Don Giovanni*) and an original Czech opera, *The Tinker,* by František Škroup.

Amateur theater, both in Prague and in the countryside, and the developing puppet theater spurred the revivalist struggle for the Czech language. In addition to adaptations of contemporary and classical dramas, puppet theaters presented original puppet plays (*The Hudlice Fair, Mr. Franz of the Castle*). At the turn of the nineteenth century, Matěj Kopecký carried on the tradition of traveling puppeteers made famous by the work of Josef Maizner, František Kočka, and František and Josef Dubský, and founded an extensive clan of puppeteers.

In the 1830s and 1840s, the most important Czech playwright was Josef Kajetán Tyl (fig. 73), whose dramatic work is still relevant today; it includes historical plays (*The Miners of Kutná Hora, Jan Hus,* and *Drahomíra and her Sons*), pictures of contemporary life (*Mistress Meg: The Mother of the Regiment, The Arsonist's Daughter,* and *The Poor Trickster*) and folk tales (*The Piper of Strakonice, The Stubborn Woman, Georgie's Vision,* and *The Maid of the Forest*). In December 1834 Tyl's patriotic farce, *The Shoemakers' Fair,* was performed at the Estates Theater. It premiered the song "Kde domov můj?" (Where is my home?), which was to become the future Czech national anthem (see cat. 189). In an effort to raise the artisitc standard of the Czech repertoire, Tyl formed his own troupe of Czech actors, who performed original works in the Kajetán building from 1834 to 1837. Despite its small number of amateur, often private performances, the troupe influenced the development of a Czech acting style (in addition to Tyl, Karel Hynek Mácha, Karel Sabina, the actors Josef Jiří Kolár, Anna Manetínská, and Jan Kaška got their start there).

In 1842, Johann August Stöger established the New Theater, a subsidiary stage of the Estates Theater, specializing in Czech drama. Stöger engaged Tyl and many of his actors and acquired special sets from Tobias Mössner, designer and painter for the Estates Theater (fig. 70). In addition to his own plays, Tyl staged practically all the work of Václav Kliment Klicpera, original plays by Štěpánek and Simeon Karel Macháček, and Czech translations of contemporary German and French plays.

Unfortunately, even in this theater the financially more advantageous German productions came to dominate, and in 1846, the theater closed. Tyl then became the repertory director and artistic manager for Czech performances at the Estates Theater. His effort to democratize theater and prove its national importance came to a climax in 1848–1851. Led by František Ladislav Rieger, the Czech patriots succeeded in 1845 in obtaining the government's permission to acquire a theater concession and land, and in 1850 the Subscription for the Establishment of a National Theater in Prague was instituted; money was collected for the construction of an independent theater building.

The failure of the 1848 Revolution and the cancellation of the constitution put off the construction of the National Theater in Prague, and in 1851 Tyl left Prague to work, until his death in 1856, in a country touring company. This left Josef Jiří Kolár to control the Czech repertoire at the Estates Theater. Kolár, who wrote historical plays and translated the works of Shakespeare, Schiller, and Goethe, preferred romantic theater in the grand style to the popular plays that Tyl had produced.

In 1859, a new building for Czech and German productions, the wooden New Town Theater in Prague, was opened, and the renewal of the constitution in the early 1860s brought the thoughts of the Czech intelligentsia back to the idea of an independent theater. Although some of the Young Czechs wanted to build a large stone edifice immediately, Rieger's idea of a temporary structure prevailed. Construction of the so-called Provisional Theater (officially titled the Royal Bohemian State Theater) was begun in May 1862 according to plans by architect Ignác Ullmann, and on November 18 and 20 it presented the gala productions of Vítězslav Hálek's *King Vukašín* and Cherubini's opera, *The Water Carrier.*

The repertoire of the Provisional Theater was composed of international classics (such as Shakespeare's plays), French conversational comedies, tragedies by Hálek and Kolár, plays by Tyl, and operas by its musical director, Bedřich Smetana. Original plays taken from contemporary life and from history (František Věnceslav Jeřábek's *His Master's Servant* and *The Travels of Public Opinion* and Emanuel Bozděch's *The Lord of the World in his Dressing Gown* and *Baron Goertz*) were performed, as were farces with song and dance by the actor František Ferdinand Šamberk (*The Eleventh Commandment* and *The Podskalák*). In the summer months, performances by the Provisional Theater were held in the Arena on Žofín Island, the Arena at Hradby, in the New Town Theater, and from 1876 in the New Czech Theater and in the National Arena. To this group of newly built theaters

73. Portrait of Josef Kajetán Tyl, one of the leading forces in Czech theater in the nineteenth century.

74. *The National Theater, Prague, 1868–1883. An important symbol of the nationalist movement, the National Theater is an enduring monument to late-nineteenth-century artistic standards.*

were added the theater at Kravín, the Arena at Komotovka, and the Arena at Smíchov, which were leased to touring troupes.

Amateur and professional theater outside Prague developed considerably in the second half of the nineteenth century. Independent theaters were built in Chrudim, Čáslav, Tábor, and Dvůr Králové, and regular Czech productions were started in Plzeň and in the Provisional National Theater in Brno. Directors Josef Emil Kramuel, Antonín Zollner, and František Pokorný founded traveling companies after the model of Josef Alois Prokop, who had led the first Czech traveling theater troupe, and in them trained many superb Czech actors.

One of the most important events in Czech cultural history in the nineteenth century was the laying of the foundation stone for the National Theater in 1868. The stones were brought to Prague from four historical sites in the Czech lands, and after years of public subscriptions, construction finally began.

The theater was to have had its ceremonial opening on September 11, 1881. However, to honor the marriage of Prince Rudolph, the Hapsburg heir to the throne, in June 1881, the uncompleted building was provisionally opened with the premiere of Smetana's opera *Libuše*, which he had composed to celebrate the National Theater's opening. Over the next few days, Václav Vlček's *Lipany*, Kolár's *The House of Smiřický*, and Meyerbeer's opera *The Huguenots* were also performed. Then, sadly, on August 12, 1881, the National Theater burned to the ground. The Czech nation immediately began a new subscription, and in two years the neo-Renaissance structure was rebuilt (fig. 74). On November 18, 1883, the theater was ceremonially opened again with a new performance of *Libuše*, followed by Bohumil Adámek's play *Salome*, and Dvořák's opera, *Dimitrij*.

The presence of this prestigious independent theater in Prague was the climax of centuries of effort on the part of the Czech theater to extricate itself from dependence on German theater. It also set the stage for the flourishing of Czech theatrical culture in the late nineteenth and early twentieth century.

Markéta Trávníčková

HISTORICAL MUSEUM,
THE NATIONAL MUSEUM

Czech Folk Art and Culture

Folk culture is essentially a cross-section of how a society lives from the point of view of one class—in this case rural people, particularly farming people. A folk culture reacts very sensitively to its particular environment, which includes the natural terrain, local customs and mentality of the people, the character of the time period, and social and economic development. It also selectively reflects the shared life in the community or the broader region. All these factors then create an immeasurably rich web of forms of expression, particularly in countries where culture is shaped by a variety of influences. This is the case in most of Central Europe. The Czech lands' location at a cultural and economic crossroads of Europe and Prague's role as an important center of European events since the Middle Ages have both been factors in the development of Czech folk culture.

The Czech lands have a heterogeneous terrain that encompasses high mountains and fertile lowlands; the many subregions within it possess a remarkably diverse material culture. Although almost no folk objects made before the seventeenth century survive, lifestyles of the country people were documented from the Middle Ages by the brief reports of travelers and officials, other literary descriptions, and pictures and prints. The eighteenth century, particularly the second half, was important for folk culture and its development. The abolition of serfdom in 1781 made the farmers, the mainstay of village society, a free entrepreneurial class. There had previously been people of means in villages, but political liberation gave their property and culture a social thrust. Village culture grew quickly to artistic maturity, but at the same time, there were marked regional differences, caused by the varying economic potential of the land. The expanding culture of prospering agricultural areas contrasted considerably with the more limited cultural growth of regions that were rarely affected by progress.

In general, Czech folk culture was at its zenith from the end of the eighteenth century to the mid-nineteenth century. After that time, advancing industrializa-

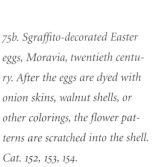

75a. Batik-decorated Easter eggs, Moravia, twentieth century. These eggs are decorated with flowers, hearts, and geometric motifs using vegetable dyes. Cat. 146, 147, 148.

75b. Sgraffito-decorated Easter eggs, Moravia, twentieth century. After the eggs are dyed with onion skins, walnut shells, or other colorings, the flower patterns are scratched into the shell. Cat. 152, 153, 154.

tion and the concomitant changes in social structure began to make the traditional rural way of life and its culture more uniform, although certain values survived for many generations. By the twentieth century, traditional cultural phenomena— dress, customs, architecture and furnishings—survived only in certain cases or only in certain areas. Traditional dress survived in west Bohemia in the small Chodsko region and in southeast Moravia in the Slovácko regions. The relics of traditional architecture remained in the upland regions and in south Bohemia. Similarly fragmentary was the survival of traditional spiritual culture. Specific family practices and local rituals were retained only in a handful of yearly customs, such as pre-Lenten Carnival festivities and the main Christian holy days, Easter and Christmas.

At the end of the eighteenth century, handcrafts developed in a variety of ways. Embroidery and the culture of dress flourished, and the style of living, reflected in home furnishings, changed in most parts of the country. In many regions, wooden buildings were replaced by stone ones, often in accordance with the instructions of enlightened rulers. The style of household possessions, particularly furniture, also changed, becoming colorful and ornamented. A number of household items, such as pottery dishes, containers, and other utensils, were developed. Crafts serving special village needs flourished.

The artifacts that characterized folk culture differed from urban work, not in quality but in their particular taste and in how they reflect a way of life that was defined by the village and its relation to nature, its congenial yet conservative outlook, and its strong accent on tradition. Many venerable elements of folk tradition reach back to its Slavic roots—in surviving talents and experience, in respect for family ties, in domestic furnishings, in clothing and in customs. It is complex but interesting to follow this process of interpenetration and growth.

Folk Dress

Clothing is eloquent evidence of culture. In Bohemia and Moravia, hundreds of types of folk dress survive. The simplest costumes, and the most recent, are from mountain areas hardly affected by development, where in some places traditional

76. Man's costume, northeast Moravia, early twentieth century. This costume, with its square-cut shirt and geometric embroidery, is typical of the upland regions of Moravia. Cat. 165.

77. Woman's costume, northeast Moravia, late nineteenth century. The embroidery, pleated skirt, and red printed scarf of this costume are typical of the Beskydy hill region of Moravia. Cat. 164.

78. Embroidered headscarf, Turnov. The white linen of this headscarf is set off with flowers and pomegranates stitched in crimson cotton thread. Cat. 170.

dress was worn until the beginning of the twentieth century. Most were simply constructed of many handmade fabrics and home-produced materials—leather, wool, flax, and hemp. Often beige in color, they display the endurance of traditional dressmaking techniques: clothing sewn from straight torn pieces of cloth and embroidered with a geometrical pattern. This is typical of the costumes of Valašsko in Moravia and the upland region of Slovácko, as well as of several pieces from the western mountains of Šumava and the Český Les.

Costumes from the foothill regions are very important. Bohemia is surrounded by a ring of mountains, below which flourished rustic cultures far removed from larger towns and their influences. For many years, the terrain limited the economy to farming, which in turn encouraged the growth of a unique local flavor. Clothing in the foothills was made from from a range of multicolored fabrics handwoven in harmonious patterns and was constructed with various types of pleating, folding, and complicated wrapping techniques. The garments of Chodsko in west Bohemia, Podkrkonoší, and Horňácko were at the same time both utilitarian and elegant.

Across the fertile lowlands, the regions of central and south Bohemia and central and southeast Moravia—Polabí, Blata, Haná, and Slovácko—interpret the clothing themes in their own way, though in their essentials they are much the same. Embroidery predominated, particularly in Bohemia where the style and quantity of ornamentation were remarkable (fig. 78). The structure of costumes throughout the lowlands is also singular, with exaggerated fullness in skirts and sleeves, elaborate headgear for single and married women, and the emphatic use of color. Certain indicators of status were accentuated. Today, these costumes are used occasionally in local celebrations and in folklore festivals.

Folk Style of Living

Rural dwellings, buildings, and household goods also contain regional characteristics, but to a lesser extent than clothing. This is because buildings are utilitarian in nature and have a more profound connection with the environment and the development of the land.

Simple dwellings with a beaten earth floor and roughly built basic furniture were relatively rare in the Czech lands; they were largely limited to nineteenth-century architecture in parts of eastern Moravia where the spurs of the western Carpathians descend. There the cultural world is shaped by long-surviving traditions that stem from different roots than the rest of the province. This land is ethnologically fascinating, as many elements of eastern and western cultures cross there; however, it is a relatively small part of the country.

For most of the Czech lands the characteristic dwellings were of a relatively high standard compared with other parts of Europe. Until the eighteenth century, wood construction, mainly log, predominated. Later development tended toward building with stone or combined materials, and timber-framed architecture was common in regions of North and West Bohemia. Many houses, however, combined both building styles.

In mountain and upland areas, many late eighteenth- to early nineteenth-century wooden houses have been preserved in a relatively pure style: log construction, joints filled with clay, walls covered with lime, and roofs of wood shingle or straw thatch. Houses in this style served for several centuries, but in the twentieth century, many gained new elements like modern types of windows and roofing. In layout and decoration, these houses differ from region to region. For example, the houses of Podkrkonoší have a characteristic gable construction (*lomenice*) with carved decoration (fig. 79).

In the flat, fertile regions, stone architecture was characteristic. One- and sometimes two-story houses, together with farm buildings, comprised a private farmstead as an enclosed unit. Depending on the nature of the terrain and the organization of the village, there were various forms of these country farms. A massive gateway and the gables of the dwelling house and granary might face the village square, or they might be arranged next to each other along a street. On the other hand, in upland areas, farmsteads were scattered across the landscape. Several

79. Timber framed cottage in the Semily district in northeastern Bohemia, late eighteenth-early nineteenth century, showing its lomenice *gable.*

80. *Masonry farm buildings from Jiřetice in the Strakonice district of South Bohemia, late eighteenth-early nineteenth century. The style of this farm can be called South Bohemian baroque, a rural carryover of the eighteenth-century Czech baroque style that was modified and used well into the nineteenth century.*

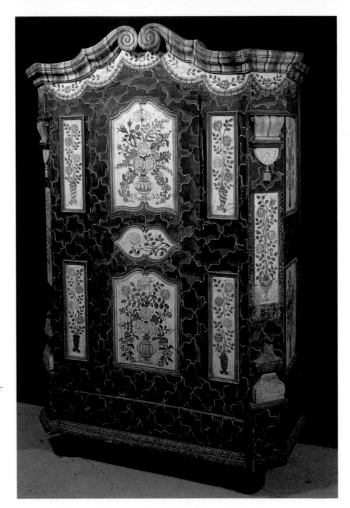

81. *Painted cupboard, foothills of the Krkonoše mountains, North Bohemia, late eighteenth century. The luxuriant decoration of Bohemian painted furniture is unsurpassed in Europe. Cat. 181.*

forms of stone houses are artistically valuable, particularly the farms of South Bohemia with their rich stucco facades in baroque and empire styles (fig. 80).

There is a strong correlation between the type of house and its household goods, especially furniture. Painted furniture became the pride of village households in the early decades of the nineteenth century. Only certain objects were painted, usually those that a bride would bring as her dowry: china cupboards, beds, and chests and wardrobes of a newer style (fig. 81). The painting style of northeastern Bohemia, incorporating floral patterns and figures, is unique in Europe. Benches and chairs had varied structures and forms. In contrast, the table as the center of the house often would not move with its owners; its form was very conventional. Country tables dating back several centuries still survive.

In the sitting room, the main dwelling space of the house, the focus was the "holy corner," generally located at the front of the room in the corner opposite the entrance and furnished with a table, chairs, and a bench. On the table often stood a small corner cupboard that stored valuable family possessions, such as the Bible and important documents. On either side, holy pictures painted on glass often hung from a ledge, and over the middle hung a carved wooden cross, symbol of the Christian family (see cat. 157).

Folk Art

Folk art is an auxiliary category that celebrates certain pieces as examplars of local decorating techniques. Most artifacts that nowadays are defined as "art" were not made with art in mind. They tended to be essential items made with natural artistic feeling, sometimes by a professional, at other times with the naïveté of an amateur.

Popular figurines, particularly with a religious theme, are an exception to this definition to a certain extent. They include carved, often polychromed crosses, sculptures of patron saints, and interpretations of biblical motifs from country chapels and wayside crosses that were produced by semi-professionals and craftspeople as self-conscious works of art (fig. 82). Many figures had special connotations. A statue of Saint Florian was frequently placed in a niche on the exterior of a house to protect the house from fire. Patron saints and the Virgin Mary were also placed in these niches. Statues were also displayed in a glass-fronted cupboard, where they were decorated with artificial flowers and rosaries and served as a small altar for the household.

Reverse paintings on glass were generally produced by artists in a workshop. They were colorfully painted on the back of a sheet of handmade glass, which was then displayed in a wooden frame. Although these vary considerably in quality, each has a distinctive period mood, ornamentation, color combination and naïveté of expression hard to emulate today (see cat. 158).

Other notable objects express spiritual aspects of the traditional way of life. Generally connected to folk customs, they employ motifs drawn from nature and

82. Madonna of Svatá Hora, Příbram region, mid-nineteenth century. Despite its somewhat primitive carving, this wooden figure has a stately quality characteristic of Czech folk art. Cat. 159.

Christianity. Many are connected to the liturgical year. Objects connected with Eastertime stand out—not just crosses, which were a general Christian symbol, but also sculptures and groups of figures depicting Calvary, Christ's tomb, the Pietà, and Christ Victorious. The most important works are Czech nativity scenes (*betlémy*). These were elaborate scenes made of hundreds of figures bearing gifts to the Christ Child, set against a background of paper rocks and a distant town. In the many types of nativity scenes, the figures were generally carved from wood and brightly painted; however, they might also be made from special materials like textiles or masterfully painted paper (see cat. 162).

Some artwork is connected to early magic practices that are hidden in typical ceremonies. Many artifacts and attributes were used in rites of passage, the most important of which was marriage. A multitude of symbols drawn from nature signified love, fertility, health, and prosperity; they were used in the bridal bouquet, wedding wreath, wedding clothing, and even the food served at the wedding feast. Baking played an important role in ritual foods, producing a range of cakes (*koláče*) with many symbolic male and female figures, birds, and stags. When served up by a modern-day housewife, these might seem to be random, humorous creations, but the motifs can be traced to ancient wedding rituals. Their individual features often represent genuine folk art and artistic capability.

Among the artifacts that display the nature and prosperity magic in folk traditions are *kraslice*, painted Easter eggs (fig. 75a, b). Young women gave them to young men on Easter Monday in return for an Easter carol and a whipping with a *pomlázka* (a whip braided from green willow stalks; see cat. 155, 156), whose symbolic purpose was to ensure health and vigor throughout the year. This custom is still practiced in some towns to the present day. The egg symbolized fertility and the beginning of life, and since Easter falls on the rise of the vegetation cycle, it represents a link between nature-based customs and a serious Christian festival. *Kraslice* represent artistic symbolism as well. They are most frequently decorated using wax batik and red coloring. The older eggs often had the same symbols that were used for weddings—figures, birds, the sun, and Christian motifs. More recent ones, made with improved decorative techniques, have a larger variety of etched and even applied patterns.

The decoration of many other types of objects overstepped the bounds of utility, giving them an exceptional artistic form, for example ceramics, artisically eloquent, though utilitarian; embroidery not only of clothing but of specialized textiles connected with ceremonies and spiritual practices; and hand tools used for farming, crafts, and household tasks. Many such pieces were made and given as tokens of love, one example being the sheaf-binders' peg, a smooth-turned wooden stake carved and inlaid with metal and mother-of-pearl that was used for binding sheaves of corn at the harvest.

Many artifacts cannot be called "art" but still testify to a past way of life. In this era of technology developed at the expense of the bond between humanity and nature, these utilitarian items are more than evidence of the past. They tell of long-forgotten principles, of a people's economical and ingenious approach to life, of their adaptation to circumstances, and their respect for natural resources. These field implements and craft tools, ordinary farm and household utensils, special-purpose and ordinary clothes, are silent witnesses to the past. They transcend their region in their usefulness but despite that—or perhaps because of it—they are the basis for understanding the rich, imaginative life of our ancestors.

Jiřina Langhammerová
DEPARTMENT OF ETHNOGRAPHY,
HISTORICAL MUSEUM, THE
NATIONAL MUSEUM

Modern Czech History

The National Revival

While the administrative reforms of Maria Theresa in the mid-eighteenth century extinguished the individuality of the Czech kingdom, the resulting struggle for political autonomy served as a starting point for Czech emancipation efforts that would culminate in the nineteenth-century Czech National Revival. In the second half of the eighteenth century, Czech interests were only represented in the Czech-speaking countryside, which shared the Catholic faith and the solidarity of the common people. The elite spoke German and considered themselves Austrians. An awareness of the dichotomy between the Czech-German and Czech peoples spread with the academic revival efforts of the intelligentsia, especially around the time of the 1792 publication of *A History of the Czech Language and Literature* by historian and philologist Josef Dobrovský. Published in German, Dobrovský's *History* was a linguistic study with no political agenda.

Two decades after the publication of Dobrovský's work, the struggle for Czech national identity grew under the influence of romanticism as part of the rising wave of Slavic political emancipation. In the first half of the nineteenth century, a number of activists, especially the Slovaks Jan Kollár and Pavel Josef Šafařík and the Czechs Josef Jungmann and František Palacký, created and defended the ideology of Czech emancipation, especially in regard to cultural identity and linguistic recognition. They first worked to codify and promote the Czech language and literature; their demands later took on a political nature. By the 1830s, the fight for Czech national consciousness sprang from the academic lecture halls and was welcomed by a group of established yet young politicians.

More books continued to be written in Czech, expressing Czech feelings and opinions. The earliest literature was plebeian in nature, more like children's rhymes than poetry, more folklore than serious prose. Its authors, the first of their families and social group to be educated, had come from the ranks of the underprivileged, indeed from the overtly poor. The Czech community and the national revival did not have its own aristocracy.

In the years preceding the unrest of 1848, when people across Europe began to demand greater political freedom, the Czech community was preparing to press its political demands. Through a prism of historical traditions (often myths), it examined its own history and developed a nationalist consciousness. This was not a revolutionary group; despite their efforts to establish an independent Czech identity, the nationalists were loyal, with a few reservations, to the Austrian overlords, who had shaped and designed European alliances for centuries. For its part, Austria was unprepared to deal with the issues of nationalism that were being raised throughout the empire and Europe. The interests of the nations making up Austria collided, even though they had in principle a common starting point: liberal democratic changes.

The 1848 revolution in the Czech lands, although not a massive success, was the first visible expression of a Czech interest in a modern solution for political problems. It could be expressed as follows: "We are here, we demand our rights, and we

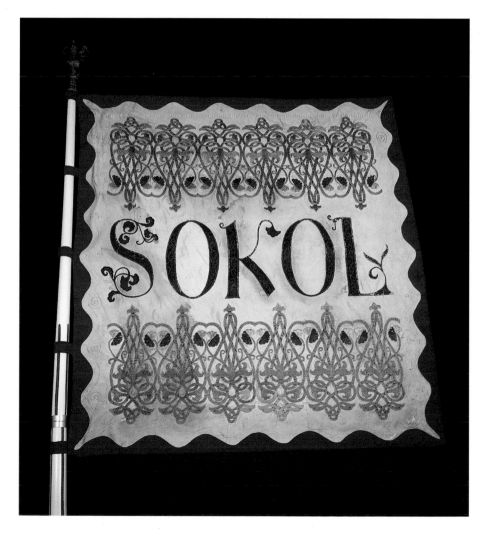

83. Sokol flag, designed by Josef Mánes, 1887. The Sokol organization, which promoted moral and physical fitness, was an important supporter of the nationalist movement. The name Sokol means "falcon." Cat. 188.

shall continue to demand them." The uprising in spring 1848 marked the first expression of a fundamental divergence between the Czech nationalists and the German-Czechs. In June 1848, the first Pan-Slav Congress was held under the leadership of František Palacký, a leading figure in Czech politics and scholarship. The mood of the congress marked a shift from Austrian allegiance to a self-aware Czech identity, insisting on its historical rights and autonomy. Czech and pan-Slavic interests were under attack from both within and outside the Empire. The Germans from the Czech lands turned for support to the German National Assembly, held in Frankfurt in May 1848. This congress strengthened links among German-speaking peoples and resulted in the decision that the Austrian problems be resolved in a pan-German framework, putting the Czechs at a disadvantage. A new danger could also be seen threatening central Europe: the influence of czarist Russia.

The uprising in Prague was quelled in 1848, and Emperor Francis Joseph I resorted to political absolutism in order to halt the nationalist movement. By 1860, this approach had been abandoned, and the emperor promised a constitutional government with autonomy for the Czech lands.

What had begun with the petitions of 1848 now continued with a series of parliamentary and ex-parliamentary negotiations, which were to guarantee Czechs equal status with Austria and Hungary under the Imperial crown. However Austria, weakened in 1866 after its defeat by Prussia at Hradec Králové, decided to bolster the existence of the empire by dividing power between Austria and Hungary. The passing of the Dualist Constitution in December 1867 created two practically independent states, Hungary and the German-Austrian part of the empire, under one monarchy. The claims of the Slav nations went unheard. The Czechs staged a series of mass demonstrations calling for their own state's rights, but it proved impossible to overcome the resistance of the Germans.

What failed to succeed politically, however, continued to smolder in the Czech community. The supporters of the Czech national cause were originally made up of individuals; after the issuing of the Dualist Constitution, numerous Czech organizations sprang up, binding their members with nationalist slogans. One group that assumed the mantle of nationalism was the physical fitness organization Sokol, founded in 1862 (fig. 83). Dedicated to the philosophy of balanced physical, spiritual, and moral development, it garnered wide popular support among the Czech people. As a civic organization playing an important role in Czech life, it was often more influential than the Church, which did not have the same weight in Czech society as elsewhere.

By the end of the 1870s, new social problems appeared that required new solutions. One problem was social unrest, causing on the one hand a wave of emigration, especially by small farmers and artisans, and on the other hand, a regeneration of the social democratic movement, which by the end of the nineteenth century had become a political and ideological force that could no longer be overlooked. Another problem was that none of the newly emerging groups could find a way to achieve its own goals and simultaneously address the issue of nationalism. This was understandable; the overwhelming Czech majority was dominated politically by the German ethnic minority, which was protected by the government. The conflict permeated all levels of society and was felt by most to be unsolvable. The generation of leaders who had led the Czech lands onto the international political scene were now venerable old men, soon to be replaced by a new generation of political realists. One of these rising politicians was the professor Tomáš Garrigue Masaryk, a principled and constructive individual (fig. 84). With several other intellectuals, he refused the self-seeking jingoism of the older patriots and brought the Czech independence movement beyond its original and in many respects narrow nationalist orientation. The turn of the century was marked by an increasing push for reform that, after the revolution of 1905, resulted in laws guaranteeing general universal suffrage in parliamentary elections.

84. Bust of Tomáš Masaryk, by J. K. Pekárek, 1921. Masaryk masterminded the formation of the Czechoslovak Republic in 1918 and served as its president until 1935. Cat. 211.

Despite these gains, the Czech dilemma of how to deal with German aspirations remained unresolved. With the outbreak of World War I, Austria-Hungary joined the German empire as a weaker ally in the battle against western Europe and the United States. Czech politicians were unprepared for war and did not have a general strategy. Abandoning the possibility of reforming the Austro-Hungarian monarchy, Masaryk proposed that the Czechs engage in anti-Austrian resistance. In close cooperation with Czech groups in the United States, he pledged himself to an independent alliance of Czechs and Slovaks.

Toward the end of the war, the Austro-Hungarian monarchy had become increasingly dependent on the Germans, confirming Masaryk's belief that the empire would not support Czech autonomy. Masaryk and his followers' struggle for independence was supported by the citizens of the future state. Among these supporters were tens of thousands of Czech and Slovak men who fought as voluntary Czechoslovak military units on the side of Allies. At the end of World War I, on October 28, 1918, the Republic of Czechoslovakia declared its independence.

The Czechoslovak Republic

Czechoslovakia in 1918 was a republic of two related Slavic peoples, 6,850,000 Czechs and 1,910,000 Slovaks, who now formed a unified Czechoslovak nation. In addition, 3,042,000 Germans and 715,000 Hungarians, Ruthenians, and Poles became Czechoslovak citizens. The boundaries of the state were delineated to include the Czech lands, Slovakia, and the small territory of Ruthenia. The western regions of the new state, Bohemia, Moravia, and Silesia, were markedly more developed economically and culturally than the eastern Slovak region.

Despite the heterogeneous origins of its population groups, the threadbare tradition of independence in Slovakia, and continuing troublesome relations between Czechs and Germans, Czechoslovakia became a democratic state. It was an important model of a modern, politically ordered society and a leader in the effort to create a contractual community of young European states with similar destinies. It inherited, however, the difficulties inherent in the national composition of the population that had plagued the Austrian empire. Masaryk summarized it thus: "The main problem here is the relationship between the Czechoslovak majority and our German citizens. If we can solve this problem, all the other language and national problems will be easily solved." While the rights of the various ethnic groups were respected, a true solution to this problem was never found.

The Czechoslovak Republic was a parliamentary democracy with universal voting rights. After the initial success by leftists, the political scene from the beginning of the 1920s took on a right-wing orientation, and the presidency became snared in the successes and failures of the state. Masaryk, president from 1918 to 1935, had both the stature and the authority to guarantee and maintain political equilibrium. His successor, Edvard Beneš, president and president-in-exile from 1935 to 1948, lacked Masaryk's charisma but was a skillful and successful diplomat for many years.

Between the wars, Czechoslovakia was an economically prosperous country, an island of democracy with a flourishing culture and respect for individual freedom—in other words, a state quite exceptional for the time in Central Europe. Nevertheless, it could not escape the consequences of its geographic location and of the European political situation. The rise of the National Socialists to power in neighboring Germany in the 1930s posed an immediate and fierce threat to Czechoslovakia. Czechoslovak Germans in the border lands felt a solidarity with the German political agenda; they united under the political leadership of the Sudeten Party and embraced Adolf Hitler's campaign for German ethnic unity. The blow came from Munich on September 29, 1938: representatives of Czechoslovakia's allies, Britain and France, in concert with Benito Mussolini of Italy, signed a contract with Hitler giving Czechoslovakia's border territories to the German Reich. Czechoslovakia had not been invited to the negotiations. After only twenty years, the Munich Conference and Agreement ended the de facto existence of the republic.

A little more than five months passed before German forces occupied the rest of Czechoslovakia. The power imbalance in central Europe had extinguished Czech and Slovak hopes for an independent existence. On March 15, 1939, under pressure from Berlin, Slovakia sued for independence; the remainder of

Czechoslovakia was occupied by the German army and renamed the Protectorate of Bohemia and Moravia.

The Czech lands found themselves in a state of war even before the beginning of the general European war. Czech-German relations acquired an new and infamous dimension. The country was occupied, yet not at war; it was threatened but could not defend itself with a mobilized army of its own. Although there was no warfare in the Protectorate during World War II, many still died violent deaths at the gallows, in prisons, and in concentration camps. In defiance, some Czechs fought against the Germans with Allied troops, while others engaged in underground resistance activities (including the 1942 assassination of Reinhard Heydrich, the occupying Protector, which the Germans punished with brutal reprisals). Still others—indeed the majority—were bound by ordinary, mostly unheroic, human concerns and endured the humiliation.

As the Allied victory approached, the Soviet army liberated the majority of Czechoslovak territory. The demarcation line of the Allied occupation zones sliced through western Bohemia. Moscow wanted to control the center of Europe. The Soviet influence penetrated to Czechoslovakia, arousing both strong enthusiasm and opposition.

At the war's end, the political elite of the Czechoslovak Republic decided to resolve some of the long-term problems of the state quickly, radically, and with the consent of the victorious powers. In accordance with the conclusions of the peace negotiations, the German inhabitants of Bohemia who had not objected to Hitler's territorial destruction of Czechoslovakia and whose attitude had thereby legitimized the occupation, were removed from the country. In its historical context, this removal seemed to have been a justifiable political step; unfortunately, there were cases of brutality that can be seen as reactions to life under German occupation. In the 1946 elections, Czechoslovak voters elected a left-wing government, removing the last impediment to Soviet influence in Central Europe.

The Communist Party of Czechoslovakia partly manipulated and partly controlled the public; once in power, they plunged Czechoslovakia into the Soviet sphere. A domestic version of totalitarianism took control of Czechoslovakia. Similar to events in the Soviet Union, a storm of political trials swept through the land; death sentences were not uncommon, and the opposition was completely liquidated. After Stalin's death in 1953, and after the XXth Congress of the Soviet Communist Party in 1956, the most drastic excesses of Sovietization lessened. The chosen path of communism was not abandoned, however; for nearly a generation Communist ideologues skillfully exploited the existing socialist sympathies, while at the same time they undermined the more fundamental democratic philosophy of most Czechs and Slovaks.

In 1968, under its new secretary, Alexander Dubček, the Communist Party of Czechoslovakia took steps to adapt socialist principles in a Czechoslovak model, independent of Soviet control. This movement garnered widespread popular, mostly nonpolitical support within the country, but was strongly suppressed by the Soviets, who responded with a military invasion on August 21, 1968. The events of "Prague Spring" came to symbolize the courage and resilience of small countries in the face of Soviet domination, and the invasion of Czechoslovakia was condemned by countries around the world. The violent response to the movement for self-determination was a phenomenon that had occurred many times in the past. Once again the interests of this small country in the center of Europe succumbed to those of the more powerful; the protesting voices were forced into exile, and a stifling silence set in.

The eventual internal disintegration of the Soviet regime and the 1989 collapse of the Czechoslovak Communist government led to the formation of a new government, made up of those who had fought for their rights in their struggle for the ideals of humanism. The essence of this new government could be summed up in one name: Václav Havel. A playwright, intellectual, and dissident who had been imprisoned under the defeated regime, Havel was elected president of the newly independent republic.

The Czechoslovak Republic calmly reached a political solution to its nationality problem. On the first day of 1993, Czechs and Slovaks ended their seventy-year long journey together: the separate Slovak and Czech Republics came into being. A fundamental portion of European history, whose contours are touched on here, is their history as well.

Stanislav Slavík
HISTORICAL MUSEUM,
THE NATIONAL MUSEUM

Catalogue

1. FLOOR TILE *Earthenware; third quarter of the thirteenth century; South Bohemia; found at Zvíkov Castle, district of Písek; h. 19.2 cm, w. 19.2 cm, d. 4 cm; H2-2.505*

The two-tailed crowned lion on this floor tile ranks among the oldest images of the symbol of the Czech state. According to legend, the lion coat of arms became the emblem of King Vladislav I in 1158; it can be documented as being used at least since the time of Přemysl I (d. 1230). The official nature of the lion image is conveyed by the text: "They call me the lion, and the kings of Bohemia do bear me." *See fig. 1, page 3.*
V B

Památky národní minulosti: Katalog historické expozice Národního muzea v Praze *(Prague, 1989), no. 142.*

2. EARRING *Copper, gilt; second half of the ninth century; Bohemia; found at Stará Kouřim, district of Kolín; h. 3.1 cm; H1-118.576*

3. EARRING *Silver; second half of the ninth century; Bohemia or Moravia; found at Stará Kouřim, district of Kolín; h. 3.6 cm; H1-118.677*

4, 5, 6

Earrings were favored by women in the upper classes of society. The finest were made from gold and silver, metals that could be fashioned using the demanding techniques of granulation and filigree. These two superb earrings come from the princes' burial grounds at the fortified settlement of Stará Kouřim, an extensive site that served as the gateway through which Great Moravian influences and traditions passed into the Czech state of the Přemyslids. *See fig. 15, page 19.* M L

M. Šolle, Stará Kouřim *(Prague, 1966).*

4. LOCKRING *Bronze; tenth century; Bohemia; found at Prague-Motol; diam. 1.3 cm; H1-55.410*

5. LOCKRING *Silver; tenth century; Bohemia; found at Prague-Motol; diam. 1.6 cm; H1-55.449*

The S-shaped lockring was a typical adornment for women between the late ninth century and the thirteenth century. Bronze, silver, and occasionally gold wire of various thicknesses were shaped into a ring, one end of which was drawn out and twisted into an S shape (hence the name). The rings were probably attached to leather bands braided into the hair. These two examples come from one of the largest early medieval burial sites in Bohemia. M L

J. Kovářík, Slovanské kostrové pohřebiště v Praze 5-Motole *(Prague, 1991).*

6. NECKLACE *Glass; tenth century; Bohemia; found at Želkovice, district of Beroun; 7 beads: diam. 12 mm; 4 beads: diam. 7–10 mm; H1-33.703*

Glass beads of various types served as adornment for women of many social ranks in early medieval Slavic society. Since beads were popular as jewelry, they are often found among grave goods. M L

J. Kovářík, Slovanské kostrové pohřebiště v Praze 5-Motole *(Prague, 1991).*

7. BUTTON *Gilded bronze; first half of the tenth century; Bohemia; found at Zákolany, district of Kladno; diam. 3.1 mm; H1-54.696*

Decorative sewn-on buttons (or ball brooches), called *gombíky*, were made in ninth-century workshops in Great Moravia, often of precious metals, and remained in favor in Bohemia through the tenth century. They adorned the dress of the upper classes. This particular button was unearthed in a burial site at Zákolany, near Budeč, an important Přemyslid stronghold. *See fig. 18, page 20.* M L

M. Šolle, "Slovanská pohřebiště pod Budčí," Památky archeologické 73 (1982): 174ff.

8. ORNAMENTAL PENDANT *Silver; late tenth century; Central Europe; found at Komárov, district of Opava; pendant: h. 3.3 cm, w. (base) 4 cm, l. 7 cm; chain: 7.3 cm; H2-9.873*

This small zoomorphic ornament probably represents a lamb in the Christian sense of the Agnus Dei, with a stylized aura around its backward-facing head. In the entire western Slav territory only a handful of comparable pieces are known, loosely related through technique (granulation and filigree) and motifs (lambs, horses, and birds). This particular lamb was one of several silver objects (only the lamb figure has been preserved) and coins of many nations buried near Silesian Komárov early in the eleventh century along a busy trade route connecting the Czech lands of the Oder Basin to the Baltic Sea. *See fig. 20, page 20.* V B

P. Radoměrský, "Poklad komárovský," Časopis slezského muzea: řada B–Historie 5 (1956): 1–9.

9, 10

9. PLOWSHARE *Iron; eighth or ninth century; Bohemia; found at Semice, district of Nymburk; diam. 25.9 cm, w. 8.7 cm; H2-100.056*

Hoards of iron implements that were buried in times of danger are important evidence of the level of agricultural technology and the importance of iron in the early Middle Ages. One item found in a hoard was this dagger-shaped wrought plowshare that was a component of the *ard*, a plow that stirred the soil without turning it. The shape of the plowshare did not change significantly from the La Téne period (from about 500 B.C.) until the high Middle Ages, when a heavy plow with a large asymmetrical share was developed. V B

M. Beranová, "Slovanský hromadný nález ze Semic," Archeologické rozhledy 24 (1972): 630–31, fig. 1c.

10. AX *Iron; end of the ninth century; Bohemia; found at Libice nad Cidlinou, district of Nymburk; l. 16 cm, w. 11.6 cm; H1-309.803*

In the early Middle Ages, wrought-iron axes were both universal working tools and important weapons for doing battle at close quarters. In a few instances, axes have been found in graves of high-ranking individuals. This was the case at an extensive gravesite at the fortified settlement of Libice, used from the end of the ninth to the eleventh century, from which this ax comes. M L

R. Turek, "Libice: Pohřebiště na vnitřním hradisku." part 1, Sborník Národního muzea, ser. A, 30 (1976), 249ff.; part 2, Sborník Národního muzea, ser. A, 32 (1978), 1ff.

11. SPUR *Iron, copper; ninth century; Bohemia; found at Hradsko near Mšeno, district of Mělník; l. 12.4 cm, w. 8.9 cm; H2-12.789*

This wrought-iron prick-spur, reinforced by a band of copper where it is riveted to the thin, horizontally grooved catch plates, typifies a type of spur used in Great Moravia during the ninth century. The use of stirrups and the custom of driving horses with a whip came from the Avars in the East; most spurs were used by warriors who fought on horseback. This particular spur was found at a major Central Bohemian stronghold, probably the one known from Frankish annals as Canburg, which in 805 was unsuccessfully besieged by Charlemagne's army. V B

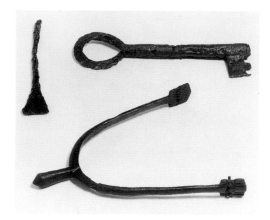

13, 12, 11

12. KEY *Iron; ninth to tenth century; Bohemia; found at Levý Hradec, district of Prague-West; l. 11.9 cm, w. (at bit) 2.7 cm; head 3.3 x 3.4 cm; H2-100.461*

This key, wrought from one piece of iron, has a sophisticated design that allowed a door latch to be secured by bolts that were released by the turning mechanism of the specific key. From the time of the Great Moravian period (ninth century), large turnkeys were used on doors of residences and small ones on furniture. V B

13. STYLUS *Iron; tenth century; Bohemia; found at Libice nad Cidlinou, district of Nymburk; l. 9.4 cm, w. 1.7 cm; H1-309.531*

A stylus was an implement with a pointed end for writing in the wax of a tablet and a broad end that could erase what was written by flattening the wax. Since priests were the only literate group in the early Middle Ages, styluses are found only in or near the ruins of church buildings. This particular one was found among the remains of a church in the fortified settlement of Libice, the probable birthplace of Saint Adalbert. M L

R. Turek, Slavníkovci a jejich panství *(Hradec Králové, 1982).*

14. RELIQUARY CROSS *Brass; eleventh or twelfth century; Kievan Russia?; found at Opočnice, district of Nymburk; h. 10.2 cm, w. 5.7 cm, d. 1.5 cm; H2-1.961*

This reliquary cross, or *enkolpion,* was cast in two parts. It is decorated with a figure of Christ on the cross, symbols of the sun and moon in relief, and two inscribed Greek inscriptions saying "Behold your son!" and "Behold your mother!" The other side bears an orant figure of the Virgin Mary and circular medallions containing pictures of the evangelists.

This cross and the two that follow are part of a rare treasure of six reliquary crosses found in Bohemia. That religious items in this single group came from two culturally different areas (enamel crosses, possibly from the Rhineland, and crosses in the Byzantine style with Greek inscriptions, probably from Kievan Russia), underscores the role of the Czech Lands as a crossroads between the Christian West and East. However, very early in the Middle Ages the Roman Catholic Church gained ascendancy, firmly incorporating the Czech Lands into Christian West-

14, 15, 16

ern Europe. Christian symbols, whether engraved or cast, and the relics they originally contained were considered to be both an expression of piety and a means of protecting the person who wore them. *See fig. 28, page 29.*   V B

J. E. Vocel, "Byzantinské kříže u Opočnice nalezené," Památky archeologické 3 (1859): 363–66, fig. 15:1a, b; B. Nechvátal, "Frühmittelalterliche Reliquienkreutze aus Böhmen," Památky archeologické 70 (1979): 213–16.

15. RELIQUARY CROSS *Bronze, enamel, gilt; eleventh or twelfth century; Meuse-Rhine region?; found at Opočnice, district of Nymburk; h. 8.4 cm, w. 5.6 cm, d. 1.2 cm; H2-1.965*

This reliquary cross is composed of two parts. The front has an enamel-decorated figure of Christ. The back has engraved braiding and foliate decoration in the shape of a cross. *See fig. 28, page 29.*   V B

J. Vocel, "Byzantinské kříže u Opočnice nalezené," fig. 15:4a, b; B. Nechvátal, "Frühmittelalterliche Reliquienkreutze aus Böhmen," 215.

16. RELIQUARY CROSS *Copper, enamel, gilt; eleventh or twelfth century; Meuse-Rhine region?; found at Opočnice, district of Nymburk; h. 9 cm, w. 7.1 cm, d. 1.1 cm; H2-1.966*

On the front of this two-part enameled reliquary cross is a figure of Christ and symbols of the sun and moon on an enamel background. On the back is a central mask and an engraved cross with arms that end in acanthus-like fronds. *See fig. 28, page 29.*   V B

J. Vocel, "Byzantinské kříže u Opočnice nalezené," 15:3a, b; B. Nechvátal, "Frühmittelalterliche Reliquienkreutze aus Böhmen," 215–16.

17. POT *Earthenware; sixth century; Moravia; found at Mikulčice, district of Břeclav; h. 14.1 cm, diam. (rim) 9.4 cm; H1-59.062*

The Slavs who settled in the fertile regions of the Czech Lands in the sixth century made simple, undecorated pottery, the chief form of which has come to be known as the Prague type. These vessels were used for storage, for food preparation, and as burial urns. The example shown here comes from the region of Mikulčice, later a center of Great Moravia. *See fig. 16, page 19.*   M L

18. POT *Earthenware; tenth century; Bohemia; found at Prague-Motol; h. 9.9 cm, diam. (rim) 10.6 cm; H1-55.436*

For the most part Slavic vessels of the early Middle Ages were richly decorated with wave patterns, grooves, and other marks made with a comblike tool. As well as being used in the kitchen, pots containing food and drink were buried with the dead to ensure that the soul had food and drink on its "last journey." *See fig. 16, page 19.*   M L

J. Sláma, Mittelböhmen im frühen Mittelalter *(Prague, 1977); J. Kovářík,* Slovanské kostrové pohřebiště v Praze 5-Motole *(Prague 1991).*

19. STORAGE VESSEL *Earthenware; late twelfth century; Ostrov Abbey workshop; found at Ostrov near Davle, district of Prague-East; h. 43 cm, w. 40 cm; H2-68.943*

This bottle-shaped, turned and joined storage vessel has applied rope and impressed foliate decorations. Discovered in a side chapel of the abbey basilica of Saint John the Baptist at Ostrov, the vessel may have been used to store wine used in the liturgy. The unique decoration echoes that of the abbey's terra-cotta floors.   V B

A. Merhautová, Skomné umění: Ostrovská zdobená terakota *(Prague, 1988), pp. 120–21, figs. 178–79.*

19

20. FLOOR TILE *Earthenware; late eleventh century or early twelfth century; Ostrov Abbey workshop; found at Prague-Vyšehrad; h. 23 cm, w. 19.5 cm, d. 4 cm; H2-14.056*

This six-sided, relief-molded terra-cotta floor tile portrays a griffin, a mythical creature that was popular in medieval art and could have either negative or positive connotations. In Prague's former basilica of Saint Lawrence in the Vyšehrad castle of the Přemyslids, the griffin and a lion symbolized the forces of good, as opposed to evil, represented by the tyrant Nero and a mythical sphinx. *See fig. 25, page 24.*   V B

D. Hejdová and B. Nechvátal, "Raně středověké dlaždice v Čechách, I." Památky archeologické 61 *(1970):109–110, fig. 2:2.*

21. FLOOR TILE *Earthenware; second quarter of the twelfth century; Ostrov Abbey workshop; Ostrov near Davle, district of Prague-East; h. 16 cm, w. 16 cm, d. 4.5 cm; H2-68.751*

This six-sided floor tile, decorated with a six-pointed star and rosettes, is from the former Abbey of Saint John the Baptist at Ostrov. There the earliest documented workshop in the Czech Lands (and quite possibly all of Central Europe) produced relief-decorated tiles for both facing and paving. Tiles from this workshop have been found in other locations, evidence both of the entrepreneurial activity of the Ostrov Benedictines and of the use of relief tiles and shaped pieces in religious architecture during the Romanesque period.   V B

A. Merhautová, Skromné umění: Ostrovská zdobená terakota *(Prague, 1988), p. 16, fig. 15.*

21

22. DENARIUS *Silver; 965–972; Prague; diam. 19 mm, mass 1.02 g; private collection*

This coin, minted during the reign of Boleslav I (r. 935–972), was the first Czech coin minted at Prague Castle for trade purposes. It was modelled after the Bavarian denarius. According to contemporary reports, it was sufficient to pay an adult man's living costs for a month. *See fig. 3, page 7.*   Z P

F. Cach, Nejstarší české mince, I *(Prague, 1970).*

23. DENARIUS *Silver; 1086–1092; Prague?; diam. 16 mm, mass 0.66 g; private collection*

This denarius was minted after Vratislav II was crowned king of Bohemia in 1086. Research suggests that the individualized features of the ruler are fairly accurate. *See fig. 4, page 7.*   Z P

F. Cach, Nejstarší české mince, II (Prague, 1972), no. 108.

24. GROSCH *Silver; 1300–1305; Kutná Hora; diam. 27 mm, mass 3.72 g; private collection*

This famous Prague coin dominated the markets of central Europe for almost 250 years. It was first minted at the rich silver mines of Kutná Hora late in the reign of Václav II (1278–1305); the last of the coins bear the mark of the year 1547. The grosch was driven out of circulation in the sixteenth century by the gradual transition to the newly introduced tolar. *See fig. 8, page 11.*   Z P

J. Smolík, Pražské groše a jejich díly 1300-1547 (Prague, 1971).

25. CHARTER OF PŘEMYSL OTAKAR II *Parchment, ink, wax; March 12, 1264; Jihlava, Bohemia; h. 10.5 cm, w. 18.0 cm; H3-a26*

In this charter Přemysl Otakar II, called the King of Iron and Gold, granted the abbey of Our Lady in Žd'ár nad Sázavou the right to use the proceeds from the gold and silver mines on the abbey's lands. Reserves of precious metals were the property of the crown, and all proceeds from mining belonged to the king. The right to mine could be passed to landowners or miners (either aristocrats and burgers), in return for a special payment *(urbur)* to the crown. The *urbur* contributed to the power of the kings of Bohemia in the thirteenth and fourteenth centuries. *See fig. 6, page 9.*   M R

26. CHARTER OF CHARLES IV *Parchment, ink; 1366; Bohemia; h. 38 cm, w. 46 cm; H3-A117*

With this charter Charles IV, Holy Roman Emperor and King of Bohemia, donated a house in Prague Lesser Town to the masters and students of Charles College, thus founding the second oldest college of Charles University—the College of All Saints or "Angel College." It was issued on July 30, 1366, concurrently with a charter for the foundation of another college in Prague Old Town. The two charters are among the oldest and most important artifacts of the university, which was founded in 1348. Of the two copies of the 1348 foundation charter of Charles University, only one has been preserved. *See fig. 11, page 13.*   M R

27. BEAKER WITH LEATHER COVER *Stoneware, leather; third quarter of the fourteenth century; Rhineland and Prague; found at Emaus Abbey, Prague; h. 17.7 cm, diam. (rim) 5.7 cm; H2-28.486*

This beaker has a shape and decoration typical of the mid-fourteenth century. Since medieval Bohemia lacked the necessary conditions to

27

manufacture salt-glazed stonewares, it was probably produced in the Rhineland, possibly in Sieburg. The case, a single piece of leather incised with floral designs, on the other hand, was probably made in a Prague workshop during the reign of Charles IV. Charles commissioned luxurious cases for both Czech and Imperial crown jewels, and the craft of incising leather cases and book bindings reached a sophisticated level in Prague far beyond that of the neighboring German-speaking countries. V B

V. Brych, "Středověké nálezy z Emauzského kláštera ve sbírkách Národního muzea v Praze," Časopis Národního muzea: řada historická, 155 (1986):14–15, 21–27, fig. 4 and 5.

28. SEAL *Brass; second half of the thirteenth century; Prague; h. 9.5 cm, diam. 7.2 cm; Archives of the National Museum*

This brass seal of the *zemský soud* (land court) of Bohemia consists of a handle in the shape of a seated lion welded to the back of a seal showing Saint Wenceslas. The *zemský soud* was the highest judicial body and with the *zemský sněm* (assembly of the land), the most important political body of the Czech aristocracy, was independent of the king. It was instituted in the second half of the thirteenth century from what originally were assemblies of Czech nobility and officials. Documents were endorsed with seals of this type up to the eighteenth century. *See fig. 5, page 8.* M R

29

29. STOVE TILE *Earthenware; second half of the fourteenth century; Bohemia; h. 16 cm, w. 16 cm, d. 9.7 cm; H2-2.542*

In Bohemia, the earliest ceramic stove tiles—with heraldic decoration in relief on the front wall and a hollow chamber facing into the body of the stove—date to the turn of the fourteenth century. The quality of this tile's decoration indicates that a trained carver rather than a potter made the mold for it. V B

30. STOVE TILE *Earthenware; fifteenth century; Prague; Vrchlický Gardens, Prague New Town; h. 20 cm, w. 20 cm, d. 9 cm; H2-131.200*

Medieval tiles with pictures of everyday life are a distinctive feature of Czech decorative arts. Here the king is seated in his bath; the queen, wearing the robes of a barber-surgeon, holds a bundle of sticks in one hand and a bucket in the other. The scene is notable for its authenticity of expression as well as its allegorical symbolism. This theme is found in illuminated manuscripts from the 1378–1419 reign of Václav IV, although it is likely that designs in tile art lagged behind those of the finer arts. V B

V. Brych, D. Stehlíková, and J. Žegklitz, Pražské kachle doby gotické a renesanční (Prague, 1990), no. 76.

30

31. PAVIS *Wood, leather, paint; last quarter of the fifteenth century; Prague; h. 98.5 cm, w. 50 cm; H2-30*

33

This oblong shield, or pavis, is decorated with the fortified gates of Prague, the city's emblem. On the back a leather grip is centered between an iron crosspiece at the top and iron brackets for chains at the edges.

The shield is one of a group of eleven with this emblem that were made by shieldmakers' guilds in Prague Old Town and New Town in the second half of the fifteenth century. The guilds were obliged to supply the town with several shields annually in return for their members being exempted from military service and general fees. From 1475, the masonry on the shield was changed from silver (white) to gold (yellow). Seven shields with yellow masonry (including this one) were made after 1475; four shields with white (silver) masonry were made before 1475. *See fig. 14, page 16.*   E Š

Památky národního minulosti: Katalog historické exposice Národního muzea v Praze *(Prague, 1989), no. 310.*

32. CHALICE *Earthenware; before 1420; Sezimovo Ústí, district of Tábor; h. 10 cm, diam. (rim) 9 cm, (base) 4 cm; H2-2.765*

Utraquist priests in the Tábor region administered the Eucharist outside churches and refused to use consecrated objects and chasubles. Simple ceramic chalices like this one symbolize the Hussite emphasis on sharing wine as well as bread in the Eucharist. This example comes from one of the first South Bohemian Hussite centers, Sezimovo Ústí, which the Hussites razed to the ground before abandoning it for newly founded Tábor. The chalice came to be a symbol of the Hussite movement. *See fig. 30, page 33.*   V B

Památky národního minulosti: Katalog historické exposice Národního muzea v Praze *(Prague, 1989), no. 267.*

35

33. STOVE TILE *Earthenware; mid-fifteenth century; Bohemia; h. 19.4 cm, w. 18.8 cm, d. 12.4 cm; H2-126.343*

Czech relief-decorated tiles with contemporary political and military themes include several featuring Hussite warriors. This example has three iron-helmeted foot soldiers, one carrying a flail and two with crossbows.   V B

J. Kouba, "Středověké kachle s husitskými bojovníky," Časopis Národního muzea: řada historická, 135 (1996): 25–34, fig. 7.

34

34. MACE *Iron, copper; c. 1500; Central Europe; l. 54.8 cm, w. (head) 14.4 cm; H2-24*

Maces, weapons of war that evolved from the club, were widely used during the Hussite Wars. E Š

35. HAUBERK *Iron; sixteenth century; Central Europe; h. 60 cm, w. 60 cm, collar, 4 cm; H2-159.265*

This sleeveless hauberk, or mail shirt, is composed of flat rings connected by rivets. Armor made of interwoven iron rings can be traced to classical times. The hauberk was the chief piece of armor of the Middle Ages; in the fifteenth to the seventeenth centuries it was used together with plate armor. E Š

36. CHEST *Spruce or fir, iron, leather, paint; c. 1500; Cental Europe; h. 72.5 cm, w. 196.5 cm, d. 78 cm; H2-17.311*

Throughout the Middle Ages, a chest was an indispensable item of furniture for storage in private homes and churches; it had both a practical and a decorative function. This chest, one of the few such pieces to survive in Bohemia, exemplifies work of the South German, Danube, and Alpine regions. The flat wood-carving technique and fantastical foliate ornament style became, in the late Gothic period, characteristic of Czech workmanship as well. V B

36

Památky národní minulosti: Katalog historické expozice Národního muzea v Praze *(Prague, 1989), no. 345. fig. 148*

37. KEY *Iron, copper; fifteenth or first half of the sixteenth century; Bohemia; l. 14.4 cm, w. 4.7 cm; H2-1.038*

This turnkey was made for a fixed lock with an improved mechanism that relied on a barrier spring with bolts and sometimes a spring catch. During the late medieval period, skilled locksmiths also began incorporating sophisticated decorative motifs on the head of the key. Gothic tracery designs, such as that on the head of this key, remained popular until the advent of the Renaissance. V B

D. Stará, "Iron," Pictorial Encyclopaedia of Antiques *(New York, 1968), pp. 379–96, fig. 518.*

38. KEY *Iron; late fifteenth or sixteenth century; Bohemia; l. 11 cm, w. 4.5 cm; H2-1.197*

This wrought-iron turnkey has a delicately cut bit and a solid head. Greater security was provided not only by the barrier lock it was made for, but also by the shape of the key axis (here a three-lobed profile). This key represents the most advanced design of the late Gothic to early Renaissance period. V B

Z. Petráň et al., Dějiny hmotné kultury, I, vol. 2 *(Prague, 1985), fig. 591.*

39. DOOR PLATE *Tin-plated sheet iron; fifteenth century; Bohemia; l. 22.5 cm, w. 22 cm; H2-9.101*

In the medieval period, doors provided a prominent place to display artistry. Plates of decorative wrought iron could be positioned between the heavy iron belts criss-crossing the front face of the door, and by us-

38, 37

39

40

42

ing negative matrices, ironworkers could ensure that the beaten plates were identical. The Moravian crown emblem, a spread eagle, was sometimes used in combination with a Czech lion or with other motifs. VB

40. BOWL *Brass; mid-fifteenth century; Dinant, Belgium; found at Vyšehrad Castle, Prague; h. 5.6 cm, diam. 25 cm; H2-1.343*

This brass dish has a die-stamped figure of a seated woman with a blossoming sprig and a garland in her hands. The theme and technique both suggest that the bowl originated in the Walloon (Dinant) area of southern Belgium.

In medieval households metal bowls were decorative luxuries. They were analogous to the christening and baptismal bowls in churches, and inscriptions suggest they were engagement or wedding gifts. The allegorical motif on this particular bowl may likewise suggest marriage. VB

J. Vocel, Grundzüge der böhmischen Alterthumskunde *(Prague, 1845); B. Frontczak, "Gotyckie, kute misy mosiezne w zbiorach Muzeum Uniwersytetu Jagiellońskiego,"* Opuscula Musealia 4 *(1990): 81–108, pl. 1*

41. CANDLEHOLDER *Brass; fifteenth century; Central Europe; h. 25 cm, w. 16 cm, d. 7.5 cm; H2-26.174*

This Gothic candleholder is in the form of man, a torch-bearer dressed as an aristocratic dandy. The schematic clothing, particularly the short, close-fitting jacket and the narrow-legged trousers, clearly depicts the fashion from the late fourteenth and early fifteenth century.

Only a few tabletop candle holders of this type, made of bronze or brass, survive in Bohemia. They may have been produced at foundries in the Czech Lands or abroad, particularly in Nuremberg, whose influence on domestic work has been suggested. *See fig. 52, page 60.* VB

J. Diviš, Antiquitäten aus Bronze, Kupfer, und Messing *(Prague, 1991), fig. 25.*

42. STOVE TILE *Earthenware; second half of the fifteenth century; Bohemia; h. 19.5 cm, w. 19.3 cm, d. 8.8 cm; H2-103.849*

A favorite genre scene on medieval tiles was a jousting tournament showing an equestrian knight and a fool. On this tile, the figures are rich in detail; the knight's tournament weaponry and the horse's ceremonial position are elaborated with remarkable precision. The first mention of tournaments in Bohemia occurs during the reign of Václav I (r. 1230–1253). VB

43. STOVE TILE *Earthenware; late fifteenth or early sixteenth century; Kutná Hora; found at Křešice manor, district of Benešov; h. 21.3 cm, w. 20.8 cm, d. 15 cm; H2-7.511*

This crenelated tile for the upper ledge of a stove is one of several that depict various occupations. The figure wears a miner's smock and cap and carries a miner's dish lamp in his hand. The tile was probably pro-

43

44

duced in a potter's workshop at Kutná Hora, the most important silver mining center in Bohemia.　v b

> Památky národní minulosti: Katalog historické expozice Národního muzea v Praze (*Prague, 1989), no. 394.*

44. STOVE TILE *Earthenware; second half of the fifteenth century; Bohemia; h. 19.1 cm, w. 18.7 cm, d. 11.8 cm; H2-2.546*

The two-tailed crowned lion on a shield, seen in relief on this chamber tile, is a late Gothic variant of the symbol of the Czech state.　v b

> Památky národní minulosti: Katalog historické expozice Národního muzea v Praze (*Prague, 1989), no. 381.*

45. STATUE OF THE VIRGIN MARY *Earthenware; fifteenth century; Bohemia; h. 7 cm, w. 2.7 cm, d 1.6 cm; H2-4.166*

On this small statue of the Virgin Mary is a suggestion of a crown; despite the limitations of the technique used, the work is surprising in the subtlety of the relief achieved. Figures of the Virgin (with or without the Christ child) and other saints were devotional objects.　v b

> V. Huml, "K hliněné plastice z výzkumu na Václavském náměstí v Praze," Praehistorica 8, Varia Archeologica 2 (1981):325–27, figs. 36:2, 3.

46. JUG HANDLE *Earthenware; fifteenth century; Prague; found at Prague Old Town; h. 12.1 cm, w. 7.1 cm, d. 7.2 cm; H2-5.310*

This fragment from the upper part of a jug handle is a rare example of the human form modeled by a potter. This tiny work of art has a striking expression. Technologically it belongs to the category of red-

45

painted ceramics that spread in Bohemia in the second half of the thirteenth century through German colonization; it was a characteristic element of Czech pottery until the early sixteenth century.   V B

Z. Drobná, "Czech Medieval Ceramics," in Medieval Ceramics in Czechoslovakia, (Prague, 1962), pp. 10–15, fig. 1.

47. BEAKER *Earthenware; fifteenth or sixteenth century; Brno; found at Bouzov, district of Olomouc; h. 17.6 cm, diam. (rim) 9.2 cm, (base) 5.5 cm; H2-21.983*

One distinctive Moravian ceramic form from the Middle Ages was the Brno beaker, manufactured in the potters' workshops of the Moravian city of Brno. The elegant shape of these vessels and their dark gray, almost metallic sheen (produced by hard-reduction firing) stimulated a demand that far exceeded the supply.   V B

V. Nekuda and K. Reichertová, Středověká keramika v Čechách a na Moravě (Prague, 1968), table 67.

48. CUP *Earthenware; late fifteenth or early sixteenth century; Loštice, district of Šumperk; found in Prague; h. 18.5 cm, max. diam. 16 cm; H2-2.825*

This cup with thirteen handles, ornamented by red-painted horizontal bands, is an example of Loštice ware, a unique phenomenon in Europe. Its appearance is due to the iron oxide content of the clay that, under high firing temperatures, oxidized and left tiny bubbles on the surface of the vessel. Loštice wares, especially cups, were prized by foreign traders and collectors. Hieronymus Bosch used them in paintings to symbolize the threat of the "French disease."   V B

V. Nekuda and K. Reichertová, Středověká keramika v Čechách a na Moravě (Prague, 1968), table 73; M. Togner, "Moravská keramika a Hieronymus Bosch," Umění a řemesla 37 (1995): 47–52.

49. MADONNA AND CHILD *Linden wood; before 1500; Uhliště, Southwest Bohemia; h. 140.5 cm, base 40.5 x 30 cm; H2-60.763*

The increasing honor accorded to the Virgin Mary in the late Middle Ages is apparent from the many sculptures representing her. This beautiful example is related to a group of sculptures produced at the end of the fifteenth century in a workshop in South Bohemia, which was ruled by the Rožmberk family. The statue's form, idealized features, and the treatment of drapery and details is characteristic of all Marian statues produced by this workshop. It originally stood in the late Gothic church of Saint Linhard in Uhliště. *See fig. 51, page 59.*   M P *and* M M

F. Vaněk, K. Hostaš, and F. A. Borovský, Soupis památek historických a uměleckých v politickém okresu klatovském (Prague, 1899), 183–84, table 125; J. Homolka, "Sochařství," in Pozdně gotické

46

47, 48

umění v Čechách 1471–1526 *(Prague, 1978), pp. 199, 245 n.98; J. Homolka,*
"Pozdně gotické sochařství," Dějiny Českého výtvarného umění I, 2
(Prague, 1984), 545.

50 (reverse)

50. PANEL PAINTING, ECCE HOMO *Wood, tempera; c. 1450; Bohemia; found at the church of Saint Martin in Kostelec nad Labem, district of Mělník; h. 104.5 cm, w. 105.5 cm (including frame), d. 6.8 cm; H2-60.749*

In this scene of Christ presented by Pilate to the Jews ("Ecce homo"), the participation of the grotesque puppetlike figures in the Passion is limited to gesture, while Christ's suffering is expressed by a grid of bloody wounds covering his body. The treatment of the body and face of the unidentified female saint on the reverse side of the panel reflects an older, more formal painting style. *See fig. 50, page 58.* M P

J. Pešina, Česká malba pozdní gotiky a renesance *(Prague, 1950), pp. 17, 100, nos. 11–12; J. Pešina, "Paralipomena k dějinám českého malířství pozdní gotiky a renesance," Umění 15 (1967):253 n. 35.*

51. CHASUBLE *Brocade, thread, appliqué; after 1500; Central Europe; l. 139 cm, w. 65 cm; H2-3.546*

The early sixteenth-century embroidered cross, from the period after 1500, was sewn on a later Renaissance brocade at the end of the nineteenth century. The appliqués of Christ and three angels catching the blood flowing from Christ's wounds are in high relief, while other figures are in lower relief. The realistic conception of Christ's face, the dynamic execution of the flamboyant drapery, and the attempt at a new understanding of the figures in the space are a reflection of a late Gothic trend in art that spread from the Netherlands across southern Germany into Central Europe. The relief shaping suggests that the model for the embroidery was probably a wooden sculpture on the same theme. *See fig. 32, page 36.* V Př *and* M M

Z. Drobná, Les Trésors de la broderie religieuse en Tchécoslovaquie *(Prague, 1950), p. 31, figs. 45, 46.*

52. CHALICE AND PATEN *Silver, gilding; fifteenth century; Prague; h. (chalice) 22.5 cm; H2-6.995*

The Saint Nicholas church in Vršovice, now part of Prague, is first mentioned in a fourteenth-century source. Among the liturgical objects in its inventory was this gilded silver chalice with paten. The chalice has a six-lobed base and a smooth, slightly flared cup. The hexagonal stem is interrupted by a thick node with six

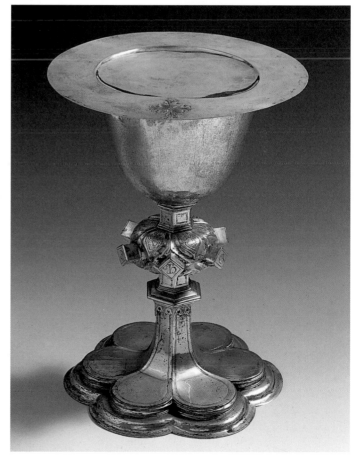

52

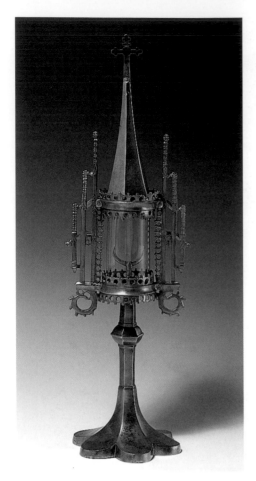

53

diamond-shaped protuberances bearing the letters "i-h-e-s-u-s" (Jesus). The stem is decorated with Gothic tracery. The smooth paten has an engraved cross surrounded by rays. Both chalice and paten were marked "CB" at a later date.   M M

A. Podlaha, Soupis památek historických, politický okres Vinohradský, vol. 28 (Prague, 1908), p. 164, fig. 204.

53. MONSTRANCE   *Brass, gilding, glass; fifteenth century; Bohemia; h. 46 cm; H2-2.079*

After the thirteenth-century incorporation of the the consecration of the Eucharist into the mass, monstrances were used in the Catholic Church to display the consecrated host for veneration. With its six-lobed base and its pinnacled flying buttress ornament echoing Gothic architectural forms, this monstrance is typical of those produced in the fourteenth and fifteenth centuries.   M M

54. PRINT OF PRAGUE   *Georg Hoefnagel (1542–1600); paper, copper engraving, watercolor; 1572; Cologne, Germany; plate mark: h. 36.0 cm, w. 41.9 cm; paper: h. 38.7 cm, w. 53.7 cm; H2-59.244*

In the upper half of this copper-plate engraving is a panorama of Prague Castle; in the lower half is part of the city of Prague as viewed from Letná Hill above the bend of the Vltava. This was a new prospect of the city, and Georg Hoefnagel superbly depicted the landscape, the castle, and the course of the river. Hoefnagel, the son of a diamond trader, followed his father in the trade but also studied with Hans Bol, an engraver and a painter of miniatures. As this merchant-artist traveled across Europe, he sketched landscapes and towns that were published from 1572 to 1618 in Cologne by Georg Braun and Franz Hogenberg under the title *Civitates orbis terrarum. See fig. 40, page 47.*   V Př

V. Hlavsa, Praha očima staletí (Prague, 1960); A. Novotný, Grafické pohledy Prahy 1493–1850 (Prague, 1946).

55. PRINT OF ZNOJMO   *Georg Hoefnagel (1542–1600); paper, copper engraving; 1561 to 1600; Cologne, Germany; plate mark: h. 32.1 cm, w. 50.3 cm; paper: h. 43.1 cm, w. 54.5 cm; H2-26.966*

The South Moravian town of Znojmo lies on the River Dyje, which since the eleventh century has formed Moravia's boundary with Austria. In the eleventh century a major Přemyslid castle replaced the older Great Moravian fortifications, making Znojmo the center of the Přemyslids' fiefdom and one of the most important towns in Moravia.   V Př

V. Richter, B. Samek, M. Stehlík, Znojmo (Prague, 1966).

56. AIDE-MEMOIRE   *Zikmund Petr Feferius; paper, ink, watercolor, leather; 1608–1644; Bohemia; h. 15.0 cm, w. 14.0 cm; H3-B.č. 12*

This aide-memoire was used by nobleman Zikmund Petr Feferius from 1608 to 1644. It exemplifies the many aide-memoires or *Stamm-*

55

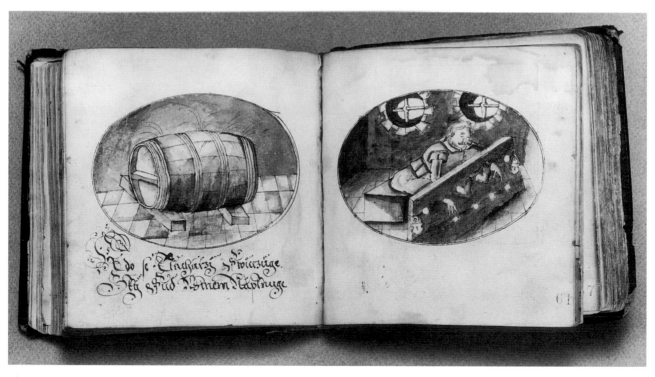

56

bücher that first appeared with the rise of humanism among aristocratic university students in sixteenth-century Western Europe and soon spread into other areas and other social ranks, particularly among burghers. Aide-memoires took on a wide variety of forms; they were not always simple volumes of blank pages for the owner to fill with thoughts and drawings. Some, like this one, had preprinted blank cartouches or engravings bound in the volume.
M R

57

57. AIDE-MEMOIRE *Regina z Berndorfu; paper, ink, watercolor, leather; 1600–1625; Bohemia; h. 10.5 cm, w. 8.5 cm; H3-B.č.22*

This aide-memoire of Regina z Berndorfu and Balthasar Reitsamen covers the years 1600 to 1625. Women's aide-memoires from this century are the exception rather than the rule, and this particular one is also distinguished by its unusually small size, which made it ideal for a woman to carry with her at all times. Like many other aide-memoires, it has decorated leather bindings.

The cartouches in this aide-memoire were probably filled in by a professional artist; the owner added a signature with a dedication and quotation or maxim. The recurrent themes in these books shed light on the life and times of the writers.   M R

58

58. WOMAN'S BELT *Silver, gilding; 1550–1600; Prague New Town?; l. 76.7 cm; H2-7.224*

This belt is made up of a flat chain and three rectangular plates decorated with small rosettes, plant motifs, and cherubim. It was shortened at some time in the past. One plate bears two stamped marks: "IBB" (possibly "TBB"), and a hallmark, perhaps of Prague New Town. In the sixteenth century, a belt or girdle was a favorite fashion accessory to which women affixed small ornaments, bags, or money pouches. The silver belt itself was considered a part of the material property of its owner, usually a noblewoman or wealthy burgess.   M M

D. Stará, "Jewelry," in The Pictorial Encyclopaedia of Antiques *(New York, 1970), p. 306.*

59. STOVE TILE *Earthenware, polychrome glaze; 1538; Bohemia; found at Opočno Castle, district of Rychnov nad Kněžnou; h. 22 cm, w. 17.5 cm, d. (existing) 2.5 cm; H2-2.620*

60. STOVE TILE *Earthenware, polychrome glaze; 1538; Bohemia; found at Opočno Castle, district of Rychnov nad Kněžnou; h. 22.5 cm, w. 19.5 cm, d. (existing) 3 cm; H2-2.621*

61

With the advent of the Renaissance, relief decoration on Czech tiles lost the originality of the previous period; new motifs were for the most part imported from neighboring German-speaking countries. Among the first of these were noble tiles, featuring high-born men or women framed by architectural elements. The occurrence of identical motifs throughout central Europe suggests that the originals and the designs on which they were based found their way along trade routes and were widely copied. One artistic and technological change during the Renaissance was the use of multicolored glazing, including stannic lead oxide, which had been used sparingly in late Gothic production. *See fig. 56, page 63.*   V B

62

Z. Hazlbauer and J. Špaček, "Poznámky k výrobě reliéfních kachlů s přihlédnutím k nálezům ve středním Polabí," Časopis Národního muzea, řada historická 155 (1986):146–66.

61. TOLAR   *Silver; 1519–1525; Jáchymov; diam. 42 mm, mass 29.65 g; private collection*

This coin from the reign of Ludvík I (1516–1526) has the Czech two-tailed lion and an inscription identifying Ludvík as ruler on the obverse, and on the reverse a relief of Saint Joachim with a staff and the escutcheon of nobleman Štěpán Šlik, who owned the Jáchymov mine. The discovery of a rich vein of silver at Jáchymov in North Bohemia at the beginning of the sixteenth century allowed Bohemia to mint a heavy silver coin based on the Saxon model. The Czech word "tolar" came from the town's German name, Joachimsthaler; later this name passed to the present American currency, the dollar.   Z P

L. Nemeškal, Jáchymovská mincovna, vol. 1 (Prague, 1964).

62. STOVE TILE   *Earthenware; second half of the sixteenth century; Moravia and Austria; h. 68.4 cm, w. 58.1 cm, d. 7 cm; H2-144.772*

The symbolic interplay of pictures from the Old and New Testaments (Christ on the cross, flanked by Abraham sacrificing Isaac, and Moses and the snake of brass) reflects the spirit of the Reformation. This iconographic arrangement is also found on several different products of Austrian or German origin, indicating that different workshops used the same model, probably from the excellent Salzburg workshops during the period 1550–1575. This green-glazed tile with a light engobe substrate represents a high level of artistic craftsmanship.   V B

J. Leisching, Sammlung Lanna. Prag, vol. 1 (Leipzig, 1909), no. 542, fig. 8.; and Y. Hackenbroch, "Stove Tiles from Austria," Metropolitan Museum of Art Bulletin (1964): 309–16.

63. JUG   *Earthenware; c. 1600; Beroun; found at Prague Old Town; h. 23.2 cm, diam. (rim) 9.3 cm, (bottom) 7.8 cm; H2-7.547*

From about 1550 to the beginning of the seventeenth century the town of Beroun, in central Bohemia, gained renown for the decorated earthenware it supplied to the capital city. On these high-speed turned wares, the ornamentation is especially characteristic: the body was first covered with a layer of slip and then decorated with slip in contrasting

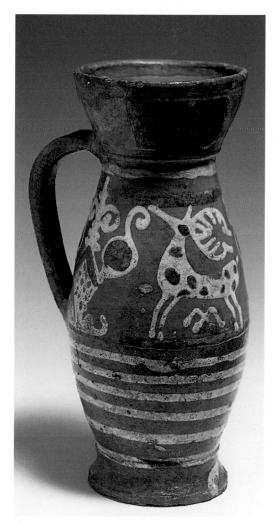

63

64

65

colors, using a little horn, or "cuckoo." Unlike ceramics of the Middle Ages, a transparent glaze was applied to both sides.　ᴠ ʙ

J. Žegklitz and J. Zavřel, "Geochemical and Petrographical Studies of the Post-Mediaeval Pottery of the Prague and Beroun Regions," Studies in Postmediaeval Archaeology, 1 *(1990):95–126.*

64. ᴘᴏᴡᴅᴇʀ ʜᴏʀɴ　*Ox horn, iron; c. 1600; Central Europe; l. 32 cm, d. 10 cm; ʜ2-327*

This flat-bodied flask is decorated on one side with hunting scenes, and on the other with concentric circles.　ᴇ š

Archaeologické sbírky v museum království českého v Praze (Prague, 1863), p. 63, item 186.

65. ᴄʀᴏꜱꜱʙᴏᴡ　*Plum wood, ivory, antler, brass, iron, hemp, wool, ink; 1607; Central Europe; l. (stock) 63 cm; span of bow 59 cm; ʜ2-31.218*

The upper and lower surfaces of this crossbow's wooden stock are covered with ivory panels engraved with human figures, mascarons, fruit, hares, caryatids, and foliage. The curved steel bow is fixed to the stock by a hemp binding, and the bow-string is braided hemp.

The oldest written record of crossbows comes from China, from the third century ʙ.ᴄ. Originally used for military purposes, in the twelfth century they came to be used as hunting weapons. They were more accurate than other bows since the stock allowed the archer to aim from the cheek.　E Š

E. Šnajdrová, "Lovecké střelné zbraně," High Life 2 (1995):97–103.

66. MORION *Iron, gilt; end of the sixteenth century; Central Europe; h. 28 cm, w. 35 cm; H2-638*

The morion, which came from either Italy or Spain and is similar to a pot helmet, was used in many European countries. Many had a narrow brim tapering to a point at the front and back. Pear-shaped morions like this one, comb morions, and helmets of a Sturmhaube type were all used by pikemen, musketeers, harquebusiers, and archers. The morion is worn to this day by the Pope's Swiss Guard. *See fig. 42, page 49.*　E Š

67. STOVE TILE *Glazed earthenware; second half of the sixteenth century; Bohemia; h. 34 cm, w. 21.3, d. 5.5 cm; H2-144.076*

The use of allegory is extremely significant in Renaissance art. Stove decorations used a whole series of allegorical themes, from Virtue, the Seasons, and the Continents, to the seven Liberal Arts (*artes liberales*), one of which, Rhetorica, is represented on this tile. At the medieval university, the liberal arts formed the general foundation provided by the faculty of arts and were divided into lower and upper disciplines; the lower were grammar, rhetoric, and dialectic, and the higher were arithmetic, music, geometry, and astronomy. After mastering this level of study, it was possible to continue at one of the higher professional faculties (theological, legal, or medical).　V B

67

68. GRANT OF RUDOLF II *Parchment, ink, gilding; 1610; Prague; h. 54.5 cm, w. 72.0 cm; H3-20/89*

In this grant Rudolf II raised Bernard Bauer to noble estate and granted him the arms depicted on the document. Such grants of arms had been issued in Bohemia since about the time of Charles IV. During the reign of Rudolf II a special official, the *comes palatinus,* was established for awarding new arms.　M R

69. TOLAR *Silver; 1588; Kutná Hora; diam. 41 mm, mass 29.06 g; private collection*

Among the outstanding artists at the court of Rudolf II was Antonio Abondio (1538–1591), an Italian renowned for his medal-making. The design for this tolar, which was struck at the Kutná Hora mint, came from his

68

70

71

72

workshop. The obverse of the coin bears the bust of emperor Rudolf II (1576–1612), and the reverse has a crowned double-headed imperial eagle. *See fig. 41, page 48.* ZP

I. Halačka, Mince koruny české *(Kroměříž, 1988).*

70. EPITAPH (*upper section*) *Argillite, with remnants of polychrome; c. 1560; Radonice nad Ohří; Originally in the church of the Raising of the Holy Cross, Radonice nad Ohří; middle panel h. 71 cm, w. 97 cm; lunette h. 58.5 cm, w. 121.5 cm; left volute h. 71 cm, w. 35.3 cm; right volute h. 71 cm, w. 37.5 cm; max. depth of all panels, 15 cm.; H2-38.146*

This Renaissance crown epitaph of Jan Bartoloměj ze Švamberka, with a relief of Christ washing the feet of his disciples during the Last Supper, surmounted by God the Father with his hands raised in blessing, is a rare example of a Lutheran architectural element of monumental character from Bohemia. Carved stone works of this type were created in the area of northwestern Bohemia after the middle of the sixteenth century, especially by sculptors from neighboring Protestant Saxony. LS

L. Sršeň, "Nástavec renesančního epitafu z Radonic nad Ohří," *in* Muzejní a vlastivědná prače *(forthcoming).*

71. WINDOW DISK *Glass, enamel paint; 1612; Chlumec nad Cidlinou; diam. 12.3 cm; H2-3.343*

Enamel painting was one of the most widespread techniques of glass decoration in central Europe during the sixteenth and the first half of the seventeenth centuries. Window disks were originally components of a larger church window. The image of Christ resurrected reflects the emphasis seventeenth-century Protestant reformers placed on Christ's crucifixion and resurrection as the only possible path to salvation. MM

72. IMPERIAL PATENT *Paper, ink; 1602; Bohemia; h. 21 cm, w. 72 cm; National Museum Archives*

In this July 22, 1602, document Rudolf II ordered the closing of Piccard, Waldensian, and Unity of Brethren congregations in Bohemia and reaffirmed a 1508 order directing that Piccard congregations be closed, their books burned, and their teachers and spiritual guides "corrected."

The Unity of Brethren, founded in 1457 in Kunvald in Moravia, had spread throughout the country by the end of the fifteenth century. Its members were persecuted relentlessly after 1620, and many, including John Amos Comenius, went into exile, particularly to Poland (Leszno), Saxony (where they founded Herrnhut), Prussia, and even America. MR

73. IVANČICE HYMNAL *Paper, ink, leather; 1576; Ivančice; h. 35 cm, w. 25 cm; 27-A-28*

Hymnals of the Czech Unity of Brethren are the oldest printed song books of the European Reformation; the first of these hymnals dates to 1501. They demonstrate the high standard of Czech printing and bookbinding during the Renaissance. The collection known as the *Ivančice Hymnal* dates from 1564; it is the work of one of the outstanding sixteenth-century figures of the Unity of Brethren, Bishop Jan Blahoslav (1523–1571). This example was printed in 1576, five years after his death.　ST *and* JF

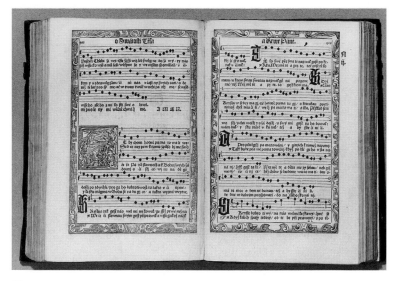

73

74. IN CANTICA CANTICORUM *Martin Luther (1483–1546); paper, ink, leather, wood; 1539; Wittenberg, Germany; h. 10 cm, w. 15 cm; Bludov 2B-38*

Martin Luther's brief commentary to the Song of Songs, *In Cantica Canticorum,* has a wood and leather binding with blind blocking. Books by Luther were brought to Bohemia by German Protestant printers. This volume is from a collection assembled by the Moravian counts of Zierotin who, almost alone in the Czech Lands, defended a non-Catholic faith as late as the second half of the seventeenth century.　PM

Verzeichnis der im deutschen Sprachbereich erschienenen Druckes des XVI. Jahrhunderts *(Stuttgart, 1988), vol. 12, L-4983.*

75. KRALICE BIBLE *Paper, ink, leather, wood, brass; 1579; Kralice, Moravia; h. 23 cm, w. 17 cm; KNM IC-4*

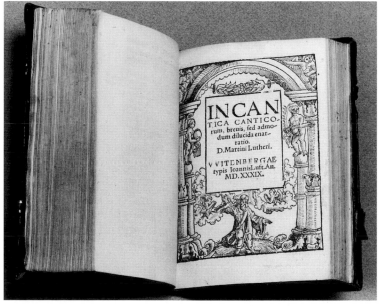

74

This first volume of the 1579 Kralice Bible was produced by the printing house of the Unity of Brethren in Kralice; it is one of the most important Czech books of all time. Translated from the original biblical languages by a group of educated theologians and philologists from the Unity of Brethren, it was the first complete translation of the Bible into a vernacular language from the original sources. For several centuries it was used to codify the written Czech language; in Slovakia "the language of Kralice" long served as the written language. As a symbol of the non-Catholic tradition in the Czech Lands, the Kralice Bible was one of the most controversial, supressed books produced prior to the Battle of White Mountain. *See fig. 31, page 35.*　PM

Knihopis českých a slovenskych tisků od doby nejstarší až do konce 18 století *(Prague, 1939–1965), no. 1107; H. Rothe and F. Scholz, eds., Kralitzer Bibel: Kralická bible: Biblia slavica, facsimile edition with commentary, 7 vol. (Paderborn, 1995).*

76

77

78

79

76. PAPPENHEIM HELMET *Iron; seventeenth century; Central Europe; h. 26.1 cm, w. 42.6 cm; H2-20.988*

The form of Pappenheim helmets shows an Asian influence. They were part of the armor of dragoons and cuirassiers, particularly during the Thirty Years' War.   E Š

77. TUCK *Alonso Louis Sahagun (active 1580–1620); iron; c. 1600; Central Europe, with Spanish blade; l. 95.2 cm, blade only: l. 75 cm, w. 2.3 cm; H2-182*

Alonzo Sahagun came from a family of smiths who worked for centuries in Toledo. Beginning in the sixteenth century, tucks or rapiers were used instead of swords as sidearms. In some armies they remained part of a dress uniform until the beginning of the twentieth century. Noblemen used lighter tucks until the end of the eighteenth century. This example was found in Blansko Castle, North Bohemia.   E Š

78. MORION *Iron, brass; c. 1600; Central Europe; h. 26 cm, w. 35 cm; H2-31.231*

This type of morion, of sheet iron with a high comb and a ridged brim and decorative brass work, was still in use during the Thirty Years' War.   E Š

79. CUIRASS WITH GORGET AND REREBRACES *Iron; 1550–1600; Nuremburg, Germany; front plate: h. 42 cm, w. 39 cm; back plate: h. 40 cm, w. 36 cm; gorget: diam. 16 cm; H2-142.969*

Armor of this type was used by foot soldiers (*Landsknechten*, the predecessors of the modern infantry) throughout Central Europe. These pieces are marked with a Nuremburg hallmark.   E Š

80. GEOGRAPHICAL INSTRUMENT *Erazim Habermel (in Prague 1595–1606); bronze, gilding; c. 1600; Prague; l. (each shaft) 49 cm, diam. (disk) 8.3 cm; H2-6.181*

This instrument is designed for measuring distance. Its maker, Erazim Habermel, who came from Nuremburg and worked also in Regensburg, was the astronomical and mathematical instrument-maker for the Prague court of Rudolf II.   E Š

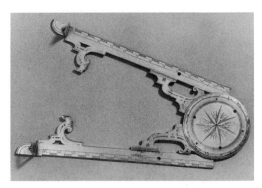

80

81. HERBARIUM *Pierandrea Mattioli (1500–1577); paper, ink, leather; 1596; Prague; h. 31 cm, w. 25 cm; KNM 31-B-2*

Pierandrea Mattioli was an important Italian doctor and botanist and the personal physician to Hapsburg archdukes Ferdinand and Maximilian II. His *Herbář aneb Bylinář* (Herbarium) was published in Czech twice in the sixteenth century. The second edition was published by the largest Czech printing house of the time, that of Daniel Adam of Veleslavín in Prague. As well as describing the appearance, manner of growth, and cultivation of plants, bushes, trees, and fruits, Mattioli emphasized their healing properties. Every herb described—both common and exotic ones, including those from other continents—was accompanied by a woodcut illustration.   P M

Knihopis českých a slovenských tisků od doby nejstarší až do konce 18. století *(Prague, 1939–1965), no. 5417.*

82. *CZECH CHRONICLE Václav Hájek z Libočan (d. 1553); paper, ink, leather; 1541; Prague; h. 28 cm, w. 19.5 cm; KNM 31-B-2*

Kronika Czeská, or the Czech Chronicle, was for years the most widely read work of Czech history. The author, Václav Hájek z Libočan, was a priest and historian. Since Hájek was a Catholic and his book could be both reprinted and read after the Battle of White Mountain, it maintained a continuity of knowledge of older Czech history among the general population. However, many modern authors regard the chronicle as

81

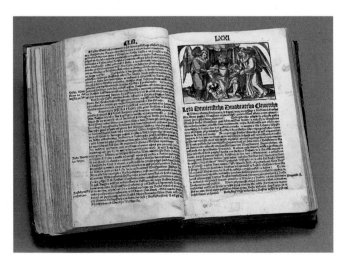

82

83

highly untrustworthy. The numerous colored woodcuts in the text were probably made by Pavel Severyn, a Prague illustrator and publisher. P M

Knihopis českých a slovenskych tisků od doby nejstarší až do konce 18. století *(Prague, 1939–1965), no. 2867*

83. PORTRAIT OF BOHUSLAV BALBÍN *Jan Jiří Heintsch (1647–1712) and assistant; oil on canvas; 1683; Prague; h. 121.5 cm, w. 98.5 cm (including frame); H2-11.802.1/2*

Bohuslav Balbín (1621–1688) was a member of the Jesuit order who played an important role in the re-Catholicization of the Czech Lands after the Battle of White Mountain in 1620. He participated in the Counter-Reformation through his hagiographical and historical essays, although he strongly condemned the devastation that accompanied the movement. L S

L. Sršeň, "Portrét Bohuslava Balbína v Národním muzeu v Praze," in Bohuslav Balbín a kultura jeho doby v Čechách, Sborník z konference Památníku národního písemnictví *(Prague, 1992), pp. 146–57.*

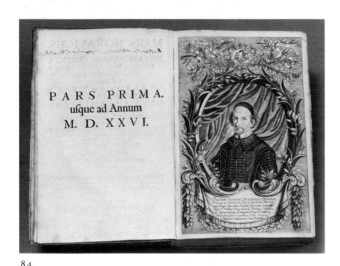

84

84. MARS MORAVICUS *Tomáš Jan Pešina z Čechorodu (1629–1680); paper, ink, parchment; 1677; Prague; h. 32 cm, w. 21 cm; KNM 42B-3*

The full title of this 500-page volume is *Mars Moravicus: Sive Bella Horrida et Cruenta, Seditiones, Tumultus, Praelia, Turbae.* It was published in Prague by the printing house of Jan Arnolt of Dobroslav. Its author, Tomáš Jan Pešina z Čechorodu, was a patriotic Catholic priest and historian. In his works, which he published in Latin and Czech, he devoted his attention particularly to Moravian history. In 1658 he was given the surname "z Čechorodu" (of Czech birth) to honor his contributions to his country. P M

Knihopis českých a slovenských tisků od doby nejstarší až do konce 18. století *(Prague, 1939–1965), no. 7032.*

85. RESPUBLICA BOJEMA *Pavel Stránský (1583–1657); paper, ink, parchment; 1643; Leiden, Netherlands; h. 11.5 cm, w. 6cm, d. 3.5 cm; 41G-2B*

Respublica Bojema (The Republic of Bohemia), a history of the Czech state, was the work of Pavel Stránský, an Utraquist student and politician who belonged to the anti-Hapsburg party. The title page bears the arms of the kingdom of Bohemia and of the other lands of the Czech crown. Following the Battle of White Mountain, Stránský refused to convert to Catholicism; from 1627, like many other non-Catholic Czech noblemen and intellectuals, he lived in exile in Protestant Saxony. This description of the Czech state was first published by the famous Elzevir publishing house in Leiden. It was frequently reprinted abroad; however, censorship prevented it from being printed in Prague until the end of the eighteenth century. P M

Knihopis českých a slovenských tisků od doby nejstarší až do konce 18. století *(Prague, 1939–1965), no. 15,740.*

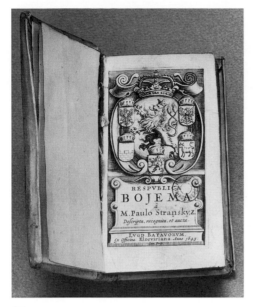

85   86

86. ORBIS PICTUS *John Amos Comenius (1592–1670); paper, ink, leather; 1728; Levoča, Slovakia; h. 17 cm, w. 10.5; 50-E-67*

The full title of this famous work by John Amos Comenius is *Orbis Sensualium Pictus; hoc est: Omnium fundamentalium in Mundo Rerum, & in Vita Actionum, Pictura et Nomenclatura.* It was used as a teaching aid that explains basic principles and terms relating to the world in several languages. Comenius, a renowned teacher, bishop of the Unitas Fratrum, philosopher, and pedagogue, spent his life from 1627 in exile. His books were printed in many cities; this one was printed in Levoča in Slovakia and is accompanied by simple woodcuts, some of which have been amateurishly hand colored.   P M

Knihopis českých a slovenských tisků od doby nejstarší až do konce 18. století *(Prague, 1939–1965), no. 4245.*

87. PAINTING OF SAINT WENCESLAS *Oil on canvas; 1719; Bohemia; h. 126.5 cm, w. 77 cm (unframed); H2-31.965*

This painting of Saint Wenceslas as a patron saint of the Franciscan order in Bohemia served as the announcement of the nomination of the Franciscan general visitator, Mansuet Förschan, as the *definitor* (land supervisor) of the Czech Franciscan province in 1719.   L S

88. PANEL PAINTING OF THE VIRGIN AND CHILD WITH SAINTS *Oil on wood; after 1685; Prague; h. 146.2 cm, w. 84.6 cm; H2-5.464*

This painting of the Virgin with saints originally hung under the choir tribune of the church of Saint Stephen, Prague. The figure of the Virgin was copied from a much-revered medieval painting, *Our Lady of Saint Stephen,* that hung in the same church. It is surrounded by figures of saints and mar-

87

89

88

tyrs. In the way it finds inspiration in medieval art and piety, this baroque picture is characteristic of certain artistic trends during the Counter-Reformation.   L S

A. Honsatko, Die Pfarrkirche des h. Stephan des Grosseren (na Rybniczku) *(Jičín, 1835), pp. 66–67; K. Chytil, "Madona svatoštěpánská a její poměr k typu madony vyšebrodské," Památky archeologické 34 (1924–1925): 63.*

89. STATUE OF A JESUIT SAINT *carver with the initials P.P.; wood, paint; 1645; South or Central Bohemia; h. 168 cm, w. 82 cm, d. 50 cm; H2-185.512/1, 2*

This statue of a young beardless Jesuit saint (possibly Peter of Canisio or John Berchmans) probably decorated an early baroque altar. Its sober form and simple style is characteristic of the uncompromising struggle for re-Catholicization following the Battle of White Mountain.   L S

90. CHERUB *Wood, paint; c. 1720; Bohemia; h. 49 cm, w. 40 cm, d. 25 cm.; H2-19.497. See fig. 58, page 65.*

91. CHERUB *Wood, paint; c. 1720; Bohemia; h. 46 cm, w. 35 cm, d. 18 cm.; H2-19.498*

Many small carved and painted statues of cherubs of this type were used in the decoration of a typical baroque church. Each figure was conceived individually, and their facial expressions and the chubby childish lines of their bodies were generally exaggerated.   L S

92. STATUE OF SAINT JOHN OF NEPOMUK *Wood, paint; mid-eighteenth century; Bohemia; h. 124 cm, w. 24.3 cm, d. 18 cm; H2-58.761*

Canon Johánek z Pomuku, who at the order of Václav IV was thrown from Prague (now Charles) Bridge into the Vltava in 1393, achieved fame after his martyrdom as Saint John of Nepomuk (beatified 1721, canonized 1729). He is generally portrayed as a canon wearing a biretta and holding a crucifix or palm spray, variations on the famous 1683 statue on Charles Bridge.   L S

93. BUST OF SAINT WENCESLAS *Attrib. Jan Bedřich Kohl-Severa (1681–1736); linden wood, paint; 1729; Prague; h. 51 cm, w. 30.5 cm, d. 26 cm; H2-17.567*

This carved bust is what remains of a life-sized baroque figure of Saint Wenceslas, made from a lath skeleton and attired in clothing of rough fabric and papier-mâché. With similar figures, it formed part of a

91

93

92

theatrum honoris (theater of glory) used in the eight-day celebration of the canonization of John of Nepomuk at the cathedral of Saint Vitus in Prague in October 1729. The carving is of high quality, although it was only used for a single festival. The *theatrum honoris* figures are attributed to the court sculptor Jan Bedřich Kohl-Severa.   L S

L. Sršeň, "Příležitostné dekorace pražských barokních slavností," in Barokní umění a jeho význam v České kultuře *(Prague, 1991), p. 154 ff; L. Sršeň, "Die Skulptur barocker Gelegenheitsfeste," Studien zur Werkstattpraxis der Barockskulptur im 17. und 18. Jahrhundert (Poznan, 1992), p. 187; L. Sršeň, "Slavnostní dekorace pražské katedrály sv. Víta r. 1729," in* Svatý Jan Nepomucký 1393–1993 *(Prague, 1993), p. 39ff. and no. 93; L. Sršeň, "Der Festschmuck des Prager Veitsdoms im Jahre 1729," in* Johannes von Nepomuk 1393/1993 *(Munich, 1993), pp. 63ff, 165ff, no. 93.*

96

94. STATUE OF A BISHOP   *Attrib. Ignác František Platzer (1717– 1787); lindenwood, paint, gilding, silver; after 1750; Bohemia; h. 60 cm, w. 26 cm, d. 14 cm; H2-5.360*

This small statue is a "modelletto," a small but detailed model that a sculptor submitted to a potential customer to demonstrate his skill. Because the left hand has been replaced, we do not know whether it was originally raised in blessing or outstretched to hold an attribute. Therefore, who the figure is cannot be determined. This carving is most likely the work of Ignác František Platzer, the most important Czech sculptor of the late rococo and classical periods. *See fig. 61, page 68.*   L S

95. MONSTRANCE   *Copper, gold- and silverplate, glass; 1789; Moravia; h. 64 cm; H2-5.188*

This monstrance's decoration, with cross-hatching, rocailles, floral festoons, and jewels of glass, conveys an impression not only of overwhelming magnificence, but also of stylistic maturity and unity. The base bears a Latin inscription dedicating the monstrance to the parish church of Nový Jičín in North Moravia. *See fig. 34, page 38.*   M M

96. CRUCIFIX   *Anonymous (Prague?) carver; wood, gilding, paint; c. 1750; Central Bohemia; h. 71.8 cm, base 8 x 17.2 cm; H2-6 844*

This rococo crucifix was part of the furnishings of the church of John the Baptist in Hořelice, Rudná, district of Beroun, consecrated in 1747. The subtle depiction of an emphatically vertical, slim body carved with a masterful knowledge of anatomy indicates that it was probably produced in Prague by a leading rococo sculptor.   L S

97. CHALICE   *Rinaldo Ranzoni (1662–1737); silver, gilding; c. 1720; Prague; h. 25.5 cm, diam. (rim) 10 cm, (base) 16.3 cm.; H2-185.534*

The partially gilded silver chalice, richly decorated with repoussé motifs of angel's heads and high baroque ornamentation, is the work of Bologna-born Rinaldo Ranzoni, who worked in Prague from 1698 until his death. It bears a maker's mark and hallmarks of Prague New Town and the Prague Hallmark Office. Ranzoni produced a significant number of liturgical objects for churches and monasteries, including the Cathedral of Saint Vitus.   M M

97

98

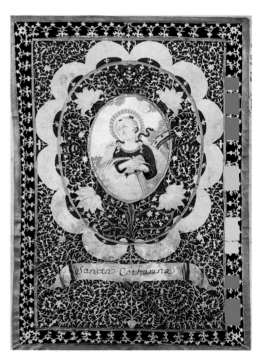

98. EX VOTO PAINTING *Parchment, gouache; 1770; Bohemia; h. 23.5 cm, w. 28.7 cm; H2-5.297*

An *ex voto* is a devotional object offered in thanksgiving to the Virgin Mary or to a particular saint. Such gifts could be in the form of pictures, decorative inscriptions, or wax or metal reliefs; they were displayed near the image of the honored saint. This ex voto is a thanksgiving offering to Our Lady of Svatá Hora by a noble couple on the birth of their child. The couple presented the painting in 1770 to the miraculous statue of the Virgin in one of the most famous pilgrimage churches in Bohemia, Svatá Hora near Příbram. L S

99. PAINTING OF SAINTS ON PARCHMENT *Parchment, gouache, paper; 1750–1800; Bohemia; h. 26.4 cm, w. 19.4 cm; H2-53.378*

The virgin martyrs Barbara and Catherine have been honored in the Czech Lands since the Middle Ages. This work has two cartouches containing their portraits, one on each side, surrounded by exceptionally delicate lacework handcut from parchment. L S

99

100. PILGRIM'S HYMNAL *Paper, ink; 1747; Bohemia; h. 21 cm, w. 16 cm; KNM R. Hlava zp. 1*

This bound manuscript is entitled *Kancionálek poutnický, který se při všech poutích mariánských pobožně užívati se může* (A hymnbook for Marian pilgrimages). The hymns it contains offer strong evidence of popular piety. E R

100

V. Bitnar, O českém baroku slovesném *(Prague, 1932); Z. Tichá, Česká poezie 17. a 18. století (Prague, 1974); Česká literatura doby baroka: Sborník přispěvků k české literatuře 17. a 18. století (Prague, 1994).*

101. TORAH POINTER *Silver; late eighteenth century; Bohemia; l. 27.5 cm; H2-5.390*

The climax of every ceremonial gathering in a synagogue was a reading from the Pentateuch (the first five books of the Old Testament) which was hand-written on a parchment scroll or *Sefer Torah*. Since the Torah was considered too sacred to be touched with the hands, a special pointer, or *yad*, was used to point out the text being read. *See fig. 39, page 45.*   L N

V. Klagsbald, Catalogue raisonné de la collection juive du musée de Cluny *(Paris, 1981).*

102. MENORAH *Brass, silver plate; late eighteenth century; Bohemia, possibly Prague; h. 18 cm, w. 27 cm, d. 8 cm; H2-1.527*

The menorah is used during the festival of Hanukkah to celebrate the liberation of Jerusalem in 168 B.C.E. (3592 by the Jewish calendar). The eight lamps commemorate how an oil lamp with enough pure oil for one day miraculously burned for eight, long enough to purify the Temple of Jerusalem. *See fig. 38, page 45.*   L N

103

103. BOWL *Pewter; c. 1800, engraved decoration dated 1804; Prague Lesser Town; diam. 29.8 cm; H2-7331*

This shallow bowl has an engraved Star of David *(Magen David)*—a religious emblem of Judaism—in the middle. The engraved Hebrew inscription around its rim indicates that this was a wedding gift from the young men's association in the Smíchov congregation (now part of Prague) to one of its members in 1804 (5564 by the Jewish calendar). It is stamped with a maker's mark and the hallmark of Prague Lesser Town. D S

104. MENORAH *Brass; late nineteenth or early twentieth century; Bohemia; h. 37 cm; H2-1.530*

This menorah has the same form as the Menorah of the Temple in Jerusalem, which was known through its depiction on the victory arch built for Titus in Rome. It was widely disseminated in Jewish iconography in the nineteenth century, although some versions date to the seventeenth century.   L N

S. Kayser, Jewish Ceremonial Art *(Philadelphia, 1955).*

105. PRINT OF THE PROCESSION OF PRAGUE JEWS *Paper, copper engraving; 1741; Prague; plate mark: h. 41.5 cm, w. 61.3 cm; paper: h. 43.5 cm, w. 62.0 cm; H2-27.131*

This engraving commemorates the April 24, 1741, procession of Prague Jews celebrating the birth of Austrian archduke and prince

104

Joseph, the future emperor Joseph II. The parade was organized by the head of the Prague Jewish community, Simon Wolf Frankel, five weeks after Joseph's birth. Frankel (no. 4) is in the middle of the sheet at the bottom. The detailed legend at the bottom of the engraving identifies some individuals who took part in this procession. *See fig. 35, page 41.* V Př

O. Muneles, Bibliografický přehled židovské Prahy *(Prague, 1952)*; N. Bergerová, Na křižovatce kultur: Historie československých Židů *(Prague, 1992)*.

106

106. IMPERIAL PATENT OF MARIA THERESA *Paper, ink; 1775; Bohemia; h. 35 cm, w. 20 cm; H3-E-1775*

By this patent, which applied to the kingdom of Bohemia, Maria Theresa regulated the duties of serfs according to their property, abolished extraordinary manorial labor, and laid down detailed guidelines for serf labor.

The worsening status of the serfs in the Czech Lands prompted the great serf uprising of 1775. After suppressing the uprising, the government moved quickly to regulate serf labor with this patent of August 13, 1775; however, it failed to resolve the basic questions of manorial labor and serfdom. MR

107. IMPERIAL PATENT OF JOSEPH II *Paper, ink; October 27, 1781; Brno, Moravia; h. 33 cm, w. 20.5 cm; H3-E-1781*

The Patent or Edict of Tolerance, issued in Vienna by order of Joseph II, granted religious tolerance to the Protestant Augsburg-Lutherans and Swiss-Calvinists and to the Greek Orthodox faith. This copy of the patent was issued by the Margravate of Moravia for the provinces of Moravia and Silesia. The edict was intended to end religiously motivated emigration and to allow a free inflow of foreign professionals of other faiths, who would bring economic benefits to the state. MR

108. TOBACCO BOX *Papier-mâché; after 1782; Bohemia; h. 4 cm, diam. 10.6 cm; H2-5.512 A-B*

This tobacco box with the word "Tollerance," the imperial eagle, and painted figures of a Lutheran, a Calvinist, and a Catholic bishop, is a contemporary response to the Patent of Tolerance by which Joseph II in 1781 legalized freedom of religion (cat. 107). The design source for the picture on the lid was probably a commemorative medal issued in Germany in 1782. *See fig. 46, page 53.* MM

109. HYMNAL *Václav Kleych (1682–1737); paper, ink, leather, wood, brass; 1727; Zittau, Germany; h. 16 cm, w. 8 cm; KNM 27D-43*

The 914-page *Ewangelický Kancyonal* (Protestant hymnal) was compiled and published by Václav Kleych. At the beginning of the eighteenth century, Kleych emigrated from the Czech Lands for religious reasons and settled in neighboring Lusatia (in present-day Germany), where he

107

109

110

111

112

published Protestant books in Czech and smuggled them into the Czech Lands. He died on one of these missions. Smuggling non-Catholic books into the Czech Lands in the seventeenth and eighteenth century was common. Such books tended to have a format designed to deceive the Jesuit missionaries who inspected travelers' goods.   P M

Knihopis českých a slovenských tisků od doby nejstarší až do konce 18. století *(Prague, 1939–1965), no. 3974.*

110. K E Y   *Iron, gilding; mid-eighteenth century; Bohemia (?); l. 19.6 cm, w. 6.5 cm; H2-1.141*

This profile-bit key has a heart-shaped head with a shield and the monograms MT (Maria Theresa) and FI (Francis I of Lorraine, her husband) on opposite sides. The key served as a mark of rank for the Imperial Chamberlain prior to the empress's death in 1780.   V B

H. Pankofer, Schlüssel und Schloss *(Munich, 1973), p. 91.*

111. B O W L   *Leonhardt Dürr; pewter; 1666; Jáchymov, North Bohemia; diam. 33 cm; H2-69.714*

This shallow bowl with finely engraved foliate decoration shows the high standard of pewter work in the mining town of Jáchymov. It bears a maker's mark and the hallmark of Jáchymov. The local pewterers produced some of the most beautiful work in Europe in the sixteenth and seventeenth centuries.   D S

112. J U G   *Haban faience, pewter; 1638; Moravia or West Slovakia; h. 21 cm, diam. 18 cm; H2-30.655*

113. JUG *Haban faience, pewter; 1673; West Slovakia; h. 13.5 cm; H2-3.034*

These faience pieces were made with techniques introduced from Italy by the superb craftsmen of the Anabaptist sect, called Habaner (from the German *Haushaben*), whose community in Moravia was founded in the sixteenth century. Although religious persecution aimed at all non-Catholics forced the Habaner to move to neighboring Slovakia after 1622, their products managed to find their way back to the Czech market. Haban ware remains well known for the high quality of its materials and its predominantly floral decoration.   MM

J. Kybalová and J. Novotná, Habánská fajáns 1590–1730 *(Prague, 1981), no. 58, 197.*

114. PADLOCK *Iron; sixteenth century; Bohemia; l. 26 cm, w. 17 cm, d. 11 cm; H2-1.072*

This heavy wrought-iron padlock, with a suspended stirrup bracket and decorative openwork, is an example of an artistically unsophisticated but useful shape from the Renaissance period. The lock was controlled by a key with a star-shaped profile axis.   VB

D. Stará, "Iron," in The Pictorial Encyclopaedia of Antiques *(New York, 1968), fig. 523.*

115. TSCHINKE (RIFLE) *Wood, iron, brass, ivory, mother-of-pearl, metal, gilding; 1600–1650; Těšín, Silesia; l. 114.5 cm; l. of barrel 86.3 cm; 14 caliber; H2-187.772*

This wheel lock rifle's barrel is octagonal for the first quarter of its length and cylindrical for the remaining three-quarters, with the transition marked by an engraved ring. Its wooden stock is richly decorated with inlaid ivory and mother-of-pearl, depicting hunting scenes, griffons, volutes, and other motifs. The tschinke was a light hunting rifle produced in the Těšín region. Most were produced in the first half of the seventeenth century; they were often exported.   EŠ

E. Šnajdrová, "Těšínka pro Národní muzeum," Starožitnosti a užité umění, *1 (1993): 15.*

113

114

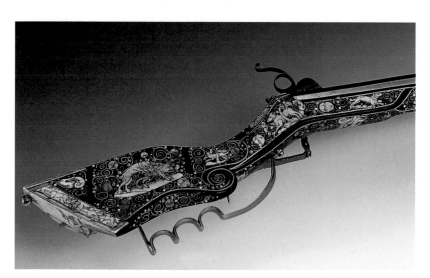

115

116

116. GAME BOX *Wood, wood inlay, brass; 1660–1700; Cheb, West Bohemia; H. 49 cm, w. 49 cm, d. 12 cm; H2-69.874*

In the seventeenth century, several carpentry workshops in Cheb began using wood inlay together with relief carving. This luxurious game box for trik-trak (backgammon) and checkers bears on its front cover the Old Testament scene of the Angel of the Lord stopping the soothsayer Balaam on his way to King Balak. The design is based on a 1616 copperplate engraving by Cornelisz Jansz de Visscher. MM

M. Mžyková, Chebská reliéfní intarzie a grafika, katalog Středočeské galerie v Praze (Prague, 1986), pp. 54–55, nos. 40, 40a, figs. 13–15.

117. HYMNAL *Václav Karel Holan Rovenský; paper, ink, leather; 1694; Prague; h. 40.5 cm, w. 29.5, d. 3.5 cm; AZ-13*

Baroque Czech hymnals from the late seventeenth century drew from an earlier tradition of popular religious song in Reformation churches and similarly recognize the exceptional power of hymns as an ideological tool. Among these works Holan Rovenský's Catholic hymnal, *Capella regia musicalis*, stands out because of its demanding compositions for one or more voices with instrumental accompaniment and interludes. DV

J. Bužga, "Holan-Rovenský: Představitel měšťanské hudební kultury koncem 17. století," Hudební věda, 4 (1967), p. 420, no. 4.

118. HYMNAL *Adam Václav Michna z Otradovic; paper, ink, leather; 1647; Prague; h. 19 cm, w. 32 cm, d. 3 cm; AZ-20*

Adam Michna z Otradovic's Christmas lullaby "Chtíc, aby spal" is among the best known of his songs to be popularized in the baroque period. The music in this hymnal, *Česká mariánská muzika* (Czech Marian

117

118

music), and in his other collections of songs, *(Svatoroční muzika, Loutna česká)* are evidence of his great poetic and compositional skills. D V

J. Bužga, "Das Tchechische Barockkomponist Adam Michna z Otradovic," in Festschrift für Heinrich Besseler (Leipzig 1961), p. 305; Antonín Škarka, Michna z Otradovic, Adam Václav: das dichterische Werk (Munich, 1968).

119. SCORE FOR *MISSA* *František Xaver Brixi (1732–1771); paper, ink, watercolor; 1760; Prague; h. 35 cm, w. 23.5 cm; XXXVII F 33*

František Xaver Brixi was among the most important composers in the Czech Lands in the second half of the eighteenth century. He composed about four hundred religious pieces, including this *Missa,* and worked as an organist in several Prague churches. In the last twelve years of his life he was the Kapellmeister of the Cathedral of Saint Vitus in Prague. *See fig. 66, page 75.* M K

120. SCORE FOR *LAUDETUR JESUS CHRISTI* *Bohuslav Matěj Černohorský (1648–1742); paper, ink, leather; c. 1728; Prague; H. 34 cm, w. 22 cm; XXXIII B 177*

Czech-born Bohuslav Matěj Černohorský was a member of the Minorite order and an excellent organist and composer. He worked in Prague and for many years in Italy. His teaching legacy can be discerned in several succeeding generations of musicians; however, this is one of a very few pieces of his work to have survived. M K

120

121. SCORE FOR *PASTORAL DUPLEX* *Jakub Valerian Paus (1705–1750); paper, ink; 1770s; Bakov nad Jizerou; h. 27.5 cm, w. 23; XV F 328*

The pastorella, a musical piece featuring the Nativity story, often in a contemporary setting, was one of the most important popular musical forms in the eighteenth century. Like many composers who used this form, Paus was a village schoolmaster; he worked in Dobrovice near Mladá Boleslav. M K

J. Berkovec, České pastorely (Prague, 1987); Mark Germer, "The Austro-Bohemian Pastorella and Pastoral Mass to c. 1780," Ph.D. diss., New York University, 1989.

122. RASTRAL *Wood, brass; eighteenth century; Prague; l. 17 cm, w. 1 cm, d. 1 cm; 32-K*

In a time when most musical materials were copied by hand, five-headed pens for drawing musical staves represented a great saving of labor and time for a note copier. E P

Hudba v českých dějinách od středověku do nové doby (Prague, 1989), pp. 209, 277–78.

121

122

123

123. PORTRAIT OF JAN ZACH *attrib. Heinrich Foelix (1757–1821); oil on canvas; mid-eighteenth century; Trier, Germany; h. 69 cm, w. 81.5 cm; 2145-F-V*

Jan Zach (1699–1773) was one of the leading figures in Czech instrumental music of the preclassical period. He worked as a composer and organist in Prague and (after 1740) abroad, particularly in the Rhineland, which is where this portrait, attributed to Heinrich Foelix, originated.   E P

124. GUITAR *Tomáš Ondřej Hulínský (1731–1788); wood, mother-of-pearl, gut strings; 1754; Prague; l. 92 cm, w. 28 cm, d. 10 cm; 1199-E*

This six-stringed baroque guitar was made by Prague master T. O. Hulínský, who also made violins, violas, lutes, gambas, harps, and other stringed instruments. *See fig. 65, page 73.*   B Č

A. Buchner, Musical Instruments: An Illustrated History *(New York, 1973).*

125. OBOE *František Čermák; boxwood, brass; c. 1800; Prague; l. 62 cm, w. 6 cm; 17-E*

This oboe is typical of instruments made by František Čermák, a famous Prague instrument maker. It has finely crafted turnings and a traditional Mozartesque five-valve apparatus of square-edged brass.   B Č

J. Keller, "Píštělníci a trubaři," Sborník Národního muzea v Praze *(1975); L. Langwill,* An Index of Musical Wind Instruments, *3d. ed (Edinburgh, 1972).*

129

126. TENOR VIOLA DA GAMBA *Wood, gut strings; 1700–1750; Prague; l. 111 cm, w. 40 cm, d. 30 cm; 1251-E*

This baroque piece is a basic member of the viola da gamba family (instruments held between the knees when played). It has six strings tuned in fourths with a third in the middle, like a lute. The sound of old viols is in general softer, finer, and less penetrating than that of the modern cello.   B Č

J. Hutter, Hudební nástroje *(Prague, 1959).*

127. BASSET HORN *Wood, brass; 1775–1800; Prague; l. 61 cm, w. 50 cm, d. 20 cm; 1763-E*

This low-pitched member of the clarinet family is made of lathe-turned wood and has a brass bell and seven valves. This form appeared around 1770 and quickly became popular throughout the Czech Lands. Wolfgang Amadeus Mozart used it in several of his compositions.   B Č

C. Sachs, Handbuch der Musikinstrumentenkunde *(Leipzig, 1930); J. Keller, "Píštělníci a trubaři," Sborník Národního muzea v Praze (1975).*

128. VIOLIN *Joseph Anton Laske; wood, gut and wire strings; 1770; Prague; l. 61 cm, w. 22 cm, d. 11 cm; 1021-E*

This four-stringed violin is one of a small number of surviving instruments made by Joseph Anton Laske, a Prague instrument maker who lived in the second half of the eighteenth century. In comparison with earlier violins, this instrument's lines are light and free.   B Č

K. Jalovec, Čeští houslaři *(Prague, 1959).*

129. SET DESIGN *Giuseppe Galli da Bibiena (1696–1756); paper, ink; 1723; Prague; h. 47 cm, w. 60 cm; H6-D15.870/S-ID-LB*

The Italian painter, architect, and engineer Giuseppe Galli da Bibiena designed sets for Johann Josef Fux's baroque opera, *Costanza e Fortezza*. The four pieces of stage machinery shown in this print were considered highlights of the production and were pointedly described in printed notices describing the performance. The two machines used in the first act were described as follows: "First from the surface of the river Tiber spouts a massive geyser and when it falls, Tiber's throne appears, from which the river god amid a choir of nymphs prophesies the defeat of the enemies of Rome."   V K

J. Hilmera, Perspektivní scéna 17. a 18. století v Čechách *(Prague, 1964), p. 38ff.; P. Toman,* Nový slovník československých výtvarných umělců *(Prague, 1947), p. 63.*

126

125   127   128

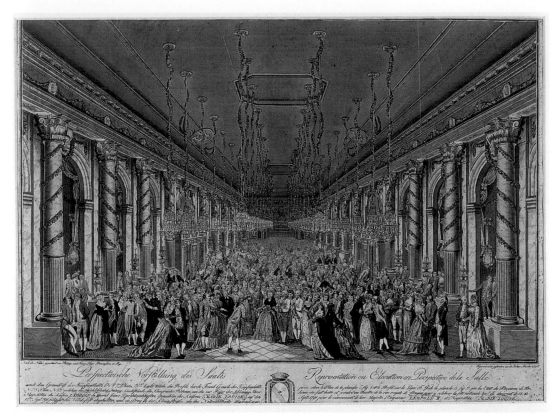

130

131

130. PRINT OF THE CORONATION BALL OF LEOPOLD II *Filip Heger, František Heger, and Jan Berka; paper, copper-plate engraving, watercolor; 1796; Prague; h. 45 cm, w. 60 cm; 115/93*

The coronation of Leopold II as king of Bohemia was accompanied by a series of festivities. One of these, a ball held at the Estates Theatre and its newly completed extension, is depicted in this engraving. Wolfgang Amadeus Mozart, who was spending his last long soujourn in Prague, attended the ball. E P

J. Petráň, Počátky českého národního obrození: Společnost a kultura v 70.–80. letech 18. století *(Prague, 1990); P. Toman,* Nový slovník československých výtvarných umělců, *vol. 1 (Prague, 1947), pp. 50–51.*

131. SCORE FOR *PARTHIA František Xaver Dušek (1731–1799); paper, ink; 1760s; Prague or Liblice; h. 24 cm, w. 31.5 cm; XXII C 149*

František Xaver Dušek was an important Czech composer, piano virtuoso, and teacher in Prague in the second half of the eighteenth century. A group of Prague artists and scientists met at Bertramka, his summer residence (now inside the city limits). This *Parthia* comes from the musical collection of Count Jan Pachta (see no. 132). M K

V. Sýkora, F. X. Dušek *(Prague, 1958).*

132. COVER FOR MUSICAL SCORE *Wood, paper, leather; 1770s or 1780s; Prague or Liblice; h. 30 cm, w. 40 cm, d. 10 cm; XXII D 96*

Count Jan Pachta's musical group was among the most important aristocratic ensembles in the second half of the eighteenth century. This rare cover for a musical score is from Pachta's music collection.   MK

M. Kabelková, *"Hudební archiv a kapela hraběte Jana Josefa Filipa Pachty," in* Hudební věda *28 (1991):329–33.*

132

133. SCORE FOR *DON GIOVANNI* *Wolfgang Amadeus Mozart (1756–1791) and Jan Křtitel Kuchař (1751–1829); paper, ink, leather; 1790s; Cistercian abbey, Osek; h. 23 cm, w. 30 cm, d. 3 cm; XXIII-F-115*

This piano arrangement for Mozart's opera, *Don Giovanni,* was written by composer Jan Křtitel Kuchař, who worked both as an organist at the Premonstratensian abbey of Strahov and as the musical director of the Nostic Theater in Prague (later the Estates Theater). *Don Giovanni* premiered at the Nostic Theater on October 29, 1787.   MK

Third-year music-history students at the Philosophical Faculty, Charles University (collective work), "Klavírní výtahy Mozartových oper v úpravě J. K. Kuchaře," manuscript, 1988.

134. SECRETARY *Wood, wood veneer, wood inlay; 1750–1775; Bohemia; h. 195 cm, w. 130 cm, d. 67 cm; H2-17.077*

This baroque secretary or écritoire is in three parts: the drawers, the extension writing surface, and the cabinet. It has an undulating bowed front, and the inlaid decoration on the front and sides consists of courtly figures, gondolas, and rocailles.   MM

133

135

134

138

135. COFFEEPOT *Johann Franz Voigt; pewter; after 1750; Karlovy Vary; h. 24.5 cm, diam. (base) 11.2 cm; H2-145.375*

This coffeepot is an example of how rococo pewter vessels copied silver models. The West Bohemian spa town of Karlovy Vary and the towns of Augsburg and Frankfurt am Main were important centers for the production of these goods, which were sold throughout Europe.   DS

136. BEAKER *Glass, gold and silver leaf; 1725–1750; Bohemia; h. 7.5 cm, diam. 7 cm; H2-31.139*

137. BEAKER *Glass, gold and silver leaf; 1725–1750; Bohemia; h. 5.8 cm; H2-3.280*

The technique of sealing gold and silver leaf between two layers of glass (termed *Zwischengoldglas*), with engraved decoration on the surfaces, dates from ancient times. Vessels made with these techniques satisfied a desire for richness and refined decoration; they were the focus of renewed interest at the end of the seventeenth century. The overwhelming majority of surviving examples originated in Bohemia during the second quarter of the eighteenth century. *See fig. 57, page 64.*　M M

139

138. GOBLET　*Glass; 1725–1750; North Bohemia; h. 15.8 cm, diam. 9.8 cm; H2-144.877*

In the first half of the eighteenth century, Czech glass gained its reputation not only in Europe but also beyond, thanks to well-organized traders. The work of North Bohemian glass-cutters was especially popular. This particular goblet, with a characteristic balustrade stem, was manufactured from clear cut glass and decorated with wheel-engraved motifs. The ornamental decoration on most high baroque Czech glass reflects the influence of French-inspired graphic designs.　M M

139. KEY　*Iron; 1711; Bohemia?; l. 13.2 cm, w. 4.2 cm; H2-1.222*

This key, with a bit on each end of the shaft and a box-shaped head that slides from one end to the other, represents an interesting device from the baroque period. The head has the monogram "MAR" (Maria) and the date 1711 cut out of one side, and the monogram "IHS" *(Iesus Hominum Salvator)* on the other.　V B

140

H. Pankofer, Schlüssel und Schloss *(Munich, 1973), p. 95.*

140. LOCK　*Iron, brass; eighteenth century; Bohemia; l. 50 cm, w. 20 cm, d. 16 cm; H2-1.134*

This baroque door lock has four horizontal bolts controlled by a vertically oriented door handle. The rich open-work decoration on the brass cover displays the Imperial two-headed eagle. Heavy locks, such as this one, were used on palace and church doors; this one comes from the church of Saint Blasius in Panenský Týnec.　V B

J. Mohr, Černé řemeslo v průběhu staletí *(Prague, 1984), p. 25, fig. 18.*

141

141. TARGET　*Spruce, paint; on left, "52"; on right, 1746; Central Europe; diam. 60 cm; H2-187.807*

This round target displays the figure of a Turk, a favorite object for target practice after the wars against the Turks in the sixteenth to the eighteenth centuries. Polychromed targets were used only from the eighteenth century; previously they were black and white. Because they were mostly the work of folk artists, only a few, like this one, have any artistic merit.　E Š

142. GRILL　*Iron; 1725–1750; Bohemia; h. 40 cm, w. 152 cm; H2-6.248*

This wrought-iron grill was originally set in a semicircular opening above the exterior doors of a palace or castle. In its original state, some of its decorative elements were probably gilded. The monogram "W" located in the center of the crown is the builder's mark.　M M

142

143, 144, 145

149, 150, 151

143. EASTER EGG *J. Haruška; eggshell, dye; 1974; Vnorovy, district of Hodonín, Moravia; l. approx. 6 cm; H4-91.309*

144. EASTER EGG *Antonín Hoffman; eggshell, wine dye; 1984; Doma- žlice, Chodsko region, Bohemia; l. approx. 6 cm; H4-103.667*

145. EASTER EGG *Ludmila Procházková; eggshell, dye; 1980; Prague; l. approx. 6 cm; H4-99.385*

A batik technique was used to decorate the shell of these blown eggs before they were dyed. The wax-covered areas remained white, forming the pattern. Decorated eggs were given by young women to young men at Easter in conjunction with the *pomlázka* ritual (see 155, 156). They symbolized fertility and new life. L R

A. Václavík, Výroční obyčeje a lidové umění *(Prague, 1959).*

146. EASTER EGG *Marie Ťoková; eggshell, dye; 1976; Ostrožská Nová Ves, Moravia; l. approx. 6 cm; H4-96.780*

147. EASTER EGG *Eggshell, dye; c. 1900; Uherské Hradiště district, Moravia; l. approx. 6 cm; H4-2.064*

148. EASTER EGG *Eggshell, dye; early twentieth century; Moravian Slovakia; l. approx. 6 cm; H4-52.498*

A batik technique of applying wax with a pipe was used to decorate the shell of these blown eggs. They are decorated with multicolored dyes in floral and geometric motifs. *See fig. 75a, page 86.* L R

149. EASTER EGG *Anna Dražilová; eggshell, straw, dye; 1974; Šaratice, Haná region, Moravia; l. approx. 6 cm; H4-91.107*

150. EASTER EGG *M. Pachtová; eggshell, straw, dye; 1980; Vyškov, Moravia; l. approx. 6 cm; H4-99.829*

151. EASTER EGG *Růžena Brodská; eggshell, paste made from river rushes, fabric; 1976; Kyškovice near Roudnice, Bohemia; l. approx. 6 cm; H4-92.992*

Some eggs were decorated with applied materials. These techniques included glueing straw on dyed eggs or covering the surface of eggs with a marrowlike paste made from river rushes in a three-dimensional pattern and decorating them with fabric. L R

155, 156

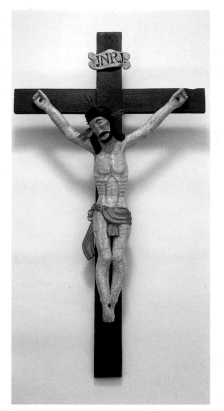

157

152. EASTER EGG *Anna Kašparová; eggshell, vegetable dye; 1975; Olšany near Prostějova, Moravia; l. approx. 6 cm; H4-91.740*

153. EASTER EGG *Eggshell, food coloring; 1920; Kostice, Podluží, Moravia; l. approx. 6 cm; H4-85.202*

154. EASTER EGG *Marie Kočicová; eggshell, vegetable dye; 1980; Uherský Brod, Moravia; l. approx 6 cm; H4-100.409*

After blown eggs were dyed with vegetable or other dyes, a decorative pattern, generally a floral motif, was scratched into the surface, revealing the white of the eggshell. *See fig. 75b, page 86.*   L R

155. EASTER SWITCH *Willow wands, ribbons; 1992; Bohemia; l. 160 cm; H4-108.699*

156. EASTER SWITCH *František Frolec; willow wands, ribbons, hair; 1992; Prague; l. 207 cm; H4-108.693*

Easter switches, or *pomlázky*, are made of willow wands braided in complex patterns and decorated with ribbons. In an Easter ritual that reflects earlier fertility rites, young men would whip young women with these switches.   L R

Č. Zíbrt, *Veselé chvíle v životě lidu českého (Prague, 1950)*, p. 259.

157. CRUCIFIX *Wood, paint, silver gilt; mid-nineteenth century; South Bohemia; h. 111 cm, w. 60 cm; H4-100.202*

This massively carved and painted Christ is attached to the simple black wooden cross, with the inscription "INRI" (Jesus of Nazareth, King of the Jews) on a carved sign picked out in white.   A V

K. Šourek, L'Art populaire en images *(Prague, 1956)*.

158. REVERSE PAINTING ON GLASS *Glass, wood, paint; nineteenth century; Pohoří, South Bohemia; h. 25 cm, w. 17 cm (framed); H4-47.387*

This reverse painting on glass is typical of the South Bohemian school. The Holy Trinity is represented by God the Father, the crucified Christ, and a dove representing the Holy Spirit.   A V

N. Melniková-Papoušková, *Československé lidové malířství na skle (Prague, 1938)*.

158

160

161

159. MADONNA OF SVATÁ HORA *Linden wood, paint; mid-nineteenth century; Příbram region; h. 54 cm; H4-94.273*

Except for the crowns, which were turned on a lathe and then glued on the figures' heads, this Madonna of Svatá Hora and the pedestal under her were carved from a single piece of wood. *See fig. 82, page 92.* AV

K. Šourek, L'Art populaire en images *(Prague, 1956); A. Vondrušková,* Tradice lidové tvorby *(Prague, 1988).*

160. BOTTLE SCENE *Glass, wood, paper, paint; end of the nineteenth century; Bohemia; h. 38 cm, w. 11.5 cm, d. 8 cm; H4-89.268*

This scene presents the crucified Christ and the instruments used to torture him. The image of Christ on the cross was cut from paper and painted, and the two saints in front of the cross and the angel under the cross are colored prints. The bottle in which these are assembled was mold-blown, and the two grooves were added before the glass hardened. AV

M. Růžička, "Jihočeské lidové montáže v dutém skle," in Československá vlastivěda, *vol. 3:* Lidová kultura *(Prague, 1968).*

161. PRAYER BOOK *Paper, ink, brass, glass; 1800–1850; probably South Bohemia; h. 18.5 cm, w. 11 cm, d. 5 cm; H4-24.830*

This copy of *Poloviční nebeklíč* (Half the key to heaven), a prayer book, lacks its title page. Its beaten and perforated brass covers, set with red and green glass, have a chalice and host on the front and a heart and cross on the back. P Š

162. NATIVITY SCENE *Wood, paper, textiles, dirt, sand, moss, glass; late nineteenth century; Králíky, Orlické hory (mountains), Bohemia; h. 50 cm, w. 77.5 cm, d. 40 cm; H4-76.576*

This nativity scene featuring the Adoration of the Magi is mounted in

162

a simple wooden box. The buildings are painted paper and the figures are carved and painted wood, probably produced in Králíky. The ground is covered with fabric to which sand, crushed glass, and moss are attached.　L R

K. Procházka, O betlémech (Prague, 1908).

163. BRIDESMAID'S DRESS *Fabric, paper, glass; 1800–1850; environs of Soběslav, Blata region, South Bohemia; h. (of woman), approx. 165 cm; H4-8.829, 17.794, 17.797, 17.799, 18.000, 18.175, 24.436, 25.999, 80.495 excluding accessories*

This ceremonial wedding outfit from Blata represents an older type of costume. The blouse with puff sleeves and ruff and the apron are decorated with primarily yellow and light brown silk embroidery. Over the blouse is a short empire-cut bodice made from colored brocade, and the skirt is made from hand-woven blue serge fabric. The headgear is characteristic of a bridesmaid's outfit. The accessories, including the low black shoes and red tights, are typical for this area.　J L

D. Stránská, Lidové kroje v Československu, vol. I: Čechy (Prague, 1940); J. Langhammerová, České lidové kroje (Prague, 1995).

164. WOMAN'S COSTUME *Fabric, leather; end of the nineteenth century; environs of Vsetín, Valašsko, Northeast Moravia; h. (of woman) approx. 165 cm; H4-96.587–96.590 excluding accessories*

This outfit is typical for the Beskydy Hills, a highland area. The shawl tied about the woman's head has a red print. The blouse with gathered sleeves is of white linen decorated with geometric blue embroidery. The pleated skirt, which is not sewn together at the front, is also made from white linen. It is covered in front by a blue print apron. The bodice is made from red cloth hemmed with green ribbon. On her feet are hand-knit woollen socks and soft *krbce* (leather sandals). *See fig. 77, page 87.* J L

V. Kovářů, Lidový kroj na Valašsku (Ostrava, 1982); J. Langhammerová, České lidové kroje (Prague, 1995).

165. MAN'S COSTUME *Fabric, leather; early twentieth century; environs of Vsetín, Valašsko, Northeast Moravia; h. (of man) approx. 180 cm; H4-84.269-84.271 excluding accessories*

This costume, typical for the upland areas, consists of long dark blue trousers and a red embroidered waistcoat decorated with braiding. The shirt has a characteristic rectangular cut and loose sleeves. A geometric pattern with a rooster motif is embroidered on the chest. The accessories, a tall hat and *krbce* (leather sandals) with woolen socks, are also typical for the mountain region. *See fig. 76, page 87.*　J L

166. LITHOGRAPH OF A COUPLE IN FOLK COSTUME *Wilhelm Horn; paper, lithography, watercolors; 1837; h. 38.5 cm, w. 48.7 cm; H4-K-4.850-A*

163

166

167

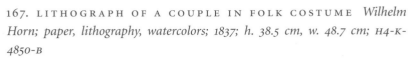

167. LITHOGRAPH OF A COUPLE IN FOLK COSTUME *Wilhelm Horn; paper, lithography, watercolors; 1837; h. 38.5 cm, w. 48.7 cm; H4-K-4850-B*

These lithographs are part of a series of prints made by Wilhelm Horn to commemorate the 1837 visit of Emperor Ferdinand V to Brno. No. 166 shows a couple in costumes of the lowland area of Mořice na Hané, district of Prostěov, that were typical of the first decade of the nineteenth century. No. 167 shows a couple in the dress of the highland region of Valašské Meziříčí, district of Vsetín; the man is holding a herder's trumpet for signaling his flock. J L

W. *Horn*, Mährische Volkstrachten *(Brno, 1837);* Československá vlastivěda, Lidová kultura *(Prague, 1968), p. 141.*

168. SHAWL *Linen, cotton; first half of the nineteenth century; Chloumek near Mladá Boleslav, Bohemia; l. 160 cm, w. 150 cm; H4-9.413*

This white linen shawl is embroidered in button stitching with white cotton and in spider-lace openwork. H B

D. *Stránská,* Lidové kroje v Československu, *vol. I: Čechy (Prague, 1940), p. 233.*

169. APRON *Linen, cotton, lace; late nineteenth century; environs of Kyjov; w. 130 cm, l. 69 cm; H4-80.688*

This apron is made from two pieces of blue batiked linen joined by a stem stitch. The edge is hemmed with braided lace. H B

M. *Ludvíková,* Moravské lidové kroje *(Prague, 1969).*

170. KERCHIEF *Linen, embroidery cotton, lace; Turnov region, North Bohemia; w. 87 cm, l. 89 cm; H4-97.484*

This white linen kerchief, embroidered with pomegranates and carna-

168

169

171

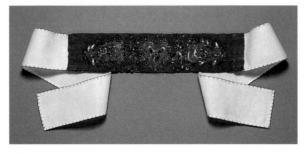

172

173

tions in crimson cotton thread, is edged with white bobbin lace. *See fig. 78, page 88.*   H B

D. Stránská, Lidové kroje v Československu, *vol. I: Čechy (Prague, 1940), p. 224.*

171. WOMAN'S CAP *Lace, garnets, beads, ribbon, thread; 1800–1850; Turnov region, North Bohemia; h. 23 cm, w. 18 cm, d. 20 cm; 114 98.288*

This woman's cap is decorated with gold lace, gold thread, red beads, garnets and gold sequins. The front is edged with white Valenciennes lace in tight concertina folds. At the back is a pink ribbon with a green and yellow woven motif.   H B

D. Stránská, Lidové kroje v Československu, *vol. I: Čechy (Prague, 1940), p. 225.*

172. FILLET *Linen, beads, ribbon, bullion; 1800–1850; Soběslavská Blata; w. 8 cm, l. 31 cm; H4-1.472*

The foundation of this fillet is a band of white linen with a red ribbon sewn in the center. It is decorated with colored beads and bullion (lace made from metal thread). A red loop stitch was used to hem the unembroidered linen.   H B

D. Stránská, Lidové kroje v Československu, *vol. I: Čechy (Prague, 1940), p. 173.*

173. CAP *Brocade, ribbon, cardboard lining; 1900–1950; Lanžhot, Podluží, Moravia; h. 23 cm, w. 19 cm; H4-103.505*

This cap, called a *rožky,* is made from a shaped band of cardboard covered on the outside with red brocade. A cockade of white, hand-painted ribbons is tied to the crown and a bouquet of artificial flowers is affixed to the back.   H B

L. Niederle, Moravské Slovensko *(Prague, 1918).*

174   175   176

174. JUG *Faience; 1825–1850; Vyškov; h. 22.5 cm, diam. (rim) 9 cm; H4-101.506*

This Moravian wine jug has a characteristic *toufar* shape. The motif is the Virgin of Mariazell (a famous Austro-Hungarian pilgrimage site) in a flower festoon. This rustic jug is the work of an anonymous Vyškov jug-maker who had mastered the technique of polychrome.   v š

K. Černohorský, Moravská lidová keramika *(Prague 1941), no. 162.*

175. BOTTLE *Glass, enamel paint, pewter; 1800–1825; Šumava region, perhaps Freudenthal; h. 17 cm, w. 8.5 cm, d. 6.5 cm; H4-41.173*

This type of bottle for spirits or liqueurs, called a *pryska,* was blown in a wooden mold and decorated with enamel. The garland circling the neck symbolizes marriage. The symmetrical composition with central reserve is characteristic of the empire period. The central flower and tulips are typical of bottles made in Freudenthal, in the Austro-Bohemian glass-making area of Šumava.   v š

F. C. Lipp, Bemalte Gläser *(Munich, 1974), pls. 217, 215, 224.*

176. TANKARD *Glass, enamel paint, pewter; late eighteenth or early nineteenth century; Šumava region; h. 22 cm, diam (rim) 8 cm; H4-423*

The enamel painted decoration of this blown-glass tankard includes a white cock crowing amidst two sprigs of flowers—a characteristic motif symbolizing marriage and fertility. Its asymmetrical composition usually is characteristic of the late eighteenth and early nineteenth centuries. v š

F. C. Lipp, Bemalte Gläser *(Munich, 1974).*

177

178

179

177. MOLD *Carver with the initials F.R.; 1820; Slavkov, Moravia; l. 24.5 cm, w. 8.5 cm, d. 3 cm; H4-56.625*

This two-sided negative carved-relief gingerbread mold, bearing a heart and a figure of a soldier, was traded from the property of gingerbread maker Košvic of Slavkov to beekeeper Arnošt Kohl from Česká Metuje in exchange for honey. L R

A. Walzer, Liebeskutsche, Reitersmann, Nikolaus und Kinderbringer *(Stuttgart 1963).*

178. BUTTER MOLD *Beech wood; second half of the nineteenth century; Bohemia; h. 7 cm, diam. 12 cm; H4-92.856*

The three motifs in this butter mold, the anchor, the heart, and the cross, are traditional symbols found on earlier objects. L R

179. DOLL *Wood, paint; early twentieth century; Skašov, district of Plzeň, West Bohemia; h. 19 cm; H4-3.478*

180. TOY HORSE *Wood, paint; late nineteenth century; Skašov, district of Plzeň, West Bohemia; h. 25 cm, base l. 16 cm, w. 7.5 cm; H4-4.448*

The bodies of these polychrome toys are lathe-turned. The doll's arms in which the baby lies are fixed to a wooden bar that passes though the body; a string attached to the bar comes out through a hole in the doll's back. When the string is pulled, the doll rocks the child. The horse's head, legs and tail are hand-carved. These toys are typical of the products of Skašov toy makers from the late nineteenth and early twentieth century. P Š

J. Brand, Z minulosti domácké výroby skašovských hraček *(Přeštice, 1989); E. Hercík,* Československé lidové hračky *(Prague, 1951).*

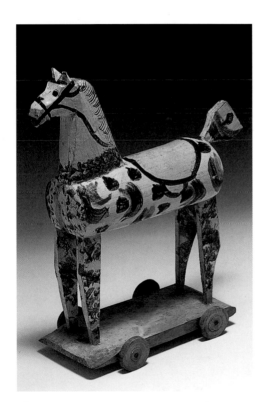

180

182

183

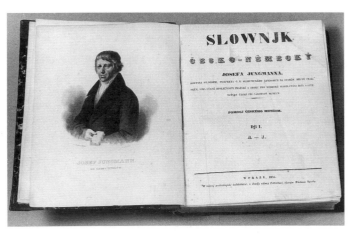

184

181. CUPBOARD *Wood, paint; 1833; foothills of the Krkonoše Mountains; h. 204 cm, w. 138 cm, d. 65 cm; H4-101.583*

This late empire-style cupboard is typical of the foothills of the Krkonoše. A costly cupboard of this type was an essential part of a peasant bride's trousseau. The painted tree of life growing out of the grail and the cornucopia are marriage symbols. *See fig. 81, page 90.*   V Š

H. Johnová, J. Staňková, and L. Baran, Lidový malovaný nábytek v českých zemích (Prague, 1989).

182. CHAIR *Wood, inlay; 1825–1850; Central Bohemia; h. 86 cm, w. 40 cm, d. 35 cm,; H4-105.718*

This plank chair has a classic European batten construction. The back is carved in an abstract version of the imperial two-headed eagle with a crown. It is inlaid with motifs that include sprigs of the tree of life growing from a grail, and a five-petaled flower symbolizing marriage. The inlay is characteristic of Central Bohemian folk furniture. The symmetrical composition of the motif and frugal use of inlay is characteristic for the post-empire styles of the second quarter of the nineteenth century.   V Š

H. Johnová and I. Večerková, Lidový nábytek v českých zemích (Prague, 1983), pl. 9.

183. NEWSPAPER *Václav Matěj Kramerius (1753–1808); paper, ink; May 24, 1800; Prague; h. 45.5 cm, w. 37.7 cm; Tresor*

German-language newspapers began regularly appearing in Prague in 1658, Czech-language ones in 1719. The most memorable of the latter is the *Krameriovy císařské a královské vlastenské noviny* (Imperial and royal patriotic news), edited from 1789 to 1808 by Czech patriot, Václav Matěj Kramerius. He was also an advocate of religious tolerance and a publisher of popular Czech entertainment and educational booklets.

This weekly newspaper was written in exemplary Czech. It focused on world news, and also covered domestic events such as nationalist festivals, Czech literature, and Czech theater.   E S

J. Herben, Matěj Václav Kramerius: Osvícený novinář a buditel (Prague, 1926); Jan Novotný, Matěj Václav Kramerius (Prague, 1973).

184. DICTIONARY *Josef Jungmann (1773–1843) et al.; paper, ink, and leather; 1835–1839; Prague; h. 27 cm, w. 23 cm, d. 6 cm (each volume); KNM 112 A 32/1-5*

This five-volume Czech-German dictionary is the greatest work of philology from the Czech national revival. Written by philologist and literary historian Josef Jungmann with the help of his friends and students, it shows the historical development of Czech and its adaption as a modern national language.   E R

Rozpravy o díle Jungmannově (Prague, 1948).

185. EMBLEM *Iron, paint; nineteenth century; Bohemia; h. 24 cm, w. 27 cm; H2-59.875*

This cast emblem signifying the kingdom of Bohemia has a large gold crown above three connected shields bearing the symbols of Bohemia (a golden lion wearing a crown on a red shield), Moravia (a red-and-white eagle wearing a crown on a blue shield), and Silesia (a black eagle wearing a crown on a gold shield).   E Š

185

186. COCKADE *Satin, tin; 1848; Prague; diam. 9.4 cm; H2-6.570*

This cockade with a central crowned Czech lion is from the uniform hat of a member of the Concordia, an armed group active in the revolution of 1848. Cockades were worn to show loyalty to the Czech nationalist cause; in Prague the chief colors for these badges were red and white. The colors and the figure of the lion were considered symbols of Czech statehood and of the historic rights of the Czech nation.   V P ř

M. Moravcová, Národní oděv roku 1848 (Prague, 1986).

187. DRAWING OF PŘEMYSL BEING CALLED TO THE THRONE *František Ženíšek (1849–1916); pastel on paper; c. 1895; Prague; h. 60 cm, w. 120 cm; frame: h. 79 cm, w. 139 cm; H2-185.150*

The legend of Přemysl and Libuše was a favorite patriotic theme of the nineteenth-century national revival. This pastel drawing shows messengers of Libuše, according to legend the princess of the Czechs, finding Přemysl and asking him to come to Vyšehrad, marry Libuše, and become prince of all the Czechs. The royal dynasty of the Přemyslids, which ruled Bohemia until 1306, took its name from this mythological figure.

186

František Ženíšek, one of the greatest Czech painters of the turn of the century, portrayed this theme five times. This picture is a replica of an oil sketch of 1895 presented as a design for a monumental lunette in the Pantheon in the National Museum in Prague. *See fig, 62, page 69.*   L S

L. Sršeň, Budova Národního muzea v Praze. Architektura, umělecká výzdoba a původní uměleckořemeslné vybavení, 1891–1991 (Prague, 1991), p. 142, fig. 72.

188. SOKOL FLAG *After a design by Josef Mánes (1820–1871); silk, silk thread; 1887; Prague; h. 157 cm, w. 140 cm; H7-10.877*

This embroidered flag of the first Prague Sokol gymnastics club is a copy of an 1862 flag designed by Czech painter Josef Mánes. Jindřich Trenkwald, a member of Prague Sokol, had it made for the twenty-fifth anniversary of the club.

The Sokol organization was founded February 16, 1862, by Miroslav Tyrš and Jindřich Fügner. Named after its symbol, the falcon, it stressed sport, outdoor activities, and Czech national pride. Its goals meshed with those of the growing nationalist movement, led by young Czechs seeking to eliminate economic and cultural dependence on the German bourgeoisie. The groundwork laid by Tyrš was the basis for a nationwide Sokol movement. *See fig. 83, page 95.*   K Š

187 (reverse)

K. Štursová, Prapory Sokola Pražského (Prague, 1992), pp. 9–12.

189

190

191

192

189. SONGBOOK *František Jan Škroup (1801–1862); paper, ink, linen; 1835; Prague; h. 20.5 cm, w. 52.5 cm, d. 1 cm; KNM XXX B 107*

The song, "Kde domov můj?" (Where is my home?) by František Jan Škroup premiered in the musical production *Fidlovačka* (The Fair) in 1834. It became popular almost immediately and would be sung spontaneously at gatherings of Czech nationalists. After the emergence of the Czech state in 1918, it became the national anthem.   MK

J. Plavec, F. J. Škroup (Prague, 1941).

190. MUSIC THEORY BOOK *Jakub Jan Ryba (1765–1815); paper, ink, leather; 1817; Prague; h. 19 cm, w. 49 cm; XV A 127*

Jakub Jan Ryba was one of the most important teachers and musicians of his day in the Czech Lands. He wrote many works on the theory of music and composed numerous religious works, including the popular Christmas mass, "Hej mistře," and instrumental pieces. This volume, *Počáteční a všeobecní základové ke všemu umění hudebnému* (Initial and general foundations of all art of music) is one of his works on music theory.   MK

J. Němeček, Jakub Jan Ryba (Prague, 1963); I. Janáčková, J. J. Ryba o svém hudebním životě (Prague, 1946).

191. BOOK OF CZECH NATIONAL SONGS *Jan Ritter z Rittersberku (1780–1841); paper, ink; 1825; Prague; h. 26.5 cm, w. 70 cm (open); I D 2*

České národní písně ("Czech National Songs"), by Jan Ritter z Rittersberku, appeared in Prague in 1825. It contains three hundred Czech and fifty German songs and fifty dances.   M K

Hudební věda *(Prague, 1988), 3:778–822; J. Markl,* Lidové písně a národní obrození v Čechách, *in* Lid a lidová kultura národního obrození v Čechách, *pamphlet no. 3 (Prague, 1980).*

192. BOOK OF MARKET SONGS *Paper, ink; 1800–1850; h. 13.5 cm, w. 9.5 cm; KNM KP ŠP. 124*

This collection of song sheets with religious and secular songs was bound by their owner into a *špalíček* or "block." Market songs were mainly written by anonymous popular composers and were sold at fairs and markets. They form an important element of Czech literature.   E R

R. Smetana and B. Václavek, České písně kramářské *(Prague, 1949); B. Beneš,* Světská kramářská píseň *(Brno, 1970); J. V. Scheybal,* Senzace pěti století v kramářské písni *(Hradec Králové, 1990).*

193. SCRIPT FOR *JAN HUS Josef Kajetán Tyl (1808– 1856); 1848; Prague; h. 21.5 cm, w. 27 cm; H6-1.175*

193

"Jan Hus, kazatel betlémský" (John Huss, Bethlehem preacher), considered to be the first Czech poetic tragedy, was written by Josef Kajetán Tyl in the fall of 1848. Its premiere in the Estates Theater on December 26, 1848, was the greatest public event to follow the unsuccessful June uprising. The author took František Palacký's interpretation of Huss and, using historical analogy, presented it as a charismatic individual's struggle to live with dignity and freedom to express the truth. The exceptional political response to the play resulted in its being banned in Prague, an edict that lasted for more than half a century.   V Pe

M. Votruba and M. Kačer, Tvůrčí cesta Josefa Kajetána Tyla *(Prague, 1961); J. L. Turnovský,* Josef Kajetán Tyl *(Prague, 1881).*

194. SET DESIGN *Tobias Mössner (1790–1871); paper, ink, watercolor, gouache; c. 1850; Prague; h. 25 cm, w. 34 cm; H6-d17.628/s-1XC-5*

The greatest designer of the Estates Theater was Tobias Mössner, who introduced principles of illusory perspective to Czech set design. He came to Prague with the theater director Stoger in 1834, and in 1836 he painted the sets for a gala performance celebrating the coronation of Emperor Ferdinand. This rustic living room shows how Mössner depicted the reality of country life in a way that suited the romantic tendencies of the time. *See fig. 70, page 79.*   V K

Dějiny českého divadla, II *(Prague, 1969), p. 258 ff.*

196   197

195. DANCING PUPPETS *Mikuláš Sichrovský; wood, fabric, metal, paint; mid-nineteenth century; Mirotice; h. 32 cm; H6-023, 24, 25, 26 /47*

Taneček (Dance) is the name given these four puppet figures from the troupe of the popular puppeteer, Arnoštka Kopecká (1842–1914). This type of puppet appeared as an encore at the end of a production, performing to music from a barrel organ. It was controlled by a specially adapted bar that allowed each pair of dancers to move in unison. *See fig. 72, page 82.*   J P

J. Toman, Matěj Kopecký a jeho rod *(České Budějovice, 1960); J. Bartoš,* Loutkářská kronika *(Prague, 1963).*

196. KAŠPÁREK PUPPET *Alessi; wood, fabric, metal, paint; 1850–1900; Prague; h. 50 cm; H6-D11.145*

Kašpárek, a clown or Punch figure, was a central character in most puppet plays. The puppet representing him was smaller than the other puppets and was always operated with strings. Puppeteers gave him lines that emphasized wit, a quick tongue, and fearlessness, which made Kašpárek a hero to spectators of all ages.   J P

J. Veselý, "Popular puppeteers," Československý loutkář *(Prague, 1957).*

197. KNIGHT PUPPET *František Wida; wood, fabric, metal, paint; 1850–1900; h. 75 cm; H6-D11.286*

In the puppet play repertoire, plays about knights were great favorites.   J P

J. Bartoš, Loutkářská kronika *(Prague, 1963).*

198. STENCIL *Cardboard; 1850–1900; h. 36 cm, w. 25 cm; H6-C30.428*

This stencil for a poster listing performances of *Jeno-vefa*, a folk play, is typical of posters popular puppeteers used to announce their performances.   J P

J. Vesely, "Plakáty lidovych loutkářů," Národopisny věstník *(Prague, 1913).*

199. COSTUME FOR *THE BARTERED BRIDE Fabric, leather; 1880s; Prague; h. 140 cm, w. 110 cm; DEP 3/41-44*

Vašek, the stuttering peasant bridegroom in Bedřich Smetana's *Bartered Bride,* is one of the great comic tenor roles in the Czech opera repertoire. Actors playing the role wore this costume in performances at the National Theater in Prague in the 1880s and 1890s and at the International Musical Exhibition in Vienna in 1892.   O M

J. Clapham, Smetana *(London, 1972), p. 93; B. Large,* Smetana *(London, 1970), p. 160.*

198

200. SET MODEL FOR *THE BARTERED BRIDE Robert Holzer (1859 –1938); wood, plywood, paint; c. 1892; w. 50 cm, h. 50 cm, d. 50 cm (approximate); H6-D22.020*

Between 1875 and 1880 Robert Holzer worked in the Vienna studios of the decorative painters Brioschi, Burghardt, and Kautsky. After a stay in Paris he moved to Prague in 1883 and began producing a wide range of stage sets that reflected actual Czech exteriors. This model for the set for the new production of Bedřich Smetana's *Bartered Bride* in 1892 is among the oldest to survive for the world-famous comic opera.   V K

V. Hepner, Scénická výprava na jevišti Národního divadla v letech 1883-90 *(Prague, 1955), p. 36; A. Chaloupka,* Česká divadelní dekorace *(Prague, 1939), p. 13;* Dějiny Českého divadla *(Prague, 1977), 3:241ff.*

201. SCORE FOR *SLAVONIC DANCES*   *Antonín Dvořák (1841–1904); paper, ink; 1878–1900; Berlin, Germany; h. 30.5 cm, w. 24.7 cm.; JPR 2/92*

When Fritz Simrock of Berlin published Antonín Dvořák's famous *Slavonic Dances* op. 46 (for piano for four hands), he reused his own original printer's plate of 1878.   M H

202. WREATH   *Silver, gilt, jewels, fabric; 1884; Prague; h. 29 cm, w. 28 cm; V I 5 III*

This silver and gilt wreath was presented to Antonín Dvořák by the members of the orchestra at the National Theater at the gala opening performance of his opera *Dimitrij* in the National Theater in Prague on April 5, 1884. Titles of Dvořák's compositions are engraved on the laurel leaves. *See fig. 69, page 77.*   M H

203. EMBROIDERY SAMPLER   *Silk, silk thread; 1800–1830; Bohemia; l. 55.5 cm, w. 28.3 cm; H2-5.802*

203

204

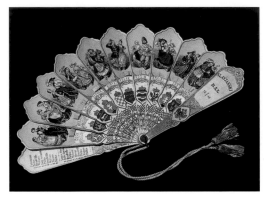

205

206

This sampler shows a variety of floral motifs embroidered in colored silk. Samplers that have been preserved in collections of Czech museums are testimony to the imagination and skill of Czech women and girls. V PŘ

204. WOMAN'S DRESS *Silk moiré, lace; c. 1855; Bohemia; jacket: l. 51 cm, w. 40 cm; skirt: l. 106 cm; cape: l. (front) 95 cm, (back) 60 cm; H2-54.181 A, B, C*

This purple and gray dress shows ladies' fashion in the period of the rococo revival, when broad skirts, attached bodices, and bell-shaped sleeves were popular. The skirt is supported by a crinoline, a cagelike structure made from birch wands or wire, that was created and promoted by fashion designer Charles Frederick Worth in Paris in the 1850s. Pavlína Metternich, the wife of the Austrian ambassador to France, helped to spread the style. V PŘ

L. Kybalová, O. Herbenová, and M. Lamarová, Obrazová encyklopedie módy, (Prague, 1973); E. Uchalová, Česká móda (od valčíku po tango), vol. 1 (Prague, 1989).

205. FAN *A. Daněk; paper, colored lithography; 1848; Vienna, Austria; l. 14.3 cm, w. 27 cm (open); tassel approx. 20 cm; H2-3.413*

This lithographed fan lists the order of dances for a February 9, 1848, Slavonic Ball. Each of the couples in the lithographs is clad in a costume of a Slav nation in the Austro-Hungarian Empire.   V Př

206. NECKLACE AND EARRINGS *Silver, Czech garnets (pyropes), almandines, small pearls; c. 1860; Bohemia; necklace: l. 40 cm, w. 6 cm; earrings: l. 5.5 cm; H2-126.422, .423 A, B*

Rich veins of pyropes in the Czech Lands made it possible to use these blood-red stones in church ornaments, embroidery, and jewelry. In the nineteenth century the Czech garnet was designated the national gem, and garnet jewelry, much of it mass-produced, became a symbol of Czech patriotism. D S

J. Durdík and Co., The Pictorial Encyclopedia of Antiques *(Prague, 1968), p. 316.*

207

207. CUP AND SAUCER *Porcelain; 1823; Slavkov; h. (cup) 10.8 cm; diam. (cup) 9.5 cm, (saucer) 15 cm; H2-126.268 A, B*

Bohemian firms finally broke the Viennese monopoly on porcelain production at the end of the eighteenth century, and several porcelain works soon opened in the Karlovy Vary region, which provided natural supplies of high-quality kaolin clay. The first stable and functional porcelain works were founded in 1792 in Slavkov, where this porcelain cup and saucer were produced. They are decorated with gold-painted designs and various views of Karlovy Vary. MM

208. CUP AND SAUCER *Porcelain; 1820–1840; Březová; h. (cup) 12.5 cm; diam. (cup base) 8.3 cm; diam. (saucer) 16.5cm.; H2-126.013 A-B*

This porcelain cup and saucer, created in the porcelain works that were founded in 1803 in Březová, was manufactured as a souvenir for visitors to Karlovy Vary; its rich decoration is more appropriate for display in a home collection than for practical use. Both pieces are decorated with gold paint, and the cup has a romantic landscape that depicts a mill near Karlovy Vary. *See fig. 63, page 69.* M M

209. VASE *Glass, enamel paint; c. 1850; North Bohemia; h. 24 cm, diam. 13.5 cm; H2-30.874*

By the 1820s Czech glassworks had perfected colored glass technology. For this vase, green glass was extruded through a layer of white enamel, facets were cut into the opaque layer to expose the transparent green base, and the surface was decorated with colored and gold paint.   M M

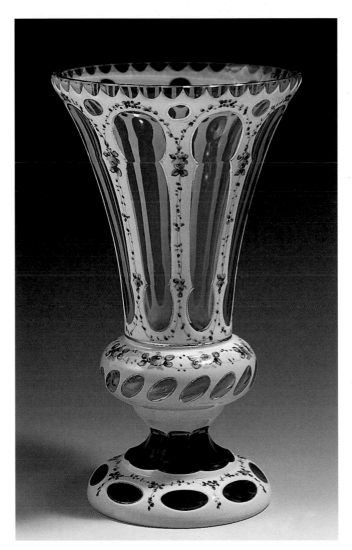

209

210

210. PRINT OF KARLOVY VARY
Vincenc Morstadt (1802–1875); paper, color etching, watercolors; V. Morstadt fec. Bei W. A. Ryba in Prag; before 1850; Prague; plate mark: h. 24.6 cm, w. 32.4 cm; paper: h. 33.0 cm, w. 41.0 cm; H2-27.020

The picturesque spa town of Karlovy Vary, in the valley of the River Teplá in West Bohemia, took its name from Charles IV, who issued a privilegium in 1370 raising the small settlement and hunting castle to the status of a town. The healing effects of the local mineral springs have been exploited since the sixteenth century. The town went on to win fame for its porcelain and its world-famous liqueur—a panacea for stomach complaints. The artist of this colored etching, Vincenc Morstadt, was known for his landscapes and accurate architectural details. V Př

O. Dostál, *Československá historická města (Prague, 1974).*

211. BUST OF TOMÁŠ GARRIGUE MASARYK; *J. K. Pekárek (1873–1930); bronze; 1921; Prague; h. 46 cm, w. 36 cm, d. 24 cm; H2-142.466*

Tomáš Garrigue Masaryk (1850–1937) was the first president of Czechoslovakia. In 1879, after studying philosophy in Vienna and Leipzig, he became a lecturer at the University of Vienna, and in 1882 he became professor of philosophy at Charles University in Prague. He was the leading figure of the "realist" faction of the Young Czech party. The public became aware of him as a result of the "Hilsner affair" when he criticized the prevailing anti-Semitism of Czech society. Shortly after the outbreak of World War I, Masaryk went into exile, and he and the others came to represent the foreign resistance to the Hapsburg monarchy. He engineered the creation of the Czechoslovak Republic in 1918 and was its first president, a post he held until 1935. This bust was cast by F. Anýž in Prague three years after Masaryk had become president. *See fig. 84, page 97.* P S

212. PRESIDENT'S FLAG *Women of the Pech family; fabric, wool embroidery, cotton appliqué; 1920; Hodonín; h. 150 cm, w. 150 cm; H8-13.108*

This flag contains the national emblem, a Bohemian lion, surrounded by symbols of other lands—Moravia, Silesia, Slovakia, and Ruthenia—and supported by two golden lions standing on golden linden boughs connected by a band of gold bearing the motto "Pravda vítězí" (Truth conquers). The flag was donated by the Pech family (the head of which was then the Sokol leader in Hodonín) to Masaryk. After Masaryk's death the flag was returned to Hodonín, and during the Nazi occupation it was buried in the Pechs' garden.   P S

212

Selected Bibliography

History

Agnew, Hugh Le Caine. *Origins of the Czech National Renascence.* Pittsburgh, 1993.

Bradley, J. F. N. *Czechoslovakia: A Short History.* Edinburgh, 1971.

Čornej, Petr. *Fundamentals of Czech History.* Prague, 1992.

Ewans, R. J. *Rudolf II and His World: A Study in Intellectual History, 1576–1612.* Oxford, 1973.

Helbing, E. C. *Österreichische Verfassungs- und Verwaltungsgeschichte* (Austrian constitutional and administrative history). Berlin, 1955.

Hermann, Adolf Hanns. *A History of Czechs.* London, 1975.

Kratochvíl, Miloš V. *History for Young People.* Prague, 1962.

Krejčí, Jaroslav. *Czechoslovakia at the Crossroads of European History.* London, 1990.

Molnár, Amadeo. *Jean Hus.* Paris, 1978.

Opat, Jaroslav, ed. *Illustrated Czech History,* series 1. Vol. 1: Jiři Sláma and Vladimír Vavřínek, *Slavic Settlement in the Czech Lands and Great Moravia;* vol. 2: Rostislav Nový, *The State of Bohemia in the Early Middle Ages (10th–12th centuries);* vol. 3: Josef Žemlička, *The Rise of Bohemia among European Powers (1173–1253);* vol. 4: Josef Žemlička, *The Czech Lands during the Reign of the Last Přemyslids.* Prague, 1996.

Památky národní minulosti: Katalog historické expozice Národního muzea v Praze (Monuments of the national past: catalog of the historical exhibition of the National Museum in Prague). Prague, 1989. English summary available.

Parrott, Cecil. *Czechoslovakia: Its Heritage and Its Future.* Newcastle, U.K., 1968.

Polišenský, Josef Vincent. *History of Czechoslovakia in Outline,* 2d ed. Prague, 1991.

Purš, Jaroslav, and Miroslav Kropilák, eds. *Přehled dějin Československa* (Historical overview of Czechoslovakia), vol. I, part 1. Prague, 1982.

Rechcigl, Miroslav. *Czechoslovakia, Past and Present.* Hawthorne, N.Y., 1968.

Renner, Hans. *A History of Czechoslovakia Since 1945.* London, 1989.

Skilling, H. Gordon. *Czechoslovakia 1918–88: Seventy Years from Independence.* New York, 1991.

Skilling, H. Gordon, and Paul Wilson, eds. *Civic Freedom in Central Europe: Voices from Czechoslovakia.* New York, 1991.

Sláma, Jiří. *Mittelböhmen im frühen Mittelalter* (Middle Bohemia in the Early Middle Ages). Prague, 1977.

Spěváček, Jiří. *Karl IV: Sein Leben und seine staatsmännische Leistung* (Charles IV: His life and political achievement). Prague, 1978.

Stone, N. and E. Strouhal, eds. *Czechoslovakia: Crossroads and Crises, 1918–1988.* Basingstoke, U.K., 1989.

Sturmberger, H. *Der Aufstand in Böhmen: Der Beginn der Dreißigjährigen Krieges* (The Bohemian uprising: The beginning of the Thirty Years' War). Munich, 1959.

Szulc, Tad. *Czechoslovakia Since World War II*. New York, 1971.

Turek, Rudolf. *Čechy v raném středověku* (Bohemia in the early Middle Ages). Prague, 1982.

Winter, E. *Die tschechische und slowakische Emigration im Deutschland im 17. und 18. Jahrhundert* (Czech and Slovakian migration to Germany in the 17th and 18th centuries). Vienna, 1956.

Winter, E. *Barock, Absolutismus, Aufklärung in der Donaumonarchie* (Baroque, absolutism, and enlightenment in the Danube monarchy). Vienna, 1970.

Zeman, Jarold K. *The Hussite Movement and the Reformation in Bohemia, Moravia, and Slovakia, 1350–1650: A Bibliographic Study Guide*. Ann Arbor: Michigan Slavic Publications, 1977.

Zöllner, E. *Geschichte Österreichs* (History of Austria), 4 vols. Vienna, 1970.

Art

Architecture in the Czech Republic. Prague, 1993.

Bachmann, Erich, ed. *Romanik in Böhmen* (The Romanesque in Bohemia). Munich, 1977.

Baroque in Bohemia: An Exhibition of Czech Art Organized by the National Gallery, Prague. London, 1969.

Bialostocki, Jan. *The Art of the Renaissance in Eastern Europe: Hungary, Bohemia, Poland*. Oxford, 1976.

Blažíček, Oldřich J. *Barockkunst in Böhmen* (Baroque art in Bohemia). Prague, 1967.

Blažíček, Oldřich J., Pavel Preiss, and Dagmar Hejdová. *Kunst des Barock in Böhmen* (Art of the Baroque in Bohemia). Recklinghausen, Germany, 1977.

Česky porcelán: průvodce expozice Uměleckoprůmyslového muzea v Praze (Czech porcelain: Guide to the exhibition of the Decorative Arts Museum, Prague). Prague, c. 1970.

Československa keramika: ze zbirek Uměleckoprůmyslového muzea v Praze (Czechoslovakian ceramics from the collection of the Decorative Arts Museum, Prague). Prague, 1962.

Czechoslovakian Glass, 1350–1980: A Special Exhibition of the Corning Museum of Glass. New York, c. 1981.

Da Costa, Kaufmann T. *Court, Cloister & City; The Art and Culture of Central Europe 1450–1800*. London, 1995.

Dekan, Ján. *Moravia Magna: The Great Moravian Empire, Its Art and Times*. Minneapolis, 1981.

Dějiny českého výtvarného umění (History of Czech fine arts). Vol. I, parts 1, 2: *Od počátku do konce středověku* (From the beginning to the end of the Middle Ages). Vol. II, parts 1, 2: *Od počátku renesance do závěrů baroka* (From the beginning of the Renaissance to the baroque). Prague, 1984–1989.

Foulds, Diane E. *A Guide to Czech & Slovak Glass*. Prague, c. 1993.

Knihopis českých a slovenských tisků od doby nejstarší až do konce 18. století (Bibliography of Czech and Slovakian books from the earliest period to the end of the 18th century). Prague, 1939–1965.

Knox, Brian. *The Architecture of Prague and Bohemia*. London, 1965.

Kutal, Albert, *L'Art gothique de Bohême* (Gothic art in Bohemia). Prague, 1971.

L'Art ancien en Tchècoslovaquie: Musée des arts décoratifs (Early art in Czechoslovakia from the Museum of Decorative Arts). Paris, 1957.

Matějček, Antonín, and Jaroslav Pešina. *Gotische Malerei in Böhmen 1350–1450* (Gothic painting in Bohemia, 1350–1450). Prague, 1955.

Merhautová, Anežka, and Dušan Třeštík. *Románské uměni v Čechách a na Moravě* (Romanesque art in Bohemia and Moravia). Prague, 1984.

Neubert, Karel. *Art Treasures of Prague: A Guide to the Galleries, Museums and Exhibition Rooms of Prague*. Prague, 1992.

Neumann, Jaromír. *Das böhmische Barock* (Bohemian Baroque). Prague, 1970.

Nová encyklopedie českého výtvarného umění (New encyclopedia of Czech fine arts). Prague, 1995.

Pesatová, Zuzana. *Bohemian Engraved Glass.* Feltham, U.K., 1968.

Pešina, Jaroslav. *Tafelmalerei der Spätgotik und der Renaissance in Böhmen 1450–1550* (Late Gothic and Renaissance panel painting in Bohemia, 1450–1550). Prague, 1958.

Poche, Emanuel. *Bohemian Porcelain.* Prague, c. 1957.

Porter, Tim. *Prague: Art and History.* Prague, 1992.

Prag um 1600: Kunst und Kultur am Hofe Kaiser Rudolfs II (Prague in 1600: art and culture at the court of Rudolf II), 2 vol. Vienna, 1988.

Renaissance Art in Bohemia. London, 1979.

Richterová, Julie. *Středověké kachle* (Medieval stove tiles). Prague, 1982.

Seibt, Ferdinand, *et al.* Gothic art in Bohemia: architecture, sculpture and painting. Oxford, 1977.

Spunar, Pavel. *Kultura českého středověku* (Culture of the Czech Middle Ages). Prague, 1987.

Von Schwarzenberg, Prince Karl, *et al.,* with an introduction by Václav Havel. *The Prague Castle and Its Treasures.* New York, 1994.

Religion

Altshuler, David. *The Precious Legacy: A Catalogue for the Traveling Museum Exhibition of Judaic Objects from the State Jewish Museum in Prague.* New York, 1983.

De Schweinitz, Eugene. *The History of the Church known as the Unitas Fratrum, or the Unity of the Brethren.* Bethlehem, Pa., 1901.

Fiedler, Jiří. *Jewish Sights of Bohemia and Moravia.* Prague, 1991.

Hrejsa, František. *Dějiny křesťanství v Československu* (History of Christianity in Czechoslovakia). Prague, 1948.

Judaica Bohemia. Prague, 1965–1990.

Kadlec, Jaroslav. *Církevní dějiny české* (Czech ecclesiastical history), 2 vols. Prague, 1991.

Kadlec, Jaroslav. *Církevní dějiny* (Ecclesiastical history), 4 vols. Prague, 1974–1976.

Kettner, Jiří. *Dějiny pražské arcidiecéze v datech* (History of the Prague archdiocese). Prague, 1993.

Kubalík, Josef. *Křesťanské církve v naší vlasti* (The Christian church in our country). Prague, 1987.

Říčan, Rudolf. *Dějiny Jednoty Bratrské* (History of the United Brethren). Prague, 1957.

Říčan, Rudolf, and Amadeo Molnár. *12 století církevních dějin* (Twelve centuries of church history). Prague, 1989.

The Jewish Museum in Prague. *Jewish Customs and Traditions.* Prague, 1994.

The Jewish Publication Society of America, *The Jews of Czechoslovakia,* 2 vols. Philadelphia, 1968–1971.

Tisíc let pražského biskupství, 973–1973 (A thousand years of the Prague bishopric, 973–1973). Prague, 1973.

Vaško, Václav. *Neumlčená. Kronika katolické církve v Československu po druhé světové válce* (Unsilencing: A chronicle of the Catholic church in Czechoslovakia after the Second World War), 2 vols. Prague, 1990.

Vilímková, Milada. *The Prague Ghetto.* Prague, 1993.

Performing Arts

Das Atlantisbuch des Theaters (The Atlantis book of Theater). Zürich, 1966.

Československý hudební slovník osob a institucí (Czechoslovakian music dictionary). Prague, 1963.

Dějiny českého divadla (History of the Czech theater), 4 vols. Prague, 1968–1983.

Gascoigne, Bamber. *World Theatre.* London, 1968.

Die Musik in Geschichte und Gegenwart (Music in history and the present), 17 vols. Kassel, 1962.

Patková, Jindra. *Das tschechische Puppentheater* (Czech puppet theater). Prague, 1975.

Pilař, V., and F. Šrámek. *Umění houslařů* (The art of the violin). Prague, 1989.

Sadie, Stanley, ed. *The New Grove Dictionary of Music and Musicians.* London, 1980.

Vondráček, Jan. *Dějiny českého divadla* (History of the Czech theater). Vol. 1: 1771–1824; vol. 2: 1824–1846. Prague, 1956–1957.

Folk Art and Culture

Československá vlastivěda (Czechoslovakian homeland studies). Vol 3: *Lidová kultura* (Folk culture). Prague, 1968.

Hasalová, Věra. *Folk Art of Czechoslovakia.* New York, 1974.

Langhammerová, Jiřina. *České lidové kroje* (Czech folk costume). Prague, 1995.

Mencl, Václav. *Lidová architektura v Československu* (Folk architecture in Czechoslovakia). Prague, 1980.

Staňková, Jitka, and Ludvík Baran. *Lidové umění z Čech, Moravy a Slezska* (Folk art in Bohemia, Moravia, and Silesia). Prague, 1987.

Stránská, Drahomíra. *Lidové kroje v Československu* (Folk costume in Czechoslovakia). Vol. 1: *Bohemia.* Prague, 1940.

Václavík, Antonín. *Výročni obyčeje a lidové umění* (Seasonal customs and folk art). Prague, 1959.

Zíbrt, Čeněk. *Veselé chvíle v životě lidu českého* (A happy moment in the life of the Czech people). Prague, 1950.